Nonprofit Kit

FOR

DUMMIES®

Nonprofit Kit
FOR
DUMMIES®

by Stan Hutton and Frances Phillips

Wiley Publishing, Inc.

Nonprofit Kit For Dummies®

Published by
Wiley Publishing, Inc.
111 River Street
Hoboken, NJ 07030
www.wiley.com

Copyright © 2001 by Wiley Publishing, Inc., Indianapolis, Indiana

Published simultaneously in Canada

For general information on our other products and services or to obtain technical support, please contact our Customer Care Department within the U.S. at 800-762-2974, outside the U.S. at 317-572-3993, or fax 317-572-4002.

Wiley also publishes its books in a variety of electronic formats. Some content that appears in print may not be available in electronic books.

Library of Congress Cataloging-in-Publication Data:

Library of Congress Control Number: 2001089318

ISBN: 0-7645-5347-X

Manufactured in the United States of America

10 9 8

1O/RV/QR/QU/IN

About the Authors

Stan Hutton cofounded a nonprofit organization in 1976. This marked the beginning of his continuing involvement with nonprofits as an executive director, fundraiser, consultant, writer, and volunteer. He has served as development director of Cogswell College and executive director of the Easter Seal Society of San Francisco and the Executive Service Corps of the Bay Area. At present, he works at the San Francisco Study Center, is a program consultant for the Clarence E. Heller Charitable Foundation, and writes for and manages the Nonprofit Charitable Organizations Web site at About.com. He is past president and member of the board of directors of Small Press Traffic Literary Arts Center.

Frances Phillips began her career in nonprofit organizations working for a National Endowment for the Humanities curriculum project at San Francisco State University when she was fresh out of graduate school. She has been a partner in the public relations and fundraising firm Horne, McClatchy & Associates; director of the Poetry Center and American Poetry Archives at San Francisco State; and executive director of Intersection for the Arts, San Francisco's oldest alternative arts organization. Currently she is a program officer at an independent foundation, the Walter and Elise Haas Fund, and director of The Creative Work Fund, which awards grants to collaborations between artists and San Francisco Bay Area nonprofits. She also teaches grant writing and creative writing at San Francisco State University; co-edits *Reader,* the journal of Grantmakers in the Arts; serves on the boards of the Poetry Center and Kelsey Street Press; and volunteers with the Bay Area Book Reviewers Association.

Dedication

We dedicate this book to the devoted nonprofit managers, staff members, volunteers, and board members who are working long hours to improve living conditions, advance the arts and learning, and protect the environment.

And to our daughter, Alice, who is also a writer and who probably will have the good sense not to bore her own children at the dinner table with details of her latest book.

Authors' Acknowledgments

This book started with our agent Maureen Watts, who had the idea and connected us with Wiley Publishing, Inc. Many thanks to her, to our acquisitions editor, Holly McGuire, and to the professionals who guided us through shaping and revising our manuscript — our project editor, Norm Crampton; technical editor, Paul Pribbenow; copy editors, Tina Sims and Ben Nussbaum; and the builders of the CD, directed by Laura Carpenter.

We owe much of our knowledge of the nonprofit sector to a remarkable array of professionals with whom we have worked. Lori Horne, Jean McClatchy, and Ginny Rubin showed Frances the satisfaction of raising money for good causes. She is grateful to the boards of The Poetry Center at San Francisco State and Intersection for the Arts for giving her a chance to move beyond fundraising to play all the rolls required of an executive director.

Stan wants to add thanks to Arthur Compton, with whom he started his first nonprofit organization and, as a result, discovered he was more interested in nonprofit management and fundraising than the practice of speech pathology; Louise Brown and the late Neil Housewright, whose support and guidance were invaluable in helping him to understand the fundamentals of fundraising; staff and volunteers at the Easter Seal Society, from whom he learned something new every day; and his present colleagues at the San Francisco Study Center, About.com, and the Clarence E. Heller Charitable Foundation, all of whom have been supportive of this project in many ways.

Terrific workshop leaders and trainers who have helped improve our skills include Jan Masaoka of CompassPoint, John Edie of the Council on Foundations, Janet Camarina of The Foundation Center's San Francisco library, Ross Connor of the Evaluator's Institute, and Sue Stevens of the Stevens Group, Inc.

Special thanks to our current colleagues, particularly Bruce Sievers, who provided wisdom about the big picture of civil society, and to Susan Clark, Bruce Hirsch, Anne Focke, and Amy Dawson, who provided valuable leads.

Acknowledgment also is due to Stan's readers at nonprofit.about.com, whose questions over the past four years have helped us understand the problems people face in starting and managing nonprofit organizations.

We owe deep appreciation to our family and friends who, in fact, have not seen much of us over the past year. Thanks for your understanding and support.

Publisher's Acknowledgments

We're proud of this book; please send us your comments through our online registration form located at www.dummies.com/register.

Some of the people who helped bring this book to market include the following:

Acquisitions, Editorial, and Media Development

Project Editor: Norm Crampton

Senior Acquisitions Editor: Holly McGuire

Copy Editors: Tina Sims, Ben Nussbaum

Technical Editor: Paul Pribbenow

Senior Permissions Editor: Carmen Krikorian

Media Development Specialist: Megan Decraene

Editorial Manager: Pam Mourouzis

Media Development Manager: Laura VanWinkle

Editorial Assistant: Carol Strickland

Cover Photo: PHX-Hagerstown

Production

Project Coordinator: Dale White

Layout and Graphics: Amy Adrian, LeAndra Johnson, Julie Trippetti, Jeremey Unger, Erin Zeltner

Proofreaders: John Greenough, Nancy Price, Marianne Santy, TECHBOOKS Production Services

Indexer: TECHBOOKS Production Services

Publishing and Editorial for Consumer Dummies

Diane Graves Steele, Vice President and Publisher, Consumer Dummies
Joyce Pepple, Acquisitions Director, Consumer Dummies
Kristin A. Cocks, Product Development Director, Consumer Dummies
Michael Spring, Vice President and Publisher, Travel
Brice Gosnell, Publishing Director, Travel
Suzanne Jannetta, Editorial Director, Travel

Publishing for Technology Dummies

Richard Swadley, Vice President and Executive Group Publisher
Andy Cummings, Vice President and Publisher

Composition Services

Gerry Fahey, Vice President of Production Services
Debbie Stailey, Director of Composition Services

Contents at a Glance

Cartoons at a Glance

By Rich Tennant

page 71

page 301

page 315

page 191

page 5

Cartoon Information:
Fax: 978-546-7747
E-Mail: richtennant@the5thwave.com
World Wide Web: www.the5thwave.com

Table of Contents

Part IV: The Part of Tens 301

Chapter 20: Ten Myths about Nonprofit Organizations 303

Chapter 21: Ten Tips for Raising Money 309

Introduction

· ·

Maybe you have an idea that will help solve a problem in your community, and you believe that starting a nonprofit organization is the best way to put your idea into action.

Maybe you serve on a board of directors and wonder what you're supposed to be doing.

Maybe you work for a nonprofit and need some ideas about fundraising, managing your organization, or working with your board of directors.

Or maybe you're curious about the nonprofit sector and want to learn more about it.

If you're one of these people, we think this book will answer your questions.

In this book, we talk about the mission of a nonprofit organization and how important it is to be committed to its charitable purpose. It may sound corny, but we feel a certain sense of mission when it comes to nonprofits. We have started them, directed them, raised funds for them, consulted for them, volunteered for them, given money to them, and written about them. We've been associated with nonprofits in one way or another for more years than we care to remember.

Why have we continued to work for nonprofit organizations? Yes, we care about others and want to see the world a better place — our values are important to us. But, to be honest, that's not the reason we've worked for nonprofit organizations for so many years. We believe the reason is that we can't think of anything more interesting or more challenging to do.

Starting a new program is exciting. Getting your first grant is thrilling. Working with the multifaceted personalities that come together on a board of directors is fascinating. Learning a new skill because there is no one else to do it is fun. Seeing the faces of satisfied clients, walking along a restored lakeshore, hearing the applause of audiences — all are gratifying.

That's why we do it.

About This Book

We try to cover the gamut in this book — everything you need to know to start and manage a charitable organization. We also attempt to give a bird's-eye view of the economy's nonprofit sector. When it comes to financial resources, for example, nonprofits are much like the rest of the world: Most of the wealth is held by relatively few nonprofit organizations; a respectable number of them are in the middle; and many more struggle to make ends meet.

We try to be honest about the difficulties you'll sometimes face. You probably won't be able to achieve everything you set out to accomplish, and you'll always wish you had more resources to do more things.

Still, we can't imagine doing anything else. Maybe you'll feel the same way once you jump into the nonprofit world.

How This Book Is Organized

Nonprofit Kit For Dummies is organized into six parts. You don't need to read it from cover from cover but can dip in for reference at any point — jumping from Part IV to Part II to Part V if you like. We won't tell anyone.

Part I: Getting Started with Nonprofits

Read Part I if you want an introduction to nonprofits and information about establishing a nonprofit organization. You'll also find a chapter to help you answer the question "Do I want to start a nonprofit organization or not?" If you decide that the answer is yes, we provide guidance for setting up a legal structure and winding your way through the IRS requirements.

Part II: Managing a Nonprofit Organization

This part covers the nuts and bolts of managing an organization — finding and hiring employees, setting up procedures (and responsibilities) for boards of directors, and recruiting and retaining volunteers. Planning and budgeting are two important aspects of keeping a nonprofit on track and in the black. And if you're managing a building or thinking of buying one for your organization, you can find some tips here.

Part III: Raising Money and Visibility

Raising money and public awareness of your work go together, so we put all those topics in Part III. Start by creating your fundraising plan and then implement it by raising funds from individuals, writing grant proposals, running annual campaigns, and, if you're really ambitious, launching a capital campaign. And you need to tell people how you're using all this money, so we tell you how to reach the media.

Part IV: The Part of Tens

This is the famous Part of Tens, containing a little whimsy on philanthropic organizations and some quick, practical advice on a topic that's dear to everyone's heart: raising money.

Part V: Appendixes

In this part, you'll find a glossary of commonly used terms in the nonprofit sector, along with a bibliography of organizations, a list of reference books and Web sites that can help you continue learning about all aspects of working and volunteering in nonprofits. You'll also find information about using the CD that comes with this book.

On the CD

We collected examples of just about everything we could think of — letters, grants, budgets, contracts, and more — and put them on the CD in the back of this book to help guide you in your work. You'll also find some software that may be helpful, as well as a list of offices to contact to find out about nonprofits in your state.

Icons Used in This Book

We use the following icons throughout the book to flag particularly important or helpful information.

This icon is posted next to little hints and suggestions gleaned from our experience over the years.

Warnings are just what you think they might be. We alert you to information that you shouldn't forget.

You may not need this technical stuff today, but — who knows? — it may be invaluable tomorrow.

The remember icon stands watch at information that you should keep ready for application.

This icon means that you can find more helpful information and management tools on the CD that accompanies this book.

Part I

Getting Started with Nonprofits

The 5th Wave   By Rich Tennant

"Dave used his time well while waiting for the IRS to approve the 501 (c)(3) application."

In this part . . .

In this part, we introduce the nonprofit sector and the key role that it plays in our society and economy. We define different types of nonprofit organizations, focusing on the kind that can receive tax-deductible contributions.

We walk you through the steps for starting a nonprofit organization: the questions you should ask, the planning you should do, the mission you should define, and the documents you need to master. We invite you to use all your skills, from dreaming to networking to filling in the blanks for the Internal Revenue Service.

Once your organization has received nonprofit status from the IRS, you need to attend to various reports every year. Sound scary? Fear not — we show you the way.

Chapter 1

Tuning In to the World of Nonprofit Organizations

· ·

In This Chapter

▶ Tracking your everyday encounters with nonprofit organizations

▶ Defining the nonprofit sector

▶ Measuring the size and wealth of the nonprofit sector

▶ Looking at different types of nonprofits

· ·

*I*t's morning in America. The radio alarm clicks on in your rural hometown. After tuning in to the weather, news, and livestock reports, you finish the kitchen chores while listening to an interview with a poet teaching at the small college in town. You hurry your two young kids away from *Sesame Street* and into the minivan for the regular a.m. run to the co-op preschool next to the volunteer fire station. Seeing the station reminds you to unload the bag of canned goods you bought for the county food drive. You drop the bag at the firehouse door and go take on the day.

It's morning in America. The radio alarm clicks on in your big-city hometown. After tuning in to the weather and stock market reports, you finish the kitchen chores while listening to a symphony recorded at the nearby concert hall. You drag your teenagers out of bed before leaving the apartment, reminding them that you'll pick them up tonight at the youth center. You hurry down the street to the subway, grab a newspaper, and notice that the city's largest hospital has a headline — a staff physician is getting results with a startling new treatment. You read about it on the train as you head to work.

Both of these mornings are filled with nonprofit organizations. The small town offers public radio and television, *Sesame Street,* a private college, a volunteer-run preschool, and a community food bank. The city scene includes public radio, a symphony orchestra, a youth club, and a hospital. Behind those layers of nonprofit organizations is another layer: the small press publisher and distributor of the poet's latest book, the medical school where the physician was educated, the economic think tank that analyzes stocks and commodities, and the agency providing emergency preparedness training to volunteer firefighters.

The nonprofit sector is not a distinct place, not some plaza or district that you'll come upon suddenly as you weave your way through your day. It's more like a thread of a common color that's laced throughout the economy and our lives. You'll find it and its influence no matter where you are — from the wilderness to the metropolis.

So, What's a Nonprofit Organization?

People hear the term *nonprofit organization* and picture Mother Hubbard's cupboard, as in awfully bare or zero bank balance. In fact, some nonprofit organizations turn very tidy profits on their operations, and that's good, because cash flow keeps an enterprise humming, whether it's a for-profit business or not.

The main financial difference between a for-profit and a not-for-profit enterprise is what happens to the profit. In a for-profit company like Ford or Microsoft or Disney or your favorite fast-food establishment, profits are paid to the owners, including shareholders. But a *non*profit can't do that. Any profit remaining after the bills are paid has to be plowed back into the organization's service program. So profit can't be distributed to individuals, such as the organization's board of directors, who are volunteers in every sense of the word.

What about shareholders — do nonprofits have any shareholders to pay off? Not in terms of a monetary payoff, like a stock dividend. But in a broad, service sense, nonprofits do have "shareholders." They are the people who benefit from the nonprofit's activities, like the people who tune in to public radio and TV or receive free food through the county food program.

Understanding the nonprofit sector is easier if you understand the characteristics of nonprofit organizations. They are

- Private (separate from government)
- Organizations (privately incorporated)
- Self-governing (controlling their own activities)
- Voluntary (overseen — at least in part — by volunteers and benefiting from the work and contributions of volunteers)
- Not distributing profits to their owners (nonprofits have no owners, but are overseen by volunteer board members)
- For public benefit (serving a public purpose and contributing to the public good)

What's sometimes confusing is that organizations doing the same kind of work as nonprofits may be *for*-profit organizations. For example, the majority of radio and television stations are profit-making enterprises. So are most publishing establishments. Some theaters and concert halls are nonprofit, and some are for-profit. And then you have an entirely different kind of organization — *government*-run schools, youth agencies, colleges, and medical facilities. They're not part of the nonprofit sector.

Neither is that charming little store on the corner where you pick up bread and milk. It may contribute to your family's welfare, but if it was created to earn a profit for the owners, it's not a nonprofit organization — even if it's losing money! Its status depends on its intent, how it's organized, and whether it includes volunteers.

Introducing the one and only 501 (c) (3)

When we use the term *nonprofit organization* in this book, for the most part, we're talking about an organization that the Internal Revenue Service has classified as a 501(c)(3). If that term is new to you, add it to your vocabulary with pride. In no time, "five-oh-one-see-three" will roll off your tongue as if you're a nonprofit expert. There *are* other kinds of nonprofit organizations, formed to benefit their members, to influence legislation, or to fulfill other purposes. They receive exemption from federal income taxes and sometimes relief from property taxes at the local level. (Chapter 2 discusses these organizations in greater detail.)

Nonprofit organizations classified as 501(c)(3) receive extra privileges under the law. They are, with minor exceptions, the only group of tax-exempt organizations that can receive tax-deductible contributions from individuals and organizations.

Being a nonprofit organization does not mean that an entity is exempt from paying all taxes. Nonprofit organizations pay employment taxes just like for-profit businesses do. In some states, but not all, nonprofits are exempt from paying sales tax, so be sure that you're familiar with your local laws.

Charitable organizations have to be careful about *lobbying* — stating their positions on specific legislation to legislators and supporting or opposing candidates running for election. It's okay for them to let the public know how a piece of legislation might affect the cause their organization supports, but it becomes lobbying when they ask supporters to contact their legislators about it. Lobbying is not completely forbidden, but 501(c)(3) organizations have to report on their IRS tax forms how much they spend on the activity. They must demonstrate that no substantial part of their revenues went to lobbying.

A close relative of the 501(c)(3) — a kind of nonprofit cousin — is the 501(c)(4), or social welfare organization. A 501(c)(4) is not restricted from lobbying and may engage in some political campaign activity, but it may not receive tax-deductible contributions. (See Chapter 2 for details.)

You might say that the nonprofit sector is the part of a nation's economy that's composed of all these public-serving nonprofit organizations and defined by tax codes. But the sector is more elusive than that. Nonprofit voluntary groups were formed in the United States in colonial times, before they were sanctioned by or benefiting from any kind of formal, legal status. In fact, one reason that the sector is so varied and vibrant in the United States is that ways of providing assistance to those in need were needed in the colonies before the government was formed or mature. And nonprofit activities continue to crop up informally all over the world when an idea or need arises.

Some complain that the nonprofit sector is made up of a lot of old-fashioned do-gooders or a bunch of liberals, that it benefits only the poor, and that only the rich volunteer. But none of these generalizations is true: The sector reaches beyond political and religious affiliations, and its influence is felt throughout all classes in society.

A sector by any other name

Not everyone thinks that *nonprofit sector* is the best term. That's because there's an array of organizations with different kinds of nonprofit status. Some of these organizations are formed to benefit their members — like fraternities and labor unions — and do not share a broad public-serving intent. Alternative terms that may be used include the following:

- ✔ **Voluntary sector:** This term emphasizes the presence of volunteer board members and the significance of voluntary contributions and services to the work of 501(c)(3)–type organizations. In this definition, it's not the organizations alone that represent the meaning of *nonprofit,* but the vast web of their supporters who participate as volunteers and donors.

- ✔ **Independent sector:** This term emphasizes the public-serving mission of these organizations and their volunteers and their independence from government. (Independent Sector is also the name of a nonprofit organization that sponsors research, publications, and public programs about the sector. You can find it at www.indepsec.org.)

- ✔ **Charitable sector:** This term emphasizes the donations these organizations receive from individuals and institutions.

- ✔ **Third sector:** This term emphasizes the organization's important role alongside government and the for-profit business economy.

We're going to use the term *nonprofit sector* throughout this book, but we want you to understand its limitations and be familiar with other commonly used terms.

Sometimes it's easiest to remember what a nonprofit *is* by recognizing what it *isn't:*

✔ It isn't a government agency with a mandate to serve all citizens with equity and the ability to collect taxes to implement programs.

✔ It isn't a for-profit business whose purpose is to return profits to its owners by creating and selling products or services.

Getting inspired

The nonprofit sector is exciting and inspiring. It encourages individuals with ideas about solving social problems or enhancing arts, culture, the environment, or education to act on those ideas. It creates a viable place within our society and economy for worthy activities that have little chance of commercial success. We think that it combines the best of the business world with the best of government, bringing together creativity, zeal, and problem solving from the business side with a call to public service from the government side.

We also find volunteerism inspiring. Everyone has heard stories of tightly knit communities where neighbors gather to rebuild a barn. That spirit of pitching in to help is the best part of the essence of a community in which values and ideas are shared.

Many people live in communities that contain people from a wide variety of backgrounds. The nonprofit sector provides an array of institutions in which all people can come together, with both those who resemble them and others who are unlike them, to work toward the common good. Volunteerism enables everyone to pitch in to rebuild "the barn" in a wide variety of contexts.

Some compare the role of the nonprofit sector to the ancient practice of maintaining a *commons* — an area of land between farms and villages that was shared and maintained by and for the benefit of an entire community. The commons was a place to turn when one needed a passageway, one's own fields were overgrazed, or one's house burned.

So the nonprofit sector provides common ground for creative, sometimes small-scale, often labor-intensive, and yet innovative approaches to solving problems and enhancing quality of life.

Bigger Than a Breadbox

The nonprofit sector is larger than many people realize. Here are some facts and figures from the National Center on Charitable Statistics about U.S. non-profits' size and scope in 1999:

- ✔ Their annual budgets combined total more than $700 billion.

- ✔ They contribute 8 percent to the country's gross domestic product, or GDP. That percentage has been growing since the 1960s, when they represented 3.6 percent of the GDP.

- ✔ They employ 10.2 million people as full-time or part-time workers, and their employees represent 11 percent of the entire workforce of the United States.

- ✔ In the United States, 93 million people volunteer 20.3 billion hours in total time helping nonprofits. The value of that contributed time and effort is more than $200 billion.

- ✔ Many nonprofit organizations are very small — only one-third have annual revenues of $25,000 or more.

One distinctive feature of the nonprofit sector is its dependency on contributions. We devote many pages of this book — most of Part III — to advice about getting contributions.

Gifts from individuals of money, goods, services, and property make up the largest portion of that voluntary support. This is also the oldest part of the voluntary tradition in the United States and goes back to colonial times. Since the late 19th century, private philanthropic foundations have emerged as another major source of support, and in the 20th century — particularly after World War II — the federal government and corporations became important income sources. Many nonprofits also sell some kind of service, and a trend in the sector shows earned income becoming a larger portion of total revenues.

Tables 1-1 and 1-2 give you a quick picture of nonprofit revenue sources. Over the past 30 years, private contributions (18.9 percent) have come to represent a smaller portion of overall revenue for nonprofits as the portions derived from government (31.7 percent) and revenues from service fees (38.6 percent) have increased.

Among private, nongovernmental sources of support (the 18.9 percent item in Table 1-1), gifts from living individuals — as opposed to bequests from people who have died — have always represented the largest portion of total giving, but philanthropic giving by foundations and corporations has been growing. Table 1-2 outlines sources of private contributions in 1999.

Table 1-1	Nonprofit Funding in the United States: 1996
Source of Income	*Percentage of Total Income*
Dues, fees, and charges	38.6%
Government	31.7%
Private contributions	18.9%
Other revenues	10.8%

Source: America's Nonprofit Sector in Brief

Table 1-2	Sources of Private Contributions: 1999	
Source of Income	*Amount of Total Giving*	*Percentage of Total Giving*
Individuals	$143.71 billion	75.6%
Foundations	$19.81 billion	10.4%
Bequests	$15.61 billion	8.2%
Corporations	$11.02 billion	5.8%
Total	$143.5 billion	100%

Source: America's Nonprofit Sector in Brief

Calling All Nonprofits

The Internal Revenue Service tax code describes allowable purposes of 501(c)(3) nonprofit organizations as serving religious, educational, charitable, scientific, and literary purposes. This broad definition encompasses a wide variety of organizations — from those conducting medical research to those providing free legal services to low-income families to those preserving historic sites. It also includes corporations and foundations founded to support such activities.

We've organized a quick overview of categories and kinds of activities.

Arts, culture, and humanities

This category probably makes you think of museums and concert halls. You're right, but that's not all. They belong here along with these organizations:

- Organizations and activities that further enjoyment and understanding of all kinds of arts
- Media and communications organizations
- Groups furthering the understanding of history and genealogy
- Halls of fame
- Historic preservation
- Organizations offering services to artists, writers, and performers
- Organizations for the training and education of artists, writers, and performers

Did you think of heredity-based organizations (such as Sons of the Revolution or Daughters of the Confederacy)? They belong here, too — along with non-profit circuses!

Education

You thought schools belonged in the education category, and you were right. This category is made up of formally constituted educational institutions (except art schools) and organizations that administer or support those institutions. It also includes the following:

- Libraries
- Continuing education centers
- Other activities supporting learning outside formal schools — such as literacy and language-learning programs
- Related services, including testing programs and scholarships

Environmental quality, protection, and beautification

You may have thought of beautification and open space programs, and, yes, those fit here. So do programs to control pollution and conserve natural resources. Farmlands and fisheries are classified in other categories.

Animal related

Services in this category range from humane societies and programs to protect animals from exploitation to wildlife preservation, veterinary services, and zoos. Aquariums? Yep, they fit here. So do services for training and exhibiting animals.

Health

Hang onto your hat. This wide-ranging category includes the following:

- ✔ Hospitals of all kinds
- ✔ Outpatient clinics
- ✔ Rehabilitation and therapy centers
- ✔ Public health programs
- ✔ Blood banks
- ✔ Search-and-rescue squads
- ✔ Organ and tissue donor programs
- ✔ First aid training
- ✔ Health insurance
- ✔ Bioethics
- ✔ Programs to support patients and their families with counseling, housing, or financial aid
- ✔ Mental health, crisis intervention, counseling support, and hotlines
- ✔ Health associations working on behalf of prevention or treatment of specific illnesses
- ✔ Medical research

Human services

If you thought the health category was broad, wait until you see the scope of human services. We break it down into subcategories:

- ✔ Organizations to protect the public from crime, as well as services for prisoners and ex-offenders
- ✔ Job development, training, and rehabilitation
- ✔ Food services such as Grocery on Wheels and food banks

- Farm-related projects such as animal husbandry and farm preservation
- Housing needs — encompassing development, construction, and management of housing, tenants' rights, and housing search assistance
- Programs to advance public safety, including disaster preparedness, food protection, rescue squads, and first aid training
- Recreation, sports, leisure, and athletics, including camps, playgrounds, amateur sports clubs and competitions, and physical fitness centers
- Youth development, including Boys and Girls Clubs, scouting organizations, service and future professionals' clubs, and citizenship programs
- Multipurpose organizations such as the Red Cross and Volunteers of America
- Children and youth services, including orphanages and adoption programs
- Services for families, such as parent education and violence shelters
- Personal services such as financial counseling and mediation
- Emergency food, clothing, and financial assistance
- Residential and custodial care programs
- Services to promote the independence of specific population groups such as seniors, immigrants, and persons with disabilities

Whew!

International/foreign affairs

The arena of international and foreign affairs includes the following:

- International exchange programs
- Economic development and relief
- Policy research and analysis
- Peace and security organizations, such as those promoting the control of biological weapons
- International human rights
- Migration and refugee issues
- International relations

Public, societal benefit

This broad category includes the following:

- ✔ Civil rights groups
- ✔ Voter education
- ✔ Advocacy for civil liberties such as freedom of religion
- ✔ Community improvement and economic development
- ✔ Philanthropic organizations
- ✔ Social science and science and technology research institutes
- ✔ Government policy reform
- ✔ Citizen participation groups
- ✔ Leadership development
- ✔ Telecommunications services

Religion related

Religion-related organizations are operated for the purpose of worship, religious training or study, or governance or administration of religions. They attract the largest portion of their support from individuals.

Many religious organizations conduct important charitable work by serving people who may or may not be part of their congregations. Some of them form independent nonprofit organizations to manage such charitable projects. These include AIDS hospices, refugee services, low-income housing, soup kitchens, and shelters for battered women. Many foundations, corporations, and government agencies do not award grants directly to religion-related organizations (to avoid promoting a specific religious point of view, to maintain a separation of church and state, and because churches are not required to report their finances for public or IRS scrutiny). However, grant-makers often support these organizations created by churches.

Comparing Income

Table 1-3 gives a quick overview from *Giving USA 2000* showing how the various kinds of nonprofit organizations compare in securing revenues.

Table 1-3	1999 Contributions by Type of Recipient Organization	
Organization Type	*Contributions in Billions*	*Percentage*
Religion	$81.78	43.0%
Education	$27.46	14.4%
Health	$17.95	9.4%
Human services	$17.36	9.1%
Other	$15.11	7.9%
Arts, culture	$11.07	5.8%
Public/society benefit	$10.94	5.8%
Environment	$5.83	3.1%
International	$2.65	1.4%

No matter where you wake up, in no matter what kind of community, the nonprofit sector surrounds you. With this vast array of nonprofit activities, the sector offers you many ways to become involved — as a contributor, a volunteer, an employee, or a founder.

Chapter 2

Deciding to Start a Nonprofit

Maybe you've been thinking of starting a nonprofit organization for years, or maybe an idea to solve a social problem or provide a needed service just popped into your head. It doesn't matter how or when you got the idea. It could be time to make it a reality.

Before you file your incorporation papers, you should understand both the positive and the not-so-positive factors that can make or break your new organization. You may even decide that now isn't the right time to take this important step.

In this chapter, we pose some questions that you should consider (and answer) before you begin the process. If some of your answers point to the conclusion that it's not the right time and place, we give you some alternatives to consider.

Weighing the Pros and Cons

Like starting any business, starting and managing a nonprofit organization is not a simple matter. Be prepared for lots of hard work, and even sleepless nights. If your nonprofit uses paid staff, you need to be sure that you have money in the bank when payroll is due. You may have disagreements with your board of directors, and you may be frustrated when trying to raise funds.

If we haven't scared you away yet, spend time looking at the sections that follow. Considering these points may be the most important thing you do in your quest to establish a nonprofit organization.

You've probably already thought about the positive aspects of starting a non-profit. If you haven't, this is our short list:

✔ Exemption from taxes on most income to the nonprofit

✔ For some types of nonprofits, the ability to receive contributions that are deductible for the donor

✔ The possibility of receiving grant funds from foundations and corporations

✔ The feeling that you're contributing to the solution of a problem or the improvement of society

And here are other facts about nonprofits that we want to state at the very beginning:

✔ If you're being paid a salary from the nonprofit, it will be subject to income tax just like all compensation.

✔ If your organization has revenues of over $25,000 a year, you need to file an annual report with the IRS. You must make these reports available for public scrutiny.

✔ You can't start a nonprofit organization to benefit a particular individual or family members.

✔ Competition for grants from foundations, corporations, and government agencies is tough. You'll be up against more established nonprofits with successful track records.

✔ Well over half of the nonprofit organizations in the United States either choose to operate without paid staff or do so because of lack of funds.

Keep these factors in mind as you consider the following sections of this chapter.

Checking out the competition

If you plan to open a grocery store, you probably wouldn't choose a location next door to a successful supermarket. The market will bear only so much trade. This principle holds true for nonprofits, too. You may have the best idea in the world, but if someone else is already doing it well in your community, don't try to duplicate it. Ask yourself whether your town really can support two counseling centers, two theater groups, or two preschool enrichment programs.

Most nonprofit founders bring passion to their organization. Passion can accomplish many things, but succeeding by offering the same program as an established organization is probably not one of them. Therefore, you want to do a thorough job researching the services and programs that are already available in your area.

And if there isn't a similar program in your area, ask yourself why. Maybe your community doesn't have enough potential clients or audience members to support the project. Or maybe funders don't perceive the same needs in the community as you do. Doing a needs assessment is a good way to evaluate the potential market for your nonprofit's services. You may want to use some or all of the following methods to determine community needs:

- ✔ Telephone surveys or written questionnaires to a random sample of residents in your community
- ✔ Interviews with local foundation and civic officials
- ✔ Focus groups with people who are likely to benefit from the organization

See Chapter 9 for a more detailed treatment of assessing community needs.

Finding people to help you

The more help you have, the better. Your chances for success increase if you begin with support from others. We're sure that examples can be found of the single-minded visionary who battles through all sorts of adversity to establish a thriving nonprofit, but starting and running a nonprofit organization is essentially a group activity.

You need to find people who will serve on the board of directors and support your efforts with donations of money and volunteer time. Usually, the first people identified as supporters are family and friends. How can they turn you down? But in the long run, you'll need to extend that support to others who believe in the organization's mission.

Some people hesitate to share their idea with others because they believe that someone might steal it. We think this fear is largely unfounded. You'll be better off if you invite others to join you in the undertaking, whatever it is. Take every opportunity to speak about your idea before civic groups, religious groups, and service clubs. Put on your salesperson's cap and convince the community that your program is needed.

If you're having a hard time drumming up support, it may be a sign that your idea needs refinement or that others view it as impractical. It may be time to go back to the drawing board.

Paying the bills

Funding your organization is a big issue. Even if you begin as a volunteer-run organization and work from a home office, you still need funds for letterhead, supplies, equipment, postage, and insurance. You'll also have filing fees of at least several hundred dollars for your incorporation and tax exemption applications. Many nonprofit start-ups are funded by the founder in the beginning. Are you able to pay all the start-up expenses before revenues start flowing to your new nonprofit?

Although start-up grants from foundations and corporations are available, they're not easy to get. You need to make a compelling case that your new organization will provide an important service to the community. You may solicit contributions from individuals before the organization is granted tax-exempt status as long as you reveal that your exemption is pending. These contributions will become deductible to the donor when and if you receive the exemption.

Some new organizations avoid this awkward period between start-up and receiving tax-exempt status by beginning as a sponsored program of an existing nonprofit organization. This arrangement is known as *fiscal sponsorship* and is discussed in more detail later in this chapter.

Put together a budget to help you decide whether the start-up expenses are manageable. You'll be creating lots of budgets sooner or later, so you may as well get an early start.

Looking in the mirror

Ask yourself (and answer honestly) whether you're the right person to do the job. Many services, especially those in the health and social services fields, must be provided by qualified and licensed individuals. And beyond professional qualifications, you also need to consider whether you feel confident about your management, fundraising, and communication skills.

One of the most challenging and exciting aspects of starting and working in a new nonprofit organization is the need to stretch yourself across many different skill areas. You may be dressed to the nines one day to pitch your project to the mayor or a corporate executive. The next day, you may be sweeping the floor of your office or unplugging a clogged toilet. In other words, you need to be versatile and willing to take on just about any task that needs to be done.

Potential funders certainly will be looking to see whether the organization's leadership has the background, experience, and knowledge to carry out the proposed program when evaluating grant proposals. This doesn't necessarily mean that you need to be an experienced nonprofit manager — or even have experience working in nonprofits, for that matter. But try to assess your background to see how you can apply your experience to the nonprofit you hope to start.

Planning and more planning

If there ever was a time to plan, this is it. Planning is what turns your initial idea into a doable project. It's also a good way to find potential holes in your thinking. You may believe, for example, that your community doesn't have adequate animal rescue services. And you may be right. But when you begin to break down the idea of starting an animal shelter, you may find that this project will cost more money or require more staff or facilities than you first think.

Write out a one- or two-page synopsis of your idea. What are you trying to do, and how will you do it? Make a list of the resources you need to accomplish your mission. Talk to as many people as you can about your idea. Ask for help and for honest feedback about your project. Think it through step by step.

Creating a plan is one of the first steps to take when considering whether you can turn your idea into reality. If you don't have a plan, create one before you make your final decision. If you need help in the planning process, have a look at Chapter 9.

Understanding Nonprofit Ownership

We once received a telephone call from a man who was shopping for a nonprofit. "Do you know if there are any nonprofits for sale in southern California?" he asked. Although this question doesn't come to us often, it illustrates a misconception about the status of nonprofit organizations. No one person or group of people can own a nonprofit organization. You don't see nonprofit shares traded on stock exchanges, and any equity in a nonprofit organization belongs to the organization itself, not to the board of directors or the staff. Nonprofit assets can be sold, but the proceeds of the sale must benefit the organization, not private parties.

If you start a nonprofit and decide at some point in the future that you don't want to do it anymore, you'll have to walk away from it and leave the running of the organization to someone else. Or, if it's time to close the doors for good, any assets the organization owns must be distributed to other nonprofits filling a similar mission.

When nonprofit managers and consultants talk about "ownership" of a nonprofit organization, they're using the word metaphorically to make the point that board members, staff, clients, and the community have a stake in the organization's future success and its ability to provide needed programs.

Benefiting the public

Nonprofit organizations are formed to benefit the public. In fact, nonprofit corporations are referred to as public benefit corporations. A nonprofit organization can't be created to benefit a particular individual or family, for example. If that were possible, we'd all have our separate nonprofit organizations.

You can start a nonprofit to help a particular group or class of individuals — everyone suffering from heart disease, for example, or people living below the poverty level — but you can't create a nonprofit for personal benefit or gain. This doesn't mean that you can't be paid a reasonable salary for your work, nor does it mean that a nonprofit organization can't have surplus funds, essentially a profit, at the end of year. But it does mean that the surplus money is held in reserve by the organization and not distributed to you or your board of directors, as it might be if it were a for-profit business.

Accounting to the public

Nonprofit organizations with over $25,000 in annual revenues must file a report (Form 990) each year with the Internal Revenue Service, summarizing income and expenses and reporting staff and consultant salaries over $50,000. We discuss this report in more detail in Chapter 5. States also have reporting requirements.

You can find a copy of Form 990 and other IRS documents on the CD that accompanies this book.

Although there is no absolute limit on the amount of compensation that a nonprofit employee may earn, the IRS does have the authority to penalize individuals (and organizations) who receive excessive compensation. Whether benefits are excessive depends on the situation. A staff member earning $100,000 annually from an organization with a budget of $125,000 would probably need to worry. But someone earning $100,000 from a non-profit with a $2 million budget probably wouldn't. An employee found to have received excessive compensation may be required to pay an excise tax, and in dire cases, the nonprofit organization may lose its tax-exempt status. Chapter 5 has more information about excessive compensation.

Nonprofit organizations also are required to make copies of their three most recent 990 reports, as well as their application for tax exemption, available for public scrutiny. State and local laws in your area may require additional disclosures.

So although nonprofit organizations are not public entities like governmental agencies and departments, their tax-exempt status requires them to be more accountable to the public than a privately owned business is.

Nonprofits Are Not All Alike

The words *nonprofit* and *charity* go together in most people's minds, but some nonprofits are not charitable organizations. The most common examples are business and trade associations, political advocacy groups, fraternal societies, and clubs. Although these nonprofits enjoy exemption from corporate income taxes, people who contribute to them may not claim a tax deduction for the contribution.

Most nonprofits, charitable or not, are incorporated organizations formed under the laws of the state in which they are created. Some nonprofits exist as either associations or trusts, but these are in the minority. The IRS grants tax-exempt status to a nonprofit after reviewing its stated purpose.

Don't rely on a nonprofit's formal name to determine the sort of organization it is. The Left-Handed Scissors Association is probably a nonprofit corporation, not technically an association. And the Canary Appreciation Foundation probably doesn't make grants.

Nonprofit types are identified by the section of the IRS code under which they qualify for exempt status. Nonprofit organizations that are charitable in nature and to which contributions are deductible to the donor are known as 501(c)(3)s. An organization providing music education in the schools is almost certainly a 501(c)(3). But business and professional groups, for instance, fall into the 501(c)(6) category.

Knowing them by their numbers

To get the full flavor of the various categories of nonprofit organizations, see the information at the IRS Web site at www.irs.ustreas.gov/prod/bus_info/eo/eo-types.html or review IRS publication 557. The following list summarizes IRS nonprofit types:

- **501(c)(3):** Organizations formed for educational, scientific, literary, charitable, or religious pursuits. Private foundations also are considered 501(c)(3) organizations but are in a special subclass and are subject to additional reporting requirements.

- **501(c)(4):** Organizations known as social welfare organizations that are formed for the improvement of general welfare and the common good of the people. Advocacy groups tend to fall into this category because organizations with the classification are allowed more leeway to lobby legislatures as a part of their mission to improve the general welfare. Certain employee organizations also come under this classification. Contributions are not deductible for the donor.

✔ **501(c)(5):** Labor unions and other groups formed to work for better conditions for workers are in this category. These groups also may lobby for legislation.

✔ **501(c)(6):** Business and trade associations that provide services to their members and work toward the betterment of business conditions are placed in this classification. Again, lobbying for legislation is allowed.

✔ **501(c)(7):** This section covers social clubs formed for recreation and pleasure. Country clubs and organizations formed around a hobby come under this classification. These organizations must be funded primarily by memberships and dues.

✔ **501(c)(8)/501(c)(10):** Fraternal lodges are placed in these two classifications. Health and burial benefits often are provided to members and must be available to all members.

✔ **501(c)(9):** A voluntary employees beneficiary association organized to pay insurance benefits to members and their dependents.

✔ **501(c)(19)/501(c)(23):** These categories cover veterans organizations for people who have served in the United States military. 501(c)(23)s are veterans organizations formed before 1880.

Several other 501(c)–type organizations are so specialized in nature that we won't go into them here. One of our favorites is the 501(c)(13), which covers cemetery companies.

Political committees and parties have their own special classification. They're recognized under IRS code section 527 and are organized for the purpose of electing persons to office. They have special reporting requirements and are not required to be incorporated.

Odd little rules and regulations to add to your file

Entire volumes have been written about IRS regulations and laws pertaining to nonprofits. We just want to give you an overview of some facts that may help you decide whether starting a 501(c)(3) nonprofit organization is your best choice.

Nonprofits and political activities

Nonprofits can't campaign to support or oppose the candidacy of anyone running for elected office. If you want to do this, form a political committee under IRS section 527.

Lobbying for specific legislation is less clear. Social welfare organizations and labor unions have more leeway when it comes to legislative lobbying; in fact, lobbying can be the primary activity of these organizations. These groups must inform their members what percentage of dues is used for lobbying activities. They also are barred from working toward a candidate's election.

Even charitable nonprofit organizations, the 501(c)(3)s, can participate in some legislative lobbying as long as it is an unsubstantial part of their activities. Although *unsubstantial* is undefined, we've heard that keeping expenditures in this category under 5 percent of the organizational budget is acceptable. Charitable nonprofits can spend even more money on lobbying activities if the organization chooses to elect what is referred to as the "h" designation, which refers to section 501(h) of the IRS Code. Doing so requires more financial reporting to the IRS but does allow the nonprofit to spend a greater percentage of its income on lobbying activities. More expenditures are allowed for direct lobbying (talking to your legislator) than for grassroots lobbying (attempting to influence how people vote).

Going deeper into the details of these laws and reporting requirements is really beyond the scope of this book. If your nonprofit is contemplating becoming involved in serious legislative activity, consult an attorney or tax specialist for advice. Penalties for engaging in too much political activity can include loss of your organization's tax exemption.

The situation with churches

Churches are in a category all by themselves. They are not required to file for a tax exemption, nor are they required to file annual reports to the IRS. Many churches do, however, wish to have acknowledgment from the IRS of their tax-exempt status as a 501(c)(3) organization.

Churches do this because their social service programs may include anything from preschools to soup kitchens. These programs can apply for foundation funding and government grants or contracts to help pay the costs of providing the services. But it's highly likely that grants or contracts will be given to churches that have not been recognized officially as tax exempt.

Taxes, taxes, taxes

Nonprofit organizations may be subject to unrelated business income tax, known as UBIT. If a nonprofit earns over $1,000 a year from a trade or business that's unrelated to its exempt purpose, this income is taxable. Most nonprofits don't have to worry about this possibility, but if your dance company decides to open an automobile repair shop, be prepared to pay taxes on the income.

Some states exempt some nonprofits from paying state sales and use taxes. Because these are state taxes, you need to check the laws in your state to see whether your organization is exempt. The same is true of property taxes — it depends on your local jurisdiction. Check with your nearest tax assessor.

Nonprofit employees, of course, must pay income tax on their salaries and other taxable compensation.

Nonprofits owning for-profits

Nonprofits may own for-profit businesses. We don't recommend it, especially when you're starting out, but it is possible. The business would be subject to all regular taxes just like all other for-profit businesses. Profits from the business become assets of the nonprofit and must be used to further the organization's goals and programs.

Very small organizations

If your group has less than $5,000 in annual revenues, it doesn't need to apply for a tax exemption. You can even go a bit over $5,000 in a year if your average income over a three-year period is less than $5,000.

When your income averages over that amount, however, you have 90 days following the close of your most recent tax year to file for a tax exemption.

Nonprofit compensation

One common feature of nonprofit organizations, regardless of their type, is that no board member, staff member, or other interested party can benefit from the earnings of a nonprofit. Assets are forever dedicated to the purpose of the organization. If the organization dissolves, the assets must be transferred to another organization performing a similar function.

This doesn't mean that people are required to work for nonprofit organizations for free. Nonprofits can and should pay reasonable salaries to their staff members, if they have any. But keep in mind the difference between paying a salary and splitting the profits at the end of year.

Although the IRS doesn't set absolute limits on what nonprofits may pay their employees, if it's determined that compensation is excessive, both the employee and the organization may be subject to penalties. Factors that determine whether compensation is excessive include a comparison of salaries paid in similar organizations for similar work, the duties and responsibilities of the employee, the size of the organization's budget, and whether the employee had a hand in determining his or her own salary.

The Difference between Nonprofits and For-Profits

Although this section is called "The Difference between Nonprofits and For-Profits," we want to start with the similarities between the two — and there are several. Good business practices, for example, are important to both. Good planning based on good information is also a critical factor in the success of both nonprofits and for-profits. Management skills, organizational ability, and attention to detail make a difference no matter whether you're working in a nonprofit or somewhere else. A little bit of luck doesn't hurt, either.

The term *entrepreneur* usually is used to describe someone who starts a new business. But any group that sets out to establish a nonprofit organization can be considered entrepreneurial as well. After all, you're starting out on a path that may lead to great success, and you'll assume some risks along the way. We hope that you won't risk your house or your savings account to get a nonprofit going, but you may have uncertain income for a while. In addition, you always risk the chance of damage to your professional reputation if things don't go as well as you had hoped.

Measuring success beyond cash receipts

The biggest difference between nonprofits and for-profits is the motivation for doing what you do — the "mission" of the organization. For-profit businesses exist to make money, a profit. Evaluating the success of a for-profit endeavor is easy: Did you make money and how much?

We're not saying this to cast stones at the capitalist system or in any way disparage the millions of folks who work for profit-making endeavors. The nonprofit sector depends on profits and wealth for its support. Believe us, we like profits, too.

And, of course, even nonprofits have to balance the books. It's even desirable for nonprofits to end the year with more money than they had when they started. We just don't call it profit; we call it a *surplus*.

But, to be successful, a nonprofit needs to change some aspect of the human condition; it needs to solve a problem, provide education, or build a monument. And because the goals of nonprofits are so lofty and progress toward achieving them is often slow, evaluating nonprofit success is sometimes difficult. That's why nonprofits are often said to have a *double bottom line* — the financial results and the social change they created.

Melding business and "mission"

We've been hearing a lot about social entrepreneurship in the last decade or so. An example is a printing business run by a nonprofit organization that not only provides printing services to customers but also recruits and trains former drug abusers to run the print shop.

The idea, of course, is that drug abusers are being rehabilitated and learning the printing business while at the same time earning money to support the program. Although they've come to public attention only recently, programs like this have been a part of the nonprofit world for many years.

Using a Fiscal Sponsor to Sidestep the Start-Up Hassle

You may not need to start a nonprofit to carry out the program you're thinking of starting. *Fiscal sponsorship* may be the best route to take. In this approach, your new project becomes a sponsored program of an existing nonprofit organization. Contributions earmarked for your project are tax deductible because they're made to the sponsoring agency.

If you're simply interested in providing a service, maybe you don't want to waste your time with the bureaucratic and legal matters that can complicate a new nonprofit start-up. Or maybe you have a project that will end after a year or two, or you simply want to test the viability of an idea. Why bother to establish a new organization if it's going to close when you finish your project? Many art projects, for example, are completed under a fiscal sponsorship arrangement.

Fiscal sponsorship may be the answer if you want to avoid starting a new nonprofit organization. Fiscal sponsorship is an alternative method of providing services without establishing a new organization.

Here's a hypothetical example. Joanna Jones, a paralegal for a Chicago law firm, has an interest in immigration law and wants to provide part-time assistance to recent immigrants from South Asia who are having problems with their visas. She has created an annual budget and spoken to several funders who have expressed a desire to make three-year grants to the project. However, in order to accept funding, Jones must either create a 501(c)(3) organization or find an alternative. Someone suggested that she seek a fiscal sponsor as a possible alternative.

After doing some research, she contacted the Angeline Community Center, a nonprofit organization that provides health and other services to low-income persons, including the immigrant population whom she hopes to help. The community center agreed to become the fiscal sponsor. The foundation funders made their grants to Angeline Community Center, earmarked for the immigration counseling program.

Jones now provides immigration counseling services under the auspices of the Angeline Community Center. Under this arrangement, the community center provides basic accounting services for the project and is ultimately responsible to the funders to ensure that their grants are used as they were intended.

A fiscal sponsor often is called a fiscal agent, but this term does not accurately describe the relationship between a fiscal sponsor and the sponsored project. The term *agent* implies that the sponsoring organization is acting on behalf on the project, when it's really the other way around. The project is a program of the sponsoring nonprofit.

This may seem like a nitpicking distinction, but it's an important one to keep in mind in order to satisfy IRS requirements for this type of relationship. The 501(c)(3) organization is responsible to both the funders and the IRS to see that money is spent as intended and that charitable goals are being met.

Here are important points to keep in mind if you decide to go this route:

✔ The mission of the fiscal sponsor must be in alignment with the project. In other words, if you have a project to provide free food to the home-less, don't approach your local philharmonic orchestra as a potential sponsor. Find a nonprofit that has similar goals in its mission statement.

✔ Sponsorship arrangements must be approved by the board of directors of the sponsoring organization. They are, after all, ultimately responsible.

✔ A contract or memorandum of understanding should be prepared that outlines responsibilities of each party to the agreement.

We include a sample fiscal sponsorship agreement on the CD.

✔ The fiscal sponsor customarily charges a fee for sponsoring a project, usually between 5 and 15 percent of the project's annual revenues, depending on what services are being provided to the project. Some fiscal sponsors can provide payroll services, office space, and even management support if needed.

✔ Contributions to the sponsored project should be written to the sponsor, with a notation that they're to be used for the project.

Pioneering in social entrepreneurship

Pioneer Human Services, a Seattle nonprofit organization, is an example of successful social entrepreneurship. Pioneer operates a long list of businesses, including a high-class restaurant inside the corporate headquarters of Starbucks, warehousing services, a metal fabrication business, and institutional food services. Founded in 1962, Pioneer has grown to have an annual budget of over $55,000,000.

Sounds like any successful business enterprise, doesn't it? The difference is that the people who work in the various Pioneer operations are clients of Pioneer's drug rehabilitation programs and ex-convicts, many of whom have been assigned to the four work-release programs and two group homes for juvenile offenders that Pioneer also operates.

Pioneer says that its mission is "to create opportunities for those we serve to realize personal, economic, and social development through participating in an integrated array of training, employment, housing, and rehabilitation services." Nearly all of Pioneer's revenues come from income from its business enterprises.

Finding a fiscal sponsor

If you're not sure whom in your community to ask about fiscal sponsorship, a good place to begin is at your local community foundation. Community foundations often have programs that provide fiscal sponsorship programs. Mission statements of community foundations typically are broad enough to cover any program that benefits the areas they serve.

If there is no community foundation nearby, contact a United Way Volunteer Center or other nonprofit that provides referrals and ask for help in finding the right agency to sponsor your project.

Using fiscal sponsorship as a first step

Using fiscal sponsorship as a temporary solution while a new nonprofit corporation is being established and a tax exemption is being acquired is a common approach. By doing this, you avoid the awkward period during which you have a nonprofit corporation but not tax exemption. Although you can receive contributions during this period, you must alert your donors that your exemption is pending and that their donation will not be tax deductible until your exemption is granted.

Beginning as a sponsored program also enables you to establish an organizational infrastructure and to create a board of directors in a more leisurely manner. You can pay more attention to building your program services in the crucial beginning stages of your project.

Chapter 3

Writing Your Mission Statement

*I*f you're still thinking about whether to take the step of starting a nonprofit organization, this chapter may help you make the final decision. The purpose of your organization is stated in its mission, and a mission statement is central to a nonprofit organization. In fact, it's the reason an organization exists. Use it as a touchstone to return to when making decisions about your nonprofit.

Mission statements can be one-liners or go on for two or three pages. We suggest aiming for something in between these two extremes. A mission statement contained in one line resembles an advertising slogan, and a long, rambling statement is rarely read, even by the board of directors and staff members.

Spend some time thinking about what should be in your mission statement because it defines your organization's purpose. Craft the language you use to describe your purpose so that it's clear and to the point.

In this chapter, we give you some guidance about how you can achieve a simple yet compelling mission statement.

Understanding What a Mission Statement Does

The mission statement is an organization's center. We were tempted to use the word *heart* rather than *center,* but we think that's stretching the metaphor a little. Or we could have said that mission statements are living, breathing organisms from which all organizational life flows, but that would be really crazy. People are really at the heart and bring the life to an organization. Mission statements just help give this human energy direction and form.

Can organizations operate without good mission statements? Yes, some do. We're sure that there are organizations out there doing good things that haven't looked at their mission statements since the Carter administration. But your chances of success are better if you and the people associated with your organization know what they're trying to do and how they're going to do it.

A mission statement should

- ✔ Be memorable because it's something you want to carry around with you at all times.
- ✔ Be narrow enough to focus the activities of your organization but broad enough to allow growth and expansion.
- ✔ Be written in plain language so that it doesn't need a set of footnotes to decipher it.
- ✔ State the organization's purpose, the means by which the purpose will be achieved, and who will benefit from the organization's activities. Organizational values and vision also may be included.

Working with a purpose

To say that you have to have a purpose seems almost too basic. Maybe you're thinking to yourself, "Of course I have a purpose. Why do you think I bought this book? I want to start a nonprofit to [fill in the blank]." But we bring this up because the purpose is basic to a mission statement.

Knowing and understanding your organization's purpose is essential to making the organizational decisions you'll need to make. Your purpose drives your fundraising efforts and your program planning. Without a clearly stated purpose, you'll have a difficult time explaining why your organization exists, a fundamental requirement when asking for money, recruiting board members, hiring and motivating staff, and publicizing your activities.

When thinking of your purpose, think of the end result you want. What would you like to see happen? What would the world (or your community) be like if your organization succeeded?

The next step is deciding how you're going to accomplish your purpose.

Describing how you work

Mission statements usually include a phrase describing the methods your organization will use to accomplish its purpose. There's more than one way to achieve your aim. Think about the activities and programs your organization will provide to achieve its purpose.

It's easy to confuse ends with methods. Providing a program is a method, not an end. The end (or desired result) you seek may be to ensure that all high school students have an equal opportunity to attend college. Your methods may include providing tutoring, offering scholarships, and promoting the value of a college education, to name a few.

You don't want to be so specific that you have to rewrite your mission statement every time you add a new program, but you should state how your organization will fulfill its purpose. Will you focus on providing services to your clients, or will you be involved primarily with public education? If you plan to do both, say so.

Putting the beneficiaries on a pedestal

If you've determined your purpose, you probably know the primary beneficiaries of your activities. The mission statement should include this information. If your programs are aimed at families, for example, make that clear in your statement.

Some organizations have a more general audience than others. If your purpose is preserving historic buildings, what group is the beneficiary of this activity? It could be current and future residents of a city, a county, or even a state. Again, thinking of who will benefit helps to focus organizational activities.

Adding your organizational values

People who work together in a nonprofit organization tend to share the same core values and beliefs. Nonprofits may be organized around religious principles, a certain philosophy of treatment, a belief in the extraterrestrial, or the benefits of eating four meals a day.

Whatever you believe, it's an important part of the passion that fuels your nonprofit. Include a phrase in your mission statement about your organizational values. Doing so helps remind you (and lets others know) why you're doing what you're doing.

Envisioning your future

Vision statements have become popular in recent years due in large part to the popularity of *The Fifth Discipline: The Art and Practice of the Learning Organization* by Peter M. Senge. Although vision statements can describe a future desired condition as a result of the organization's activities, they are more typically applied to the organization itself.

Simply put, a vision statement is your dream of what your organization can become. Usually, the statement includes words like "the best," "recognized as a leader," or "become financially stable." A common failing of vision statements is that they're often unrealistic.

Here's an example of a vision statement from a fictitious agricultural policy think tank.

> The ABC Agricultural Economics Institute is an organization that will continue to encourage excellence in its staff by providing opportunities for communication, collaboration, and professional development. The institute's research projects and position statements on agricultural matters will be widely reported in the media and referred to in the setting of state and national agriculture policy.

Some nonprofits include their vision statements in their mission statements, and others don't. We believe that holding a dream is a good thing and that there's some truth to statement, "If you can't conceive of doing something, you can't do it." Still, we encourage you not to spend an inordinate amount of time shaping your vision statement. Focusing on concrete ends and means is more important.

Writing broad, writing narrow

Narrow mission statements are best for organizations that work within a limited geographical area and have a single, specific purpose. But what if your vision is broader than your county? What if you hope to expand your services to a regional, state, national, or even global level?

We recommend starting in the most focused way possible and growing the organization. So, for example, if you hope to establish counseling services across the nation for parents of children who have learning disabilities, beginning close to home is the best approach. Get your program going in your hometown before branching out to other areas.

The narrower your mission statement, the easier it is to convey your organization's purpose and activities. If you start out with a mission to provide counseling service to every parent in the United States who has a child with a learning disability, you'll likely run into trouble. You're trying to run before you can walk.

Mission statements can always be changed. As your organization achieves success locally and you determine that it's time to expand, you'll probably want to review your mission anyway as a part of your organizational planning process. That's the time to consider setting a broader mission.

Writing long, writing short

In keeping with our notion that a mission statement should be easily expressed, we tend to favor short, pithy statements over long, rambling ones.

We understand, however, that some organizations want to describe their goals and programs more fully than what can be captured in a single short paragraph. For those organizations, we suggest that you begin your mission statement with a one-paragraph summary that states simply what your non-profit hopes to accomplish and how it plans to do it. You may want to prepare your longer statement first and then go back and distill the essence of your mission into a short, succinct paragraph.

This is a little like having your cake and eating it, too. Treat your pithy first paragraph as you would an executive summary of a longer report. That way, you'll still have a short, clear statement to use when you need it.

Writing the Mission Statement

Before writing the final draft, get input from everyone involved. You want to hear as many ideas as possible, and you want everyone to agree on the essence of the organization's mission. But when it comes to putting words on paper, choose your best writer and turn her loose.

We're not fans of committee-written prose. We've sat in meetings at which verb choice and the placement of commas were discussed without apparent end. The result of such efforts is usually obscure prose that requires several readings to interpret the meaning.

Your mission statement is something that you carry around with you, in your head and in brochures. You want to be able to explain quickly and succinctly what your organization does. If you have to pull out a book to explain it, your audience is going to lose interest fast.

Working in a group

If you're starting a nonprofit with a group of people, everyone needs to agree on the mission statement. In this case, we recommend a meeting to solicit input from everyone. The biggest advantage to this kind of group activity is achieving full buy-in from everyone involved. After all, you want people to believe and accept the organization's mission statement. If they don't, they probably won't stay around to help.

You probably already have a good idea of your purpose. The task before you is to refine that idea so it's simply stated in a few words.

Bring a few prewritten suggestions to the group meeting. Present them as drafts to the group and ask for feedback. If your group is larger than five or six people, consider bringing in an experienced group facilitator who will guide the discussion so that everyone's ideas are heard and the discussion remains on track.

Drafting the statement

The best advice we have about the language used in a mission statement is to stay away from jargon and flowery rhetoric. Also avoid the buzzwords that are currently popular in your field. In fact, this is good advice in any kind of writing — grant proposals, memos, letters, and so on. You don't want your audience scratching their heads and wondering, "What does that mean?"

Here's an example of a vague, unclear mission statement:

> The Good Food Society works to maximize the utilization of nutritious food groups to beneficially help all persons in their existence and health by proclaiming the good benefits of balanced nutrition.

You probably get the idea that this organization wants us to have better eating habits so that we can enjoy better health. But try reciting this to someone whom you're trying to convince to contribute to your organization. Can you say tongue-tied?

Long, multisyllabic words do not make a mission statement more impressive. If anything, they have the opposite effect. Instead of the preceding statement, try something like this:

> Believing in the value of good nutrition, the Good Food Society aims to improve public health by providing information about the benefits of a balanced diet to parents of school-age children through its public education programs.

This mission statement may not be perfect, but it states the organization's values, its long-term goal, the targeted group, and a general method for accomplishing the goal.

The statement also suggests that the Good Food Society has given some thought to how to best accomplish its mission — that is, to aim its information campaigns at parents, who presumably have some control over the food their children eat. The implied strategy is that if good eating habits are established in childhood, they will carry over into the child's adult life.

Giving your statement the elevator test

Imagine that you're riding in an elevator with someone who knows nothing about your nonprofit. You have 15 seconds to describe your organization's purpose and activities. Doing so is easy if you have a clear, short mission statement. Even if you have a longer mission statement, develop a 50- to 75-word spiel that you can recite from memory.

Our point is that mission statements should be used, not written and then stuck in a drawer somewhere and pulled out only when you're writing a grant proposal.

Getting Buy-In for Your Mission Statement

We talk a bit about buy-in in the section "Working in a group," earlier in this chapter, and we discuss it at even more length in Chapter 9. The important thing to remember is that the more involved people are in creating a mission statement, the more they will invest and believe in it.

When the founder is one person

All new nonprofits have founders. If you're setting out to start a nonprofit on your own, you'll soon discover that you need to gather more people around you. You need a board of directors and volunteers to help you move forward. We suggest that you begin by finding people who share your values and, if not your passion, at least your desire to accomplish your aims.

Bring these people together to discuss your mission. Even an hour or two spent talking about what your organization can do will help you and your supporters come together around a common theme.

When the founder is a group

If you've already assembled a group and everyone has agreed that it's time to incorporate and seek tax-exempt status, creating the mission statement should be one of the first things you do.

Having a group of like-minded people together gives you an advantage because you probably have identified your board of directors and key volunteers. But starting a nonprofit with a preformed group also carries some potential pitfalls. What happens, for example, if members of the group have different priorities?

We know of a community-based group that wanted to start a neighborhood health center focusing on environmental health risks in the community. The group hoped to provide health screening services and public education about local environmental risks and to encourage local government to clean up toxic areas in the community.

The challenge this group faced was the different perspectives held by its different members. School-based participants wanted to focus on children and respiratory problems caused by the environment. Another faction became involved because its interest was in early detection of breast cancer. And a third faction believed that prostate cancer screening was of paramount importance.

What was the solution? This group decided to make its first priority the establishment of a neighborhood meeting place where information about environmental factors in the community and all associated health risks could be presented. The group also scheduled a series of town hall meetings at which neighborhood residents could express concerns about environmental health risks and get answers to their questions.

The school-based faction had to pull back on its initial plan to provide one-to-one counseling to children and their parents about respiratory ailments in the schools. At the same time, the breast and prostate cancer prevention advocates agreed to assign a lower priority to the door-to-door campaigns that they had originally insisted be implemented as soon as possible.

Our point is that different factions almost always need to compromise in order to agree on a mission that enables the organization to use its limited resources in the most effective way. As the organization grows and more resources become available, more programs that address the concerns of the individual founders can be implemented.

Speaking of your mission . . .

An effective mission statement doesn't have to be fancy, just clear and complete. Here are a few good examples:

From a health clinic: "Our organizational mission is to establish and maintain a family health clinic to ensure access to affordable health care for the residents of Lincoln County. The clinic will achieve its mission by providing primary health care on a sliding fee basis, practicing preventive medicine, and promoting healthy lifestyles through a county-wide public education campaign."

From an organization promoting political awareness: "In order to ensure full participation in our country's political process, we inform citizens about the benefits and responsibilities of exercising their rights in a democratic society.

We fulfill our mission by publishing and distributing a magazine that provides examples of successful grass-roots civic activities and informational articles about collaboration among groups with diverse interests. We also sponsor town hall meetings at which issues of citizen participation are discussed."

From a public middle school: "Our mission is to help our students to be well prepared for the high school curriculum and to instill the desire to be lifelong learners by providing our sixth, seventh, and eighth grade students with teachers who are skilled in classroom instruction and who themselves demonstrate the benefits of continuous learning far beyond their formal education."

Getting to the compromise

For groups that are working together to establish a nonprofit organization, we recommend that you find an outside facilitator to guide the group through the inevitable discussions about priorities and the direction of the new organization. Finding a neutral person who can bring an outsider's perspective to the group's deliberations is almost essential. You can do it yourselves, but you'll be happier (and spend less time in meetings) if you get someone to help you.

See Chapter 12 for suggestions on finding help. If you aren't near a nonprofit support organization, a nonprofit that helps other nonprofits with technical assistance, ask other nonprofits near you for suggestions.

Using the statement

You need to have your mission well formulated before you take formal steps to start your nonprofit because the mission statement will appear in your bylaws. You also use your mission statement to explain your charitable purpose when you apply for tax-exempt status.

Remember that mission statements aren't carved in stone. They can be changed. We don't recommend wholesale changes in your basic purpose, but you can alter it to either narrow or broaden your organization's focus, depending on your progress toward achieving the mission and the needs you see in your community.

Nonprofits should periodically review their mission statements, certainly at the beginning of any organizational planning process and perhaps more often, to be sure that they are on track and headed in the right direction.

Looking at Your Own Mission

If you're thinking of working for a nonprofit or joining a board of directors, reviewing the mission statement of the organization in question should be high on your priority list. We can think of few things more difficult than working on behalf of an organization whose mission you do not support wholeheartedly.

Believing in the mission is essential in order for board members and staff to be effective in communicating the nonprofit's purpose to funders and contributors. If you have doubts about what the organization is trying to accomplish, move on to another project.

Of course, we're not saying that people need to put their lives on the line for their nonprofit's mission, but to do the best job, you must believe deeply in what your nonprofit hopes to achieve and the methods it uses to achieve it.

Think carefully about your own values and how they fit with the values of the organization. If you have an aversion to getting loads of junk mail and unsolicited telephone calls, don't sign up with an organization that depends on these tried-and-true fundraising techniques for the bulk of its contributed income.

In many cases, nonprofit workers have a better chance of job satisfaction because the goals of a nonprofit go beyond making money. Spend some time thinking about what you want before you take the leap.

Chapter 4

Incorporating and Applying for a Tax Exemption

*I*f you want to provide services as a nonprofit organization, you need to set up the legal structure for your organization and apply for its tax exemption. Before you begin providing services and fulfilling your mission, you must take care of those jobs, which require attention to detail and ample planning.

This two-step process usually consists of forming a nonprofit corporation under the laws of your state and then submitting a form to the Internal Revenue Service requesting that your organization be considered tax exempt. Remember, tax exempt does not mean that you won't have to pay any taxes. You won't have to pay taxes on the organization's income, and donors who contribute to your organization can claim a tax deduction. But if your nonprofit employs staff, it will be required to pay payroll taxes like any employer. And your liability for sales and property taxes depends on your state and local laws. Also, if your nonprofit has income that's unrelated to its charitable purpose, you'll be required to pay taxes on that income.

We're not attorneys, and the information in this chapter is not meant to be legal advice. We provide a guide to the incorporation and exemption process and give you suggestions about where you can go for help. Although many nonprofits are formed without the aid of legal counsel, we think that consulting an attorney is a good idea, even if it's only to review your work. After all, you'll be taking on legal responsibilities. Why not use professional help?

Creating a New "Person" — the Corporation

Thinking of a corporation as a living, breathing organism requires a stretch of the imagination, but doing so helps you to understand that a corporation is a separate entity from the human beings who create it. In fact, one advantage of creating a corporation is that the individuals who govern and work for it are separate from the abstract thing they create. Although board members can be liable for the corporation's actions if they don't exercise their duties and responsibilities in a prudent way, in most cases corporations protect individuals from personal liability. So it's helpful to think of a corporation as apart from the people who start it because, well, it is.

Also remember that you're creating an entity that's expected to continue in perpetuity. In other words, the corporation you create will go on living after you decide to do something else or after your death. Corporations can be closed or dissolved, but you must take legal steps to do so. You can't just take down your shingle and walk away.

The first legal step in creating a nonprofit organization almost always is forming a corporation. We say "almost always" because exceptions exist. In the United States, for example, associations and trusts also can operate as tax-exempt nonprofit organizations. And charitable groups with under $5,000 in annual revenues, as well as churches, are not required to apply for tax exemption. We say more about associations and trusts later in this chapter, but for now, we want to focus on the most common legal structure for nonprofit organizations: the corporation.

Looking to your state law

In the United States, corporations are created and regulated under the laws of the state in which they're formed. Although there are more similarities than differences in how a corporation is formed from state to state, you do need to create your nonprofit so that it conforms to the peculiarities of your state. Some states, for example, require a minimum of three directors; others require only one.

On the CD accompanying this book, we list information about where to go to get specifics about incorporating in your state. Usually, the secretary of state's office handles incorporations. Some states have an incorporation package that includes the forms you need to file.

A preamble about articles of incorporation and bylaws

We say more about articles and bylaws later in this chapter and on the CD, but we want to give you a little preliminary information about the governing documents of a corporation. Think of a corporation as a tiny government with a constitution and laws. When you prepare corporate articles and bylaws, you're setting down the rules under which the organization will operate.

The *articles of incorporation* make up the document that creates the organization. It names the organization and describes its reason for existence. In the case of a nonprofit corporation, it specifies that the corporation will not be used to create profit for its directors and gives the nonprofit's location and the geographic range of its operations. The articles are signed by the corporation's incorporators, usually three people, who may or may not end up being directors of the organization.

Bylaws specify how directors will be elected, the length of their terms, the officers and their duties, the number of meetings to be held, who is and isn't a member of the corporation, how many members or directors are required to be in attendance for a quorum to be present, the rules for director attendance at board meetings, and how the bylaws may be amended. They also may list the standing committees of the board and grant or limit particular powers of the trustees.

As you draft these documents, remember that you're creating the legal rules under which your nonprofit will operate. Both articles of incorporation and bylaws may be changed by following the rules of the state (in the case of articles of incorporation) or the bylaws.

A word about members of a corporation

Corporations may have members. They may even have different classes of members — voting and nonvoting, for example. Depending on state law, you usually have the option to create membership conditions in either the articles or the bylaws. If you're going to have members, we recommend adding these conditions in the bylaws, which are easier to amend than the articles of incorporation.

In general, unless you have a very good reason to do so, having members in your corporation adds additional responsibilities to the governance of the organization. If you have members, for instance, you need to have membership meetings, probably at least one per year, and the members will be involved in choosing directors for the organization.

There are good reasons for getting as many people involved in your organization as possible, and having members is one way to achieve this goal. If your nonprofit is a neighborhood improvement group, for example, including as many people as possible in the governance of the organization may be important.

Many nonprofit organizations have "members," with membership cards and special rates on admissions to performances or exhibits. Don't confuse this kind of membership, which is a marketing and fundraising strategy, with legal membership in the corporation. You're free to start a membership program of this type without amending your bylaws or your articles of incorporation.

Choosing your nonprofit's name

Choosing a name may be one of the most important things you do. A nonprofit's name is a little like a mission statement. It should suggest the types of programs and services it offers and the people it serves.

If your programs provide home health services to persons over 65, don't name your nonprofit something generic like "Services for the People." Stay away from names that are so abstract that they have no meaning at all. A name like the Reenergizing Society prompts more questions than it answers. What or who is being reenergized? How are clients being reenergized? And why are they are being reenergized? Use concrete, descriptive terms.

To avoid possible embarrassment, check the acronym that results from your organizational name. The Associated Workers For Union Labor, for example, is not a title you want to abbreviate on your letterhead.

Also be careful that you don't select a name that's easily confused with that of another organization. Before you decide on a name, do an Internet search to see whether any other companies or organizations already have that name. The state agency that accepts your application for incorporation has procedures for ensuring that two corporations do not end up with exactly the same name. These procedures won't help you uncover organizations in other states or names that are similar and could be confused with your name. To help ensure that you have a distinctive name, you may want to include the name of the city or region where your organization is located — Tap Dancers of Happy Valley, for example.

If you find a name you like for your organization but then decide that you're not totally pleased with it, you can register a DBA, which stands for "doing business as." The original corporate name will continue to be your organization's legal name, but you can use the DBA name on letterhead, annual reports, and press releases — everywhere except legal documents. A county office usually handles this type of transaction. Check your local laws.

Writing the Articles of Incorporation

We assume that you have the papers you need from the appropriate state office. (If not, use the state-by-state list on the CD for contact information.) That office may even have sent sample articles of incorporation and instructions about how to prepare your own. Pay close attention to the instructions. Follow them step by step. It may be as simple as filling in the blanks. In the following sections, we give you some general guidance on drafting your articles.

The articles need to be signed by the incorporators of the corporation. In some states, three incorporators are needed; in others, you need only one. If the articles need to be notarized, the signatures must be added in the presence of a notary public. Most states charge a fee for filing for incorporation. Include a check or money order with the articles if one is required.

Before the articles

Put a heading on your articles so that they can be identified. The heading should be something like this:

Articles of Incorporation of the XYZ Theater Company, Inc.

Sometimes you're required to add a short paragraph after the heading stating that the incorporators adopt the following articles under the [cite the state code number under which you're filing] of [give the state name].

Article 1

This is where you insert the name you worked so hard to choose. It's as simple as writing the phrase, "The name of the corporation is the XYZ Theater Company, Inc."

Could it be any easier?

Article 11

Some states require that you state that the corporation is perpetual. If yours does, put it here and say something like this:

This corporation shall exist in perpetuity unless dissolved.

Chances are that the state will give you the language to use if it's needed.

Article III

This is a good place to state the organization's purpose. This article is probably the most important because state authorities and the Internal Revenue Service will review it to help them determine whether your organization qualifies as a charitable entity.

Remember that 501(c)(3) organizations must be organized for a charitable, religious, educational, literary, or scientific purpose. You've already done your mission statement, right? So it shouldn't be too hard to state your purpose. Using the XYZ Theater Company, Inc. as an example, you might say this:

> This corporation is established to provide theatrical productions of new and classic plays. It also will work to strengthen the theater arts, support emerging playwrights, and encourage persons to enter the acting profession by providing scholarships and grants to theater arts students and by promoting the benefits of dramatic entertainment to the general public.

This article must also include a statement of exempt purpose under the IRS code:

> This corporation is organized exclusively for charitable, literary, and educational purposes, including for such purposes, the making of distributions to organizations that qualify under section 501(c)(3) of the Internal Revenue Code, or any corresponding section of any future federal tax code.

You must state that no proceeds of the corporation will enrich any individual, except that reasonable compensation may be paid for services to the corporation. Also add that if the corporation is dissolved, any assets remaining will be distributed to another corporation serving a similar purpose and qualifying as a tax-exempt, charitable organization under the provisions of 501(c)(3) of the Internal Revenue Code.

This may be the most critical article for getting your nonprofit corporation established and, ultimately, approved for tax exemption by the IRS. If your state doesn't provide good examples of the language required in this article, ask a lawyer about the requirements in your state.

Article IV

All articles of incorporation identify the name and address of an *agent of the corporation,* someone to whom mail can be addressed. This address is considered the address of the corporation until changed. Include the person's name and street address. Post office boxes usually aren't allowed to be used as addresses.

This person, by the way, doesn't need to be a director or incorporator of the corporation. The agent of the corporation can even be your attorney.

Article V

Put the initial directors' names and addresses in this article. Most nonprofits start with three initial directors. If you're incorporating in a state that requires only one director, we still recommend having three.

Article VI

List the incorporators' names and addresses in this article. *Incorporator* simply refers to the person or persons who are creating the corporation. Often, the incorporator and the initial director are one and the same. And again, whether you need one or more depends on your state requirements.

Article VII

If you want your corporation to have members, here's where you define the qualifications for membership. You can define classes of membership — voting and nonvoting, for instance — but we don't recommend it. If you don't want members, all you have to say is, "This corporation has no members." Better yet, refer the question to your bylaws, which are easier to amend if you change your mind. If that's what you decide to do, you can say, "Members in this corporation are defined in the bylaws."

Corporate members are not the same as the subscribers to a PBS station or the members of a museum or zoo, for example. Members of a corporation have the right to participate in governing the organization.

Article VIII

You may not need an Article VIII. Some forms have a blank space here to add additional provisions. We don't recommend doing so unless you're sure you know what you're doing. Maybe your group is adamant that all future directors must be elected by 85 percent of the membership. Such a provision probably would ensure that you'd never elect new directors, but who knows? Use this blank space cautiously.

Signed, sealed, and delivered

The articles must be signed by the incorporator(s) and mailed to the appropriate state office with the required fee, if any, enclosed. Some states offer an opportunity to expedite processing for a surcharge. Usually only the original articles are mailed to the state office, but sometimes one or more additional copies are required.

Your next step is to wait. It's hard to say how long the response will take — it depends on the efficiency of the state office and the volume of incorporation papers it receives.

Creating a nonprofit corporation alone doesn't make your organization tax exempt. You also need to get recognition from the Internal Revenue Service (see the section "Going for Your Tax Exemption," later in this chapter) before your nonprofit is a "real" nonprofit.

If the articles are in order and your corporate name passes muster, you'll receive a certified copy of the articles, stamped with an official seal. Guard this piece of paper as if it were gold. Make copies and put the original away for safekeeping in a fireproof box. You've taken the first step toward starting your nonprofit.

When you receive your certified copy of the articles of incorporation, you may want to purchase a corporate seal from your local stationery shop. These neat little gizmos emboss a seal containing the name of your organization and the date of incorporation on a piece of paper. Sometimes, formal papers such as property leases call for a corporate seal. You can probably can get along without one, but we think they're fun to have.

Getting Your EIN

The first thing to do after you complete your incorporation is to apply to the Internal Revenue Service for an EIN, or Employer Identification Number. Even if you don't plan on hiring employees anytime soon, you need this number for your application for tax exemption and for all your state and federal reports. The EIN is a little like a Social Security number for organizations. It will be attached to your nonprofit forever. No fee is required to get your EIN.

Getting this number is easy. Submit IRS Form SS-4, which you can download at www.irs.ustreas.gov/prod/bus_info/eo/eo-tkit.html. You can also find a copy on the CD accompanying this book. As IRS forms go, this one is simple and straightforward and only one page long.

The name of the applicant is not your name; it's the name of your new organization. As with the incorporation papers, you need to identify an individual as the principal officer and include his Social Security number on the form. If your organization is a church or church-controlled organization, check that box in section 8a. If it's not, check the Other Nonprofit Organization box. Specify what sort of nonprofit organization you are. In most cases, "charitable" should suffice.

You'll be asked in what state your organization is incorporated and when the business was started. Use the date on your incorporation papers as the start date. You'll also be asked how many employees you expect to hire in the next 12 months. If you don't expect to hire anyone, put in a zero. Your principal activity (line 15) will be charitable. Also state the general area in which you'll be working, such as social services, education, or the arts.

The IRS estimates that you'll receive your EIN in four to five weeks. If you want a faster turnaround, you can take advantage of the Tele-Tin program. Call 800-829-1040 to find the correct phone number for your area. The person named as the principal officer on the form must make the call. Be sure that you have completed the SS-4 Form before you call. An IRS officer will take your information over the phone and assign an EIN to your organization. You must fax or mail the form to the appropriate IRS office within 24 hours of making the call.

Even if your organization is an unincorporated association or a trust, you still need an EIN number if you plan to apply for a charitable tax exemption.

Developing Your Organizational Bylaws

Bylaws are the rules by which your organization will operate. As with articles of incorporation, different states have different requirements about what needs to be included in the bylaws, so it's important to contact the agency in your state to get the specific information you need.

In general, bylaws guide the activities of your organization and the procedures of your board of directors — how many directors, the length of their terms, how they will be elected, what constitutes a quorum, and so on.

Bylaws are divided into articles just like the articles of incorporation. Because more detail is included, however, the articles themselves are divided into sections (and subsections, if needed) to address various aspects of the articles. Bylaws can always be changed. Almost always, however, amending the bylaws requires more than a simple majority; usually two-thirds of the directors must agree to a bylaw change.

If you review the bylaws of ten different organizations, you'll find variation in the order in which articles are presented. You may find the board of directors specified in Article III or Article V. Bylaws also vary in how specifically they spell out what's required. Some bylaws specify the number and type of standing committees; others give this responsibility to the board president.

If you don't address a particular question in your bylaws — setting a quorum, for example — most states have a default position in their code that applies to the governing of nonprofit corporations.

Check the Chapter 4 contents on the CD for a general guide to creating bylaws for your new nonprofit.

Holding Your First Board Meeting

Your organization's first board meeting is more or less a formality, but documenting it is important because it officially kicks off your new nonprofit corporation. If you've named directors in your articles of incorporation, they should be present at the meeting. The first order of business is to elect the officers of the organization. A resolution should be passed authorizing the board or its designate to open the necessary bank accounts, because you'll need a copy of this resolution to open an account.

Minutes of the meeting should be prepared and kept with your articles of incorporation. We say more about keeping records in Chapter 5, but this is a good time to start a *board book* — a loose-leaf notebook containing a copy of your articles of incorporation, bylaws, and the minutes of your first board meeting and every board meeting to follow.

Applying for Tax Exemption

The final step in becoming a tax-exempt charitable organization is to apply for tax exemption from the Internal Revenue Service.

You request what's known as a *letter of determination* — a letter from the IRS stating that it has determined that your organization qualifies as a tax-exempt organization under the applicable sections of the IRS code. Send copies of this letter to foundations, government agencies, and state tax authorities — in short, to anyone to whom you need to prove that yours is a tax-exempt nonprofit organization.

Take a deep breath and relax! You're about to do battle with an IRS form, Form 1023 to be exact, the application for recognition of your organization's tax-exempt status. We include a copy of the form and its instructions on the CD accompanying this book. If you prefer, you can download this material directly from the IRS Web site at www.irs.ustreas.gov/prod/bus_info/ eo/eo-tkit.html or order through the mail by phoning 800-TAX-FORM.

Note: Form 1023 is the application for 501(c)(3) organizations. If you're using this book for another type of nonprofit organization, you need to submit Form 1024.

Getting along until the exemption comes

After you file your application, your organization will be in never-never land for a while. You don't have your exemption yet. Although making an accurate prediction is difficult, the IRS can take between two and six months to act on your application. The process may take longer if the application is returned for corrections.

During this period, your organization can operate and even solicit contributions. You must tell donors that you have applied for a tax exemption. Assuming that your application is approved, if your organization is newly incorporated (15 months or less), your tax-exempt status will be retroactive to the date of incorporation. If your organization had been operating for a longer period before you submitted Form 1023, the exemption may be retroactive only to the date on which the application was submitted.

Who doesn't need to apply

If your organization is a church, a church auxiliary, or an association of churches, you don't need to apply for tax-exempt status. Also, if your non-profit had an income of less than $5,000 in any previous year in which you operated, and if you do not expect your revenue to grow beyond this limit, you're not required to submit this application.

Keep in mind that you still may apply for tax exemption even though you're not required to do so. Having a determination letter from the IRS acknowledging your tax-exempt status has some advantages. For example, you need to show proof of your exemption to get a bulk mail permit from the U.S. Postal Service. It's also a public acknowledgment that contributions to your organization are deductible to the donor.

Collecting the other materials

In addition to the completed application, you need to submit conformed (exact) copies of your articles of incorporation and the certificate of incorporation if your state provides one. If bylaws have been written for your organization, submit them, too, but bylaws alone don't qualify as organizing documents.

Present this material as attachments to your application. Put your organization's name, address, and EIN (Employer Identification Number) on each attachment and specify the section of the application that each application refers to. The application package you receive from the IRS has a checklist of the materials that must be included.

Every nonprofit applying for tax exemption must have an organizing document. Usually, this document is the articles of incorporation, because most nonprofit organizations are incorporated. However, in the United States, associations and trusts also may apply for and receive tax-exempt status. An organizing document for an association may be the articles of association or a constitution; a trust is usually organized by a trust indenture or deed.

Paying the fee

The fee for filing IRS Form 1023 is $500 for organizations that have had or anticipate having revenue of over $10,000 per year. If your organization has been operating without a tax exemption and has income of less than $10,000 per year, or if you anticipate having less than $10,000 per year in the future, the fee is set at $150.

Obtain IRS Form 8718 (`www.irs.ustreas.gov/prod/bus_info/eo/eo-tkit.html`) to submit the fee. (Fees may change at any time, so be sure to get the latest form.) Attach the form to your application, along with your check or money order for the correct amount. If you choose to pay the lesser amount, sign the form to certify that the organization income is, in fact, under $10,000 or is expected to be under that amount.

We don't recommend trying to save $350 on the application fee unless you're very certain that revenues to your organization will remain under $10,000. We understand that the $350 difference in the fees can loom very large for a start-up nonprofit, but why play with fire? Although the penalties for misstating your income aren't clear, we wouldn't want you to find out the hard way.

Understanding the difference between public charities and private foundations

Public charities and private foundations are both 501(c)(3) organizations, but you should understand the important differences between them before you begin completing the application. Private foundations have different reporting requirements than public charities and may be required to pay excise taxes on their income. Many private foundations are set up by families or individuals to work toward their philanthropic goals. Special rules are in place to ensure that this system is not abused.

Contributions of private foundations are deductible, but not to the same extent as contributions to public charities. Actually, this issue isn't too important to most of us because the limits on deductibility are high for both. A donor can claim charitable deductions up to 50 percent of adjusted gross income for contributions to a public charity, but only up to 30 percent for contributions to a private foundation. Few people are able or willing to contribute more than 1 or 2 percent of their income, so we doubt that you would lose many contributions because of this limitation. Still, the reporting requirements are more onerous, and then there's that pesky excise tax.

So one important determination that the IRS will make based on your application for tax-exempt status is whether your organization is classified as a public charity or a private foundation. Keep this in mind because, until proven otherwise, 501(c)(3) organizations applying to the IRS are considered private foundations. For more information about this issue, see "Establishing public charity status."

Establishing public charity status

Several measures applied by the IRS determine whether an organization is a public charity. Generally, for a nonprofit to be considered a public charity, it must receive one-third of its revenues from public sources. It's complicated, and we can't cover all the nuances and technicalities. But, fundamentally, it comes down to how much of your total organizational income you get from the public.

A tale of two nonprofits

Imagine two nonprofits. The first is a small, storefront historical museum that intends to get most of its revenues from grants and contributions from the public. The second is a chamber orchestra that also receives grants and contributions but gets half its income from ticket sales and performance fees.

Both organizations probably can qualify for public charity status, but under two different IRS code sections. The museum must apply for public charity status under IRS code section 509(a)(1). The orchestra must apply under section 509(a)(2).

Both of these organizations will undergo what's referred to as the public support test. To pass this test, the museum needs to demonstrate, over a four-year average, that one-third of its revenue comes from contributions from the general public, support from government agencies, or grants from organizations that get their support from the public, such as United Way. So if your museum's average revenue is $60,000 per year and at least $20,000 a year comes from donations, state grants, and support from United Way, you're home free.

But what if that's not possible? Fortunately, the organization may be able to qualify under another test that gives more leeway on the percentage of public support. Under this test, only 10 percent of total revenue needs to come from those public categories. But the organization also must demonstrate that it has an ongoing fundraising program that's reaching to the public for more donations. Other factors also are considered. If the museum's contributions come in many small gifts rather than a few large ones, it's more likely to be given public charity status. It's even better if the museum's board of directors is broadly representative of the community. And if the organization makes its facility available to the general public, as we're sure this museum would, that's another feather in its cap.

The chamber orchestra is expecting contributions, too, but more of its income will come from selling tickets to its concert series and from fees it receives from performing at schools and retirement homes. For nonprofits that expect to generate significant income from fees for services related to their exempt purpose, the IRS allows those fees to be calculated as public support. In other words, contributions from the public *and* their earned income must make up one-third of their revenues. The orchestra needs to be sure that it gets less than one-third of its total income from business unrelated to its charitable purpose and investments. As long as it maintains this distribution of income, it should keep its public charity status.

Big fat gifts may come with tax strings

You should be aware of some of the potential pitfalls of large gifts. Suppose that you've found a benefactor who wants to support your work and makes a gift of $50,000 to your nonprofit. Nice, huh? Well, maybe not. A single gift can't be counted toward your public support if it's more than 2 percent of your total income over the previous four years. At $60,000 a year for four years, your total is $240,000. Your major gift of $50,000 makes up almost 21 percent of this total. Because of the 2 percent rule, only $4,800 of the $50,000 can be counted as public support. So now your income is $240,000 plus $50,000 for a total of $290,000. And the revenue that you can consider as public support is $80,000 plus $4,800 for a total of $84,800. Your average public support over the four-year period has dropped to less than 30 percent, or less than one-third.

What should you do? Give the money back? Not necessarily. There's a chance that this large gift can be considered an unusual grant. In other words, it's not typical of your general public support, and you could ask the IRS officials to exclude it from their calculations when they review your financial report for that year.

When you get to Part III of Form 1023, you need to check a box indicating which public charity classification you seek. For Question 9, if you think that your nonprofit is more like the museum, a (509)(a)(1), you'll probably want to select the "h" box; if you're closer to the chamber orchestra, a (509)(a)(2), the "i" box is yours. If you're not sure — and, frankly, who would be? — you can let the IRS decide which category you fit by selecting the "j" box. Boxes "a" through "g" are for churches, schools, and other specialized classes. If your organization is one of those, be sure to include the appropriate schedule along with your application.

Every IRS rule has an exception or two, and qualifying as a public charity is, well, no exception. Churches, schools, hospitals, public safety testing organizations, and a few others are automatically considered public charities. If you have an intense interest in this, read Chapter 3 of IRS Publication 557. If you think that your organization falls into one of these categories, check the appropriate box (a through g) and answer the questions on the appropriate schedule included with Form 1023. But we don't recommend doing so unless you're absolutely certain that you know what you're doing.

Take schools as an example. To apply as a school, you have to submit Schedule B. Your school must provide regular instruction and have a student body and a faculty. In other words, you can't just start an organization and call it a school.

Describing your activities

You have almost a full page on Form 1023 to explain in some detail your charitable activities and how you plan to carry them out. You must provide more detail here than you have in your articles of incorporation or in your mission statement. The IRS wants you to list what you're going to do in order of importance, approximately how much time you will devote to each activity, and how each activity fulfills your charitable purpose.

When you're filling out this form, you haven't started operating yet, so you're simply listing *proposed* activities. If you've done a business plan, refer to the plan to make sure that you cover all your activities. If you've been operating your organization, explain what you've been doing and how it relates to your charitable purpose.

A nonprofit that provides family counseling and public education about strengthening families might say something like this:

> The charitable purpose of the Claremont Family Counseling Center is to promote the benefits of positive family interaction in the following ways:
>
> The primary activity will be to provide professional family counselor services, on a sliding scale fee basis, to families in Claremont County and surrounding counties. No family will be refused service due to the inability to pay for services, and services will be available to all members of the general public. (75%)
>
> The center will maintain a Web site that provides referral information, suggestions for strengthening family interactions, reference materials concerning families, and e-mail and bulletin board posting capabilities. (10%)
>
> Staff members will present information about families to local schools, service clubs, and churches through multimedia presentations. (10%)
>
> Brochures will be prepared and distributed on request. (5%)

When to file

Don't put off filing for your exemption. If you file within 15 months of the time your organization was founded, your exemption will be retroactive to your founding date. Filing sooner rather than later makes life simpler.

There are always exceptions, of course. For example, suppose your organization is a church, or has had less than $5,000 in annual revenues while it's been in existence, or has been operating under a group exemption letter from a parent organization. In other words, if your organization wasn't required to file earlier, you can indicate which category you fall into, and you should be just fine.

But if you procrastinate, the situation gets more complicated. You may be able to receive an exemption retroactive only to the date of your filing. If you've had no contributions or income, this probably isn't a big loss. However, if you've had contributions prior to filing for your exemption, those donations won't be deductible for the donor. In addition, your organization may be liable for corporate income taxes on your earlier income. The IRS tries to help by giving you ways to extend the deadline. If you've received bad advice, for example, you may be able to get an extension on your filing date. As a last-gasp measure, the IRS even gives you the option of requesting

501(c)(4) status (for more on this status, see Chapter 2) between the time your organization was formed and the time you filed for your public charity exemption.

But make things as easy as possible. Don't delay in filing Form 1023.

Dealing with financial information

The IRS wants to see financial information. (Surprise, surprise.) For new organizations, this means estimating your income and expenses for three years — the current year and two years following. Making financial projections sends shivers down the backs of many folks, but it's really not that difficult. Ideally, you will have made plans for your nonprofit already, and you can take the figures from your business plan. If you haven't written a business plan, now's a good time to do so. See Chapter 9 for planning information and Chapter 10 for help in creating a budget.

When you estimate your income, keep in mind the requirements for qualifying as a public charity. Diverse sources of income are important, both for qualifying as a 509(a)(1) or (2) organization and for the stability of your nonprofit.

You also need to choose your annual accounting period. This is usually referred as your fiscal year. It can be any 12-month period you desire. Most organizations choose as their fiscal year either the calendar year (January 1 through December 31) or the period from July 1 to June 30. Most government agencies operate on a July 1 through June 30 fiscal year, and nonprofits that get support from government grants and contracts often prefer to operate on the same basis. Some organizations offering services to schools set the fiscal year to correspond with the academic year. But the choice is yours. You can set your fiscal year from November 1 to October 31 if you like.

Your first accounting period doesn't need to be a full 12 months; in fact, it probably won't be. If you form your organization in September and select a calendar year as your fiscal year, your first accounting period will cover only four months, September through December.

If you have an accountant, seek advice about the best accounting period for your organization. Remember that your fiscal year will determine when future reports are due to the IRS, and also when you prepare year-end financial reports for your board of directors. The annual 990 report is due, for example, five and a half months after the close of your fiscal year. So if your fiscal year is the same as the calendar year, the report is due on May 15. If you always spend early May traveling to the Caribbean, you may want to pick another accounting period.

Advance versus definitive rulings

If your nonprofit is new, the IRS has little evidence to determine whether your organization qualifies as a public charity. Therefore, it's not uncommon for newly formed organizations to receive what's known as an advance ruling. If your nonprofit has been operating for less than eight months, an advance ruling is your only option.

An *advance ruling* means that your organization will be treated as a public charity for five years. At the end of that period, the IRS will review your status. If the sources of your revenue qualify you as a public charity, you'll receive a new determination letter recognizing your public charity status as definitive. Getting a definitive ruling doesn't mean that you can go off and do anything you want with your nonprofit, of course. You still need to continue to show the appropriate sources of income, over any four-year period, to maintain public charity status.

Advance rulings may seem tenuous, but they offer nonprofits an opportunity to develop the appropriate revenue streams and to become well-established organizations. Don't be put off by an advance ruling. The IRS isn't picking on you; it's standard operating procedure.

If you've been operating for over eight months, you have the choice of asking for an advance or definitive ruling. If you're in this situation, we suggest that you seek professional advice before making the selection. If you do request an advance ruling, submit two copies of IRS Form 872-C along with your Form 1023 application.

Tackling Form 1023

We assume that you've already looked at Form 1023. Yes, it's long (nine pages!), and yes, it's a little scary. If you can get help from your accountant or attorney, we certainly recommend that you do so. Don't discount getting help from your friends and associates, either. Two heads are usually better than one.

Read the instructions carefully. The application package includes line-by-line explanations as well as the various schedules that you may need to submit if you're applying as a church or school, for example. If a schedule isn't required for your type of nonprofit, don't submit a blank one. Toss it into the round file.

Send the form with all the appropriate attachments and schedules. Don't forget the application fee with its accompanying Form 8718. In fact, that's where you find the address to send the application. Keep a copy of everything for your records. Then take a break! You deserve it.

Chapter 5

Safeguarding Your Nonprofit Status

In This Chapter
- ▶ Making public disclosures
- ▶ Avoiding trouble over pay and politics
- ▶ Preparing IRS Form 990

*K*eeping your nonprofit status isn't hard if you follow the rules. Nonprofit organizations are private organizations, but because they are granted special tax status and presumably are acting on behalf of the public, they're required to disclose more information than privately held for-profit companies are. Nonprofit status is a privilege.

Maybe a good way to think about it is to compare nonprofits to companies that sell shares of stock to the public. These companies must follow the rules and regulations set forth by the Securities and Exchange Commission about disclosing financial information. Nonprofits in the United States must follow the rules of the Internal Revenue Service to make financial information available for public scrutiny. In some cases, state and local governments also have disclosure rules.

Your nonprofit organization can get into trouble with authorities in a few ways. This chapter lays out the reporting requirements that you need to follow and some pitfalls to avoid in order to maintain your 501(c)(3) status. We don't aim to scare you! Just keep good financial records and stick to your mission.

Disclosing What You Need to Disclose

Disclose is a funny word, isn't it? It seems to imply that you're hiding something that must be pried from your clutches. Don't think of it that way. The IRS regulations that lay out the rules for disclosure refer to "the public inspection of information." That's much more genteel.

What information must be disclosed to the public? (Sorry, we can't help our-selves. We like the word.) It's simple, really. It's your three most recent filings of IRS Form 990 and your application for exemption — if you filed for your exemption after July 15, 1987.

If you have a question that this chapter doesn't cover, refer to IRS Publication 557 (www.irs.ustreas.gov/prod/forms_pubs/pubs.html). We also have put a copy of that publication on the CD.

Form 990 is the annual report that you must file with the IRS. We talk more about filing the 990 later in this chapter, but in a nutshell, it's a report of your annual finances and activities as a nonprofit organization. Don't panic! We've filled them out many times and survived.

Current IRS regulations state that the three most recent 990 reports and some attachments to the report must be available for public inspection at the orga-nization's primary place of business during regular business hours. A staff member may be present during the inspection, and copies may be made for the person requesting them. If you make copies on your own copier, you can charge the same as the IRS charges: $1 for the first page and 15 cents for each additional page.

The information provided in this chapter is about 501(c)(3) organizations that are considered public charities. If your organization is a private founda-tion, special disclosure rules apply especially to you. Check with the Council on Foundations (www.cof.org) about disclosure requirements.

If you work out of your home or you really have no primary place of business, you can arrange to meet at a convenient place or mail copies to the person who requested them. You have two weeks to do so. The information also can be requested in writing, and if it is, you have 30 days to respond.

If you applied for your exemption after July 15, 1987, you must include your application for exemption and all the supporting materials submitted with it in the information you make available for inspection. Although the IRS does-n't say so, we assume that this includes your articles of incorporation as well as your bylaws, if they were attached to your application.

It's important to know the rules and regulations about public inspection of non-profit materials, but frankly, in the many years we've been working for nonprof-its, no one has ever asked to see our 990 forms. This doesn't mean that you won't be asked, however. Follow the Boy Scout motto and be prepared.

What you don't need to show

You don't need to reveal your donor list. Donors who contribute over a cer-tain amount must be named on a schedule attached to your 990 report, but this document is excluded from the disclosure requirements.

How to avoid having strangers in your office

You can avoid the hassle of photocopying Form 990 for walk-in visitors by placing the required information on the Web. Yes, even the IRS acknowledges this as an alternative, although the IRS still calls it the World Wide Web. If you do so, be sure that you post an exact copy of the materials, not a summary or a retyped copy. We suppose that you could scan material with a scanner and put it on your Web site as a graphic, but the best way to do it is to put the materials in PDF format by using Acrobat Reader, available from Adobe (www.adobe.com/products/acrobat/readstep.html).

GuideStar (www.guidestar.org) and the National Center for Charitable Statistics (nccs.urban.org/990) are engaged in a joint project to put PDF files of 990 returns on the Web. The California Attorney General's office (http://caag.state.ca.us/charities/index.htm) has a similar project for California nonprofits. Don't count on these projects to take care of your disclosure responsibilities, however. They're works in progress. Remember that you need to make available your three most recent 990 returns and your application for exemption.

The public disclosure rules offer a nice tool for anyone who gets a bee in his bonnet and wants to harass your organization. So if you start getting request after request after request, check with the nearest IRS office. IRS officials have the authority to relieve you of the disclosure responsibilities if they agree that harassment is occurring.

Other items that may remain private include the following:

- ✔ Trade secrets and patents
- ✔ National defense material
- ✔ Communications from the IRS about previous unfavorable rulings or technical advice related to rulings

IRS regulations go into more detail, but we think these three items sum up the major points. If you have a question about an item, consult your attorney or tax adviser.

Also, you don't need to make available board minutes, contracts, or salary information unless these materials are required in filing your 990 return.

Double-checking local law

Check your state and local government requirements about whether your nonprofit must make other information available under local laws. Ensuring the accountability of nonprofit organizations has attracted increasing public and media attention.

San Francisco, for example, requires nonprofit organizations that have contracts with the city with a value of $250,000 or higher to have two board meetings a year that are open to the public. These groups also must make additional financial information available for public inspection.

When You're Paying and Politicking Too Much

Paying excessive compensation and engaging in campaign politics can get a charitable nonprofit organization in trouble. It doesn't happen often, but you should be aware of the rules.

Determining a reasonable amount of pay and benefits

In past years, if the IRS discovered wrongdoing in a nonprofit, it had little recourse but to take away the organization's exempt status. Under the new tax laws passed in 1996, the IRS established "intermediate sanctions" in cases of excess benefits for nonprofit staff or disqualified persons associated with the nonprofit. Board members and their family members — really anyone who can influence the organization's activities — are disqualified persons.

Excess benefits can include excessive salaries for a staff member or a business deal arranged to benefit a disqualified person in which the nonprofit overpaid for a service. So if you sit on a board of directors that decides to rent office space from your uncle at two or three times the going rate, you and your uncle may be in trouble.

An excessive benefit for a nonprofit staff member is any sum that's above a "reasonable amount." You're probably thinking, "What's a reasonable amount?" and you're right to ask the question. In the case of executive compensation, it's up to the board of directors to find out what a fair salary is for nonprofit managers in your area and for an organization of your size and scope.

If the IRS finds that someone in your nonprofit has received an excessive benefit, the financial penalties are severe. A 25 percent excise tax is levied, and the full amount must be paid back to the organization in less than a year. If payment is not received, the tax can go up to a healthy 200 percent.

Here are three tips on avoiding excess benefits problems:

- ✔ No board member should participate in a board decision that benefits herself or her family. Certainly, no executive director should participate in setting her own compensation.
- ✔ Rely on credible independent information about reasonable costs in business deals and compensation matters.
- ✔ Document the reasons why you make the decisions you make.

We don't want to frighten you with visions of huge tax bills. We're not saying that you can't pay nonprofit staff well or that you have to undertake a scientific study to determine fair compensation. Use your head, be reasonable, and exercise caution.

 Document board decisions by keeping minutes of board meetings. You don't need to keep a verbatim record of board deliberations, but your minutes should reflect the discussions that take place and the decisions that are made. Maintain what's known as a *board book* — a loose-leaf notebook that contains copies of your articles of incorporation, bylaws, amendments to bylaws, notices sent to announce board and membership meetings, and a chronological record of your board meeting minutes.

Getting involved in politics

We won't say that you shouldn't get involved in politics, because it's your right to do so if you wish. If you want to give your personal support and endorsement to a candidate, by all means do it. But be sure to separate yourself from your nonprofit organization when you do. Nonprofits can't support or endorse candidates for political office.

If you want to talk to your legislator about the passage of a bill that benefit your clients, go ahead and make an appointment. But if you find yourself traveling to your state capital or to Washington, D.C., on a regular basis, step back and consider how much organizational time and money you're spending on the activity. Charitable nonprofits can spend an "insubstantial" amount on direct lobbying activities. If it's 5 percent or less of your organizational budget, you're probably within the limits allowed, according to the people who pay attention to these things.

Be more cautious with what's known as *grass-roots lobbying,* or attempting to influence the general public to vote in a particular way. If lobbying is important to your overall mission as a 501(c)(3) public benefit nonprofit, you can elect the "h" designation, which requires more financial reporting to the IRS but allows you to spend more money on these activities. To do so, file IRS Form 5768 after you have a look at the regulations in IRS Publication 557.

Sending in Form 990

The formal name for this report is Return of Organization Exempt From Income Tax, but everyone refers to it as the 990. It *is* IRS Form 990, after all. With some exceptions, this basic report must go to the IRS each year to report on your nonprofit organization's finances and activities.

The report must be postmarked on the 15th day of the fifth month after the end of your annual accounting period; in other words, after the close of your fiscal year. When you filed your application for exemption, you selected your accounting period. Many nonprofits use the calendar year as their fiscal year. If that's your case, your 990 should be out the door on May 15.

We won't try to tell you that the 990 report is simple. At first glance, it's an imposing form with many spaces to fill in and instructions presented in small type. Here are some tips on filling it out:

✔ Take your time.

✔ Seek help when you need it.

✔ Prepare a rough draft before you fill in the final copy.

Completing Form 990 is similar to doing your own tax return, except that you don't need to send a check.

Who doesn't need to file a 990?

How do you know whether you need to fill out a 990? Let's start with the easiest case first. If your organization is a church or a church-related organization, you don't need to file. You can if you want to, but doing so isn't required.

Also, and this applies to many nonprofits in the United States, if your organization normally has revenues of no more than $25,000 per year, you are excused. Skip directly to the fundraising chapter. Just kidding.

Even if your income is below $25,000, some states still require that you file a 990. Check your state laws.

Other nonprofits are excused as well, but they typically aren't 501(c)(3) organizations. If you're interested in finding out what they are, take another look at IRS Publication 557 if you aren't bored with it by now.

Private foundations are 501(c)(3) organizations, but they file Form 990-PF.

Using the 990-EZ return

If your nonprofit had less than $100,000 of gross receipts (all income before expenses are subtracted) in your last fiscal year, and if it has total assets of less than $250,000, you can use the 990-EZ form. It's a shortened version of the 990, only two pages long, although if you have one or more large contributions, you may have to file Schedule B. More about that later in this section.

Fill in the identifying information at the top of the form. If you've filed in past years, you should receive a package of forms in the mail with a peel-off label that you can use for your name and address. Be sure to add your Employer Identification Number (EIN). Also check the correct box to indicate whether you're using a cash or accrual accounting method. If you need help with that question, see Chapter 10.

All 501(c)(3) organizations that file either the 990 or the 990-EZ must attach Schedule A, which reports employees and contractors who earn more than $50,000 per year. Even if you have no employees, or no employees who earn more than this amount, you must file this schedule. If it doesn't apply to your organization, just fill in the identifying information and write "Not Applicable" where appropriate.

If your 501(c)(3) organization received in the past year a contribution of cash, a grant, or property that was valued at over $5,000, *and* if that gift totaled more than 2 percent of your total grants and contributions, you must file Schedule B with your 990 or 990-EZ. If a single individual gives you two gifts of $2,500 within the year and the total constitutes at least 2 percent, you must file the schedule. This schedule is not available for public inspection. If you don't have grants or gifts in this range, be sure to check Item L on the 990 and 990-EZ forms.

Parts 1 and 11

In Part I, you report your financial activities over the past year. Chances are that the two lines that have the highest amount of revenue are line 1 (contributions, gifts, and grants) and line 2 (program service revenue, including government fees and contracts). You may have some income from membership fees for line 3 and income from investments or interest on a savings account for line 4.

Lines 5 through 8 deal with income from sales of materials or assets and income from special events. You're asked to report the costs and expenses associated with the materials sold and any direct expenses associated with special events. In other words, the IRS wants to see a net amount for sales and special events. The total you end up with on line 9 is your total revenue for the year.

How the IRS decides that income is unrelated

The IRS definition of unrelated business income is based on three questions: Does the income come from a trade or business? Is it regularly carried on? Is it not substantially related to the organization's exempt purpose?

What does this mean? Consider an extreme example. The Juniper Avenue Young People's Club, a 501(c)(3) nonprofit with the mission of providing recreational opportunities, mentoring, and job skill training to adolescents, decides to open a shoe repair business. They rent a store-front space, purchase equipment, hire employees, and begin soliciting business. The shoe repair shop does very well. In fact, in the first year of operation, income exceeds expenses by $10,000. The club uses the money to pay some costs incurred in working with young people in the neighborhood. The problem is that the shoe repair shop has no relationship to the club's charitable purpose. In this case, the club probably would be required to file Form 990-T and pay appropriate taxes on the $10,000. That's okay, however, because the club realized a profit that can be applied to some of its program costs.

However, what if the club opens the shoe repair shop with the purpose of providing training in the shoe repair trade to adolescents in the neighborhood? In that case, chances are good that any income from the business would be considered "substantially related to the organization's exempt purpose," and tax (known as UBIT) would not be due on any proceeds.

Your total revenue is not the same as your gross receipts. Gross receipts include all the income you received from sales and special events before you subtract expenses. You may have total revenue of less than $100,000 but gross receipts over that amount. If you do, you can't use Form 990-EZ. You need to file the long form. Sorry.

Report your expenses on lines 10 through 16 in their appropriate categories and total the amount on line 17. Subtract line 9 from line 17, and you have your surplus (or deficit) for the year. This amount goes on line 18. We come back to line 19 in just a minute.

Part II includes lines 22 through 24, which is where you report your assets — cash, savings, or investments as well as property and equipment. (Equipment should go on line 24, other assets, with a description. Attach a page with an equipment list if you need to.) Total these figures for line 25.

Enter your total liabilities on line 26. They could include accounts payable, outstanding loans, and vacation time owed to employees, for example. Subtract line 26 from line 27, and you have your net assets or fund balance. Put this amount on line 27. If you paid off all your bills and sold all your assets, this is what you would have left over — in theory.

Notice that you need to report asset and liabilities for the beginning of the year and the end of year. (If this is your first 990 report, you provide only end-of-year totals.) Refer to the form you submitted last year for these figures.

Now go back to line 19 in Part I. Enter your net assets from last year's form on this line. If there was an adjustment to your net assets during the year (usually done by an accountant), enter the figure for this adjustment on line 20 and attach an explanation. On line 21, enter the amount of your net assets at the end of the current year.

That's it for reporting your financial activities on the 990-EZ form. It was easy, wasn't it?

Parts III, IV, and V

Part III asks you to state your primary exempt purpose. This doesn't need to be a long statement like the one you wrote for your Form 1023 application; a few words will do. You also need to describe your programs, say how many people you served, and give a total cost for each program. You'll find spaces for three separate programs, but if you have only one program, that's fine. If you have more than three, attach an additional sheet describing them.

Part III includes a space to report grants in each program area. This refers to grants made *by* your organization, not grants *to* your organization. You probably didn't make any grants, but if you did, report them here.

Part IV requires a list of your directors, with the board officers identified, and key employees and their addresses. The only key employee you need to report here is the executive director, if you have one. You also need to state how much time is devoted to each position each week and record any compensation received, including salary, retirement benefits, and expense allowances. If you have more than three people on your board of directors, attach an additional sheet.

Part V, the last part, hurrah! You will likely be able to check no to the questions in this section or leave items blank. But several things may need your attention. Line 35 refers to income that may have come to your organization through activities not related to your charitable purpose. This is called *unrelated business income,* and if it totals more than $1,000, you must report it on Form 990-T. You may be liable for taxes on this income.

If you've amended your bylaws or articles of incorporation since you filed your last report, check that item and include a copy of the amended document when you send in the form.

Near the bottom of page 2, report who has custody of the organization books and provide that person's address and phone number. The president or secretary of your board of directors should sign the form.

The 990 report

If your organization had gross receipts over $100,000 in the last year, you must use the long 990 form. Don't despair. It's just a longer version of the 990-EZ form. We won't go through this form line by line. Refer to the detailed line-by-line instructions that come with your form.

If possible, work with an accountant to complete this form. Some of the financial reporting requirements are technical, and you would be wise to seek professional assistance.

Your 990 needs to be postmarked on the 15th day of the fifth month after the close of your financial year unless you request an extension.

Reporting to Your State and Local Governments

You'll have reporting requirements for your state and possibly your local government, especially if you provide services under contract. Sometimes reporting to the state is as simple as completing a one-page form, attaching a copy of your 990, and paying a small fee.

More and more states (and some local governments) require registration for fundraising activities. Be sure to check local laws.

Some states require a separate financial form, although we think that most of them follow the federal form closely. You'll probably get all the needed reporting information when you ask for the incorporation packet, but if you didn't or you aren't sure, check with your state office that regulates nonprofit corporations. You can find contact information for these offices on the CD.

Part II
Managing a Nonprofit Organization

The 5th Wave By Rich Tennant

"I've had a lot of experience running non-profit organizations. My last three positions were managing Internet companies."

In this part . . .

In this part, we introduce the major aspects of managing a nonprofit. Chapter titles, such as planning programs, devising sound budgets and financial oversight, choosing and maintaining facilities, attending to insurance, and hiring and supervising employees, may sound familiar to anyone who has run a for-profit business. But some important skills are found only in the nonprofit sector: How many profit-making businesses depend heavily on volunteers to meet their goals? Part II answers that question, too.

Chapter 6

Building Your Board of Directors

In This Chapter

▶ Finding out about the role of a board of directors

▶ Recruiting board members

▶ Getting the most out of your board

Some boards of directors do miraculous things. Others just muddle through. But no nonprofit organization has an "ideal" board of directors all the time. We say this because you may get the impression that your board is so disorganized that you may as well close up shop and go fishing. Don't despair. Boards can always get better, and many nonprofits do excellent work with boards of directors that would send shivers down the backs of most nonprofit consultants. The purpose of this chapter is to help you understand how nonprofit boards work in a perfect world. We don't live in a perfect world. Keep that in mind.

Understanding a Nonprofit Board of Directors

A board of directors, which we refer to as "board" from here on, is a group of people who have agreed to accept responsibility for a nonprofit organization. A board has a president and other officers, usually including a vice president, a secretary, and a treasurer. Board members almost always serve without compensation. They are volunteers and have no financial interest in the nonprofit's business. A board meets to make decisions about the organization, set policy to be implemented by staff or volunteers, and oversee the nonprofit's activities. Raising money for the nonprofit is another responsibility that many, but not all, boards assume.

A nonprofit organization doesn't have owners like a for-profit business does. So a board of directors guides and oversees the organization like an owner might. Look at it this way: No one owns city, state, and federal governments, either. So the country hands over the responsibility of running the government to elected officials. We expect them to govern the affairs of our city, state, and nation. The job of a nonprofit board is similar; in fact, it's referred to as nonprofit *governance*.

Key board role: Preserving public trust

A board's primary governance responsibility is *fiduciary,* or to uphold the public trust. Laws in the United States give special rights and privileges to non-profits, primarily the right to exemption from corporate income tax and the right to receive contributions that are tax deductible for the donor. A board's duty is to ensure that these rights and privileges are not abused. Nonprofits are given this special status because they provide a public benefit. A board's volun-tary leadership and oversight keep the focus on that public benefit.

Suppose that a nonprofit is formed with a mission to rescue stray cats. People who support this idea make contributions to the nonprofit with the belief that their money will be spent for programs to help the plight of stray cats. But, unknown to the donors, the nonprofit begins to spend its money on programs to support preschool education. Supporting preschool education is a worthy goal, but it's a long way from the original purpose of helping stray cats. So, in this example, even though contributions are being used for a good cause, they're not being used as the donors intended or to fulfill the organiza-tion's original purpose.

Even worse would be a nonprofit that collected funds for helping stray cats but, instead, used the funds for the personal benefit of the board members and staff. This is a serious and possibly criminal activity. And aside from potential felony fraud charges, it violates IRS rules and could result in revoca-tion of the nonprofit's tax-exempt status.

Board members and staff — or anyone, for that matter — can't personally benefit from nonprofit funds except for compensation for services provided or reimbursement of expenses. In a for-profit business, net earnings (profit) at the end of the year may be shared among the company's owners or stock-holders. If nonprofit board members decide to divide surplus funds among themselves, this is considered *inurement,* a big word that can be more or less defined as personal enrichment. So a board must ensure that the nonprofit is doing what it set out to do, and it must make sure that funds are spent prop-erly. If it does nothing else, it must do this.

Remember that these responsibilities are legal responsibilities. The National Center for Nonprofit Boards (NCNB) outlines three duties for nonprofit boards: care, loyalty, and obedience. Although they sound like vows one might take when entering a monastery, they actually describe established legal principles.

> ✔ **The duty of care** refers to the responsibility to be a prudent board member. In other words, board members must pay attention to what's going on and make decisions based on good information.
>
> ✔ **The duty of loyalty** means that a board member must put the organization's welfare above other interests when making decisions.
>
> ✔ **The duty of obedience** requires that board members act in accordance with the nonprofit's mission and goals.

Guiding strategy and other board tasks

In addition to the legal and fiduciary responsibilities, a nonprofit board performs other roles. A board should guide the overall planning and strategy of a nonprofit organization. At the most basic level, this means reviewing the organization's mission statement and goals on a regular basis. Every nonprofit should have an organizational plan. Have a look at Chapter 9 for more information about planning.

One role of a nonprofit board is to hire the executive director. Of course, many nonprofit organizations operate without paid staff, but if your nonprofit does have employees, finding the right executive director is one of the board's most important tasks.

A board works with its executive director to set goals and objectives for the year. Board members should not look over the director's shoulder every day. However, a board should have a good idea of the executive director's work plan and ensure that that plan is in line with the agency's purpose.

Your board should reflect your organization's character and mission. A community organizing group dedicated to collective decision making may want board members who work well together as a collective. A neighborhood development organization clearly wants board members from its focus area. A youth leadership organization may want to invest in future leadership by creating positions for youth members on its board.

A board also must ensure that the organization has the resources to carry out its goals. As part of this duty, many boards are active in fundraising. But a board also is responsible for reviewing the organization's budget and staying informed of the organization's financial situation. Nothing is more dismal than finding out, for example, that an organization hasn't been paying its payroll taxes. Insist on good financial reporting. At a minimum, quarterly financial reports should be prepared and distributed to your board.

Many people get involved on boards because they care about and understand the nature of the service the organization provides. They may not be trained in bookkeeping and accounting. It's important that they don't let their eyes glaze over when the financial report is passed around at the board meeting, assuming that everyone else understands it. It's the job of board members to understand finances. They should ask questions of staff and other board members and study Chapter 10 on nonprofit finances.

To go deeper, if your organization uses an outside accountant or bookkeeper, boards can ask for a brief meeting with him to explain how the information is presented. Many nonprofit service organizations (see Appendix A) offer affordable workshops on nonprofit finances and record keeping; others have organizations that place volunteers from businesses into nonprofits.

Maybe the problem is more than lack of comprehension. Maybe the financial information could be presented more clearly. If one board member doesn't understand the information, you can be sure that many other board members don't understand it, either.

Some organizations form advisory boards, which don't have governance responsibilities. Two types of advisory boards exist:

✔ Those that have members who actually provide advice because of their professional expertise

✔ Those that are formed so that prominent names can be listed on the organization's letterhead

Many people think that a board member's primary role is to raise money. A popular slogan addressed to board members who aren't raising funds is "Give, get, or get off." Harsh, isn't it? It's true that nonprofits can't fulfill their purposes effectively without money. And it's important for board members to take an active interest in the organization's financial vitality. But a board member's role is broader than fundraising. It includes staying well informed about the organization's work, selecting leadership, setting policies, planning, overseeing, and serving as an ambassador for the organization. Many highly skilled volunteers think that they shouldn't serve on boards because they aren't wealthy, and this misconception represents a real loss to nonprofit organizations.

Some people are reluctant to serve on boards for other reasons, including personal and financial liability. In many states, people who serve on the board of an organization that encounters financial or legal difficulties are well protected from personal liability if they've been attending meetings and staying informed. Laws regarding board member liability vary by state.

Some organizations protect their boards by purchasing directors and officers insurance (see Chapter 11). Generally, the organization's creditors can't come after its board members' personal wealth for payment. An exception is that the Internal Revenue Service can make board members financially account-able when organizations fail to pay payroll taxes. But even the IRS will work with an organization to develop a payment plan and schedule to catch up on taxes. People are right to take the responsibility of board service seriously, but nonprofit board work also can be fun and satisfying.

Splitting and sharing responsibilities

Defining roles causes problems for a number of nonprofit organizations. Should the board of directors be involved in day-to-day management deci-sions? No, probably not. An executive director and her staff don't need board members to approve every management decision that comes along. The board must trust the staff to run the organization. To put it simply, the board sets the overall goals and policies, and the staff implements them.

But (and this is a big but) many nonprofits have limited staff or even no staff at all. What happens when the organization's work is done by the board and other volunteers?

In the case of volunteer-run organizations, board members must develop split personalities, or, if you prefer, they must wear two hats. When they meet as a board of directors, they must see the larger picture and make group deci-sions that benefit the organization and its programs and clients. And most important, they must exercise their fiduciary responsibilities. However, when it comes time to do the hands-on work that's needed to provide the services and do the day-to-day tasks of running a nonprofit, board members must act as if they're employees. They may even hold regular, unpaid volunteer jobs with job descriptions and scheduled hours. Confusing, isn't it? Still, this dis-tinction should always be in the minds of those who serve as both board members and staff.

In any organization, building in practices that create checks and balances is a good idea. These practices are particularly important when board members also act as staff. For example, you'll have better financial oversight and con-trol if one person approves bills for payment, a different person signs checks, and yet another person reviews the canceled checks and monthly bank state-ments. You don't *have* to use this system; it's just one way to make sure that money is spent properly.

Titles are sounding more corporate

Although executive director is still the most common title for the top staff person in a nonprofit organization, some nonprofits have begun to follow the corporate style and have given their executive directors the title of president and chief executive officer (CEO). In these organizations, the president of the board is called the chairman of the board. The acronyms float down in the organizational hierarchy. The accountant, for example, might be called the CFO, for chief financial officer, and the CEO's right-hand person might be called vice president and COO, for chief operating officer.

The usual rationale for this change in titles is that it places nonprofit executives on more equal ground with corporate executives when the two groups meet to discuss sponsorships and joint marketing ventures. We don't really have a preference about nonprofit titles. You can call yourself whatever you like.

Finding the Right People for Your Board

You don't want just anybody to serve on your board. You want the wealthiest, most generous members of your community who believe in what you're doing, will come to all meetings, be advocates for your programs, and sweep the floor on weekends.

But you won't find many board members who fit this description. Even so, two of the above traits are critical to the success of the organization. Which two? Believing in your mission and being a good advocate on behalf of your programs. Sure, having rich members who will do the dirty work when it's needed is nice, but the most important thing is to find board members who understand and believe deeply in what you're doing. Showing up for board meetings is a nice habit, too.

You also should think seriously about the skills that board members will bring to your organization. Do you need an accountant to help with financial statements? A public relations specialist to help with media campaigns? An attorney to help with legal matters? Yes, you probably do. But don't expect the accountant to do your audit or the attorney to represent you in court. You need a disinterested professional to do that work.

If you already have a board and you're thinking of recruiting new members, drawing a grid is sometimes helpful. Along the top, list the skills you think you need on your board. Along the side, list your current board members and place check marks under the skills they bring to the board. This exercise helps you visualize the skills you need to fill when you're looking for new members.

Where do you find board members? Start with your address book. Who do you know who might make a good member and be willing to serve? Ask your friends. Ask your funders. Who benefits from your agency's work? Who are your agency's neighbors? Some cities have nonprofit support organizations that can help in this regard. Look at Appendix A for a list of these agencies.

Although having a friend or two on the board is fine, be careful about overloading the board with golfing buddies and carpool partners. Boards need diverse opinions and honest feedback from members.

Keeping the board fresh

Board building should be a continuing process. Therefore, we highly recommend that your organizational bylaws specify terms of service. Two three-year terms or three two-year terms are the most common terms of board service. Almost always, bylaws allow reelection to the board after one year's absence. Limiting terms of service helps to keep fresh blood on the board. You want new ideas, which are more likely to come from people who are new to your organization.

Is it easier to keep the same people on your board year after year? Sure. But if you don't turn over your board members, you run the danger of becoming a stagnant group that spends all its time doing things the way they've always been done. And, frankly, terms of service help you recruit new board members because they know that their time commitment is temporary.

Even if you don't specify board terms, continuously recruiting new board members is important. As time passes, board members' lives may change in ways that draw them away from your organization. Many nonprofit organizations lose vitality when their boards don't refresh themselves with new members.

Big boards, little boards, and medium-sized boards

Opinions differ about the ideal number of board members. One school of thought holds that big boards are better because the work can be divided among more people, more diverse viewpoints can be considered, and outreach into the community is more extensive. Other people say that smaller boards are better because maintaining a working relationship with a smaller group is easier, and decision making is better because fewer opinions need to be considered. Those who support small boards also say that board members can easily become invisible in a large group, meaning that no one will notice if they don't do their share of the work.

We think that there really isn't one right answer to the board size question. Nonprofits vary widely in size, function, and type, so what works for one non-profit may not work for another. This is truly a case where the phrase "one size fits all" doesn't apply.

Following are some points to consider when setting board size:

✔ Start-up nonprofits tend to have smaller boards than more mature orga-nizations. Start-up budgets tend to be smaller, and building a board of directors takes time.

✔ Boards that are actively engaged in major gift and special event fundrais-ing tend to be larger because both fundraising techniques are fueled by personal contacts and friendships. The more board members you have, the more personalized invitations you can send to your next event. Some large cultural and arts institutions have 50 board members or more.

✔ Boards that govern nonprofits funded mostly by grants and contracts tend to have fewer members, perhaps an average of 10 to 18 members.

Selecting board officers and committees

Board officers are usually elected to two-year terms. Most nonprofit boards have a president, vice president, secretary, and treasurer. Sometimes the positions of secretary and treasurer are combined into one office.

Table 6-1 outlines the responsibilities of board officers.

Table 6-1	Duties and Responsibilities of Board Officers
Office	*Duties and Responsibilities*
President	Presides at board meetings, appoints committee chairpersons, works closely with executive director to guide the organization, and acts as public spokesperson for the organization (but also may assign this responsibility to the executive director)
Vice-President	Presides at board meetings in the president's absence and serves as a committee chairperson as appointed by the president
Secretary	Maintains the organization's records, records board meeting minutes, and distributes minutes and announcements of upcoming meetings to board members
Treasurer	Oversees the organization's financial aspects, makes regular financial reports to the board, and serves as chairperson of the board finance committee

If the board has standing (permanent) committees, the board president appoints committee chairpersons. Typical standing committees are finance, development or fundraising, program, and nominating committees. Other possible committees that may be either standing or ad hoc — a temporary committee organized to deal with time-limited projects — include planning, investment, and facilities.

Table 6-2 outlines the responsibilities of common standing committees.

Table 6-2	Responsibilities of Standing Committees
Committee	*Responsibilities*
Development	Sets fundraising goals and plans fundraising activities for the organization
Finance	Assists the treasurer in overseeing financial activities and making budgets
Nominating	Recruits new board members and nominates board officers for election to their positions
Program	Oversees the program activities of the organization

Board committees make regular reports to the full board about the organization's activities in their particular areas. Board officer terms and the number and type of standing committees are written into the organization's bylaws.

Executive committees are standard groups on some larger boards of directors. Usually, the members of the executive committee are the officers of the board. The executive committee may hold regular meetings to set the agenda for the meetings of the full board and to advise the board president, or it may come together on an as-needed basis. Sometimes an organization's bylaws empower the executive committee to make decisions on behalf of the full board in an emergency or other special circumstances.

Introducing new board members to the organization

Boards of directors exhibit all the characteristics of small groups, maybe even families: Friendships develop, alliances form, and disagreements occur. Over time, the group develops routines and habits that help to make members feel comfortable with one another and help to guide the board's work. When a new member joins the group, the existing members need to make that person comfortable and share the collective wisdom that has accumulated.

Invite a prospective board member to observe at least one board meeting before electing her to membership. That way, the new member gets a chance to see how the board operates, and the current members have an opportunity to size up the new person. If the nonprofit provides on-site programs, new board members should take a tour either before or soon after they join the board.

A packet of background materials about the organization and board procedures helps the new member get up to speed quickly. The following information is useful in orienting new board members:

- ✔ Organization's mission statement
- ✔ Bylaws
- ✔ Board minutes for the last two or three meetings
- ✔ Financial audit or financial statement
- ✔ Names, addresses, and phone numbers of other board members
- ✔ Organizational plan (if one is available)
- ✔ Description of programs
- ✔ Calendar of organization's events and scheduled board meetings
- ✔ News clippings about the organization

This may seem like a lot of reading — and it is. But even if a new board member doesn't read everything from cover to cover, she at least has the reference material when she needs it.

We also suggest that the board president and/or the executive director meet with a new board member soon after she begins serving on the board, both to welcome her and to answer any questions she has.

Putting Staff Members on the Board

As a general rule, paid staff should not be board members. This situation can just get too complicated. For example, conflict of interest is always a potential problem. These awkward moments are likely when board and staff have different priorities, such as when staff members want raises but the board says no.

However, there are exceptions. In fact, many nonprofits probably have at least one staff member on their boards. In start-up nonprofits, for example, founders frequently play both roles. This situation shouldn't be surprising. Who is better suited to bring the vision and passion needed to create a new organization than the person who caused it to be formed in the first place? In many new nonprofits, of course, paying the staff isn't even possible; resources are so limited that all work is done on a volunteer basis.

Another example of an exception is an organization formed to support an artist or group of artists — a string quartet, for instance — where separating the artistic vision from the organizational mission is difficult.

Having a staff member on your board doesn't appear to be against the law. For example, under California nonprofit corporation law, up to 49 percent of the members of a nonprofit board of directors is allowed to receive compensation from the nonprofit. The standards of philanthropy set forth by the National Charities Information Bureau say that a board should have no more than one paid staff member on it. This group also says that its standards should be taken with a grain of salt (it doesn't use those words exactly) for nonprofit organizations that are less than three years old or with budgets under $100,000 a year.

The CD includes a list of state offices where you can get information about nonprofit corporation law in your state.

Using the Board to Full Capacity

If you spend any time around nonprofit staff, you'll probably hear a few complaints about boards of directors. "I can't get my board to do anything." "I wish I could get them to show up at meetings." "No one wants to raise money." These common criticisms of boards sometimes are simply water cooler remarks. Work is hard, and having an "enemy" about which you can gossip and complain feels good and relieves stress.

But, in more cases than not, boards of directors care very much about the organization they govern and want to do the best they can in helping the agency fulfill its mission. Whether or not your nonprofit has paid staff members, you can take steps to help the board do its work well.

If your nonprofit has an executive director, the working relationship between the executive director and the board president is key to having both an effective board and an effective organization. Ideally, the relationship between these two leaders is one of respect and trust.

Making board meetings effective

Most board work is done in meetings, either of the full board or in committees. We can't think of anything that damages board effectiveness more than poorly organized meetings that don't stay on topic and continue late into the night. Nonprofit board members are volunteers. They aren't being paid by the hour. The board president is responsible for ensuring that meetings are well organized and begin and end at a scheduled hour.

If the organization has an executive director, the president may delegate some responsibilities for setting up meetings. Ultimately, however, it's the president's job to see that board members have the information they need to make good decisions and that they do so in a reasonable amount of time.

Here are some tips on ensuring good meetings:

✔ Ten days to two weeks before a board meeting, send an announcement of the meeting to all board members. Include the minutes from the last meeting and an agenda for the coming meeting. Also include any committee reports, financial statements, or background research that will be discussed at the meeting.

✔ Limit the length of meetings to two hours, less if possible. After two hours, especially if the meeting is being held in the evening, attention will begin to wane. If you must go longer, take a break. Refreshments are always nice.

✔ Try to find a conference room for the meeting. Holding a discussion around a conference table is much easier than holding one in someone's living room. The table offers a place to set papers, and people won't argue over who gets the recliner.

Avoid holding meetings in restaurants and cafes if possible. The noise levels are too high to make good discussion possible, and all the activity is a constant distraction. In addition, you have no privacy. Believe us. We've tried it.

✔ Stick to the agenda. Don't allow people to wander off the topic. Some agendas allow time for discussion after each item. You don't have to do this, but if your meetings have been veering off course, this technique may work for your board.

✔ Follow *Robert's Rules of Order.* You don't need to be overly formal in your meetings (and many board meetings are very casual), but having a basic knowledge of when to make a motion and when to call the question is helpful.

Some hyperorganized boards schedule board meetings at the beginning of the year for the entire year. By entering these dates in their appointment calendars months in advance, board members are less likely to schedule other events on the same days and more likely to attend the meetings. For example, if you meet monthly, you might schedule your meetings for the second Tuesday of each month.

If you're not this organized, always schedule the next meeting before the end of the present meeting. Doing so is much easier than trying to schedule a meeting by telephone.

The CD includes samples of common agenda types to use as models.

It's difficult to say how often a board of directors should meet. The glib answer: as often as it needs to. But a meeting schedule really depends on the organization's needs and the amount of business conducted in board meetings. Some nonprofit boards meet only once a year, the bare legal minimum. These tend to be small but stable organizations with one or two employees, at least one of whom is almost certainly a member of the board. Most nonprofit boards meet more frequently than once a year; some meet quarterly, some meet every other month, and others schedule monthly meetings.

The advantage of more frequent board meetings is that board members are more engaged in the governance of the organization. The disadvantage, especially if the agenda doesn't include much business, is that board members may be more tempted to skip meetings. Of course, the board president may call a board meeting at any time if special business needs to be handled.

Point of order!

Unless you're presiding over a very large and formal meeting, you probably don't need to delve too deeply into parliamentary rules. In fact, if you do find yourself in that situation, you should hire a professional parliamentarian to help keep the meeting in order.

In the 19th century, U.S. Army officer Henry Robert saw the need for a uniform set of rules to be used to manage the give and take of meetings. He published the first edition of *Robert's Rules of Order* in 1876. The book is now in its 10th edition and is one of the best-known books in the United States. It's also probably one of the least-read books.

For the purposes of most nonprofit board meetings, only a few basic rules are needed:

✔ Calling a meeting to order simply announces the formal beginning of the meeting and the point at which minutes will begin to be recorded. If you have a gavel, this is the time to use it.

✔ Making a motion is when a member suggests a policy or action that the board will vote on. A motion must be seconded by another member of the group.

✔ If discussion is needed to consider a motion, it should come after the motion has been moved and seconded.

✔ Calling the question is an announcement made by the board president. It signals the end of discussion. It's now time to vote yes or no on the motion.

✔ To be strict, a motion is needed to adjourn the meeting. Most nonprofit boards don't follow this practice and adjourn the meeting when they reach the end of the agenda.

Getting commitment from board members

How to persuade members of a board to pull their weight is sometimes a problem that can't be solved. It's unlikely that every board member will contribute equally to the work involved in governing a nonprofit organization. If everyone on your board shows up at every meeting, reads all the materials, studies the financial statement, and contributes to fundraising activities, consider yourself fortunate.

Here are some techniques that encourage full board member participation:

- ✔ **Board contracts:** Some nonprofits ask new board members to sign an agreement that outlines expectations for board service. The contract might include a commitment to contribute financially to the organization, attend all board meetings, and serve on one or more committees.

  Check out a sample board contract on the CD.

- ✔ **Bylaws:** Organizational bylaws can state the requirements for board participation. For example, a board member might face dismissal from the board if she misses three consecutive board meetings.

- ✔ **Job descriptions:** Just like employees, board members often do better if they know exactly what they're supposed to do. Creating job descriptions for officers, committee chairpersons, and individual board members may clarify responsibilities and make it easier to fulfill them.

- ✔ **Self-evaluation:** Sometimes encouraging a board to look at itself motivates board members. The National Center for Nonprofit Boards (www.ncnb.org) sells a self-assessment kit for boards of directors.

- ✔ **Reliance on board members:** Solicit opinions from members between board meetings. Use their expertise and recognize their contributions.

Not all board members contribute equally to the work of the board, a possible result of time constraints, business travel, or just plain laziness. Give each member some slack. But if a board member's lack of participation impacts the full board, it's up to the board president (often in partnership with the executive director) to ask the member to reconsider his commitment to the organization.

To a great degree, each board member's board work reflects his commitment to the organization's mission. Board members who truly believe in what you're doing do everything they can to help you succeed.

Chapter 7

Getting the Work Done with Paid Staff

*S*ome nonprofits have paid staff from the very beginning. This may be true, for example, for nonprofits that start out with grant funding to operate a program. Other nonprofits may start more slowly, with the board of directors and other volunteers initially doing all the work and paid employees being hired later. And many nonprofits never have paid staff. These organizations may use consultants or temporary employees to help raise money or catch up on filing, but they never have the budget for regular full-time employees.

There's no rule about when a nonprofit organization should employ paid staff. The amount of work to be done and the nonprofit's resources are often the deciding factors. In other words, the organization must determine whether there's enough work to justify a paid staff and whether the organization has the resources (that is, the money) to pay salaries and associated expenses. You probably won't wake up one morning and say to yourself, "Hey, it's time to hire some staff." New nonprofits often begin by hiring part-time staff or consultants before bringing on full-time employees.

Hiring your first staff member should be cause for celebration. It means that your nonprofit has reached a milestone in its development. But it also means that the organization (and the board of directors) will have more responsibilities to raise funds and ensure that proper personnel policies are in place and followed. This chapter covers the details.

Deciding That You Need Help

Knowing when to take the leap into being a boss isn't easy. Hiring employees creates responsibilities for the employer, not the least of which is paying a salary every two weeks. You'll also need to pay payroll taxes and provide a workplace, equipment, and, don't forget, guidance and supervision. Expect to have more bookkeeping duties because you'll need to keep track of payroll records, vacation time, and sick days and decide which holidays your organization will observe. The last one should be a snap, right?

We don't know of any foolproof sign that lets you know when it's time to hire your first paid staff member or expand your existing staff. At least three situations, however, may signal that it's time to get serious about personnel matters:

- ✔ The work has been done solely by board members and volunteers, but people are getting tired and the work isn't getting done as well as it should.

- ✔ The organization was founded by two people who have worked with a small board of directors to build program services gradually. The founders have been paid irregularly. Resources have increased to the point that regular salaries can now be paid.

- ✔ The nonprofit has a paid director and office manager but recently received funding to establish a program that will require hiring four additional staff members.

Hiring employees should be a long-term commitment. For this reason, the organization should have sufficient cash flow to ensure regular payment of salaries, benefits, and payroll taxes.

Doing the Preliminary Work

Before you begin placing want ads, invest time in writing a job description for the position you want to fill. Going through this exercise helps to clarify the skills needed for the job and serves as a job blueprint for the new employee.

A job description usually includes the following information:

- ✔ A short paragraph describing the job
- ✔ A list of duties and responsibilities
- ✔ A list of skills and abilities needed for the job
- ✔ Experience and education required
- ✔ Special qualifications required

We include several standard job descriptions on the CD.

Work in nonprofit organizations can be split into three broad areas: providing services, handling administrative functions, and fundraising.

- ✔ **Services** are the reason the organization exists in the first place. They might include providing telephone referral services for a particular illness or disability, providing home visits to seniors, or organizing after-school activities for children. This list is almost unlimited.

- ✔ **Administrative functions** include bookkeeping and accounting, office management, property or building management, clerical services, benefits administration, and contract management. You can add to this list as needed — it depends on the size and complexity of your organization.

- ✔ **Fundraising** goes under various names, including resource development and advancement. Depending on the size of your organization and the extent of its fundraising activities, the number of people doing this work can go from less than one-full time person to 25 or more.

The larger these areas (or departments) are, the greater the specialization within them. A large development department, for example, may have a director (or vice president), corporate/foundation director, special events coordinator, major gifts director, planned giving specialist, annual fund director, and support personnel to help these people do their jobs.

But in small nonprofits, one person probably has job responsibilities in more than one area, perhaps even in all three areas. In other words, this sole staff person could be performing service, administrative, and fundraising functions. Obviously, this situation occurs in single-employee organizations. Even so, it's important to create a job description that captures the fundamental elements of the job.

When you add paid employees to your organization, you assume legal responsibilities that begin with the recruitment process. We recommend that you consult *Human Resources Kit For Dummies* by Max Messmer (Hungry Minds, Inc.) to be sure that you cover all the bases.

Hiring the first staff member

Here's an example of a nonprofit that's hiring its first employee. Founded five years ago, the Appleton Community Theater produces plays performed by local amateur actors. The theater has received several small grants from foundations and has put on three plays a year for the past five years. Other income from ticket sales and donations brings its budget to about $75,000 a year. The board of directors has decided that the organization has grown to the point that it can support an office manager who will be responsible for bookkeeping, ticket sales, and general clerical work, such as preparing fundraising letters, maintaining a list of donors, and writing final reports for foundation grants.

For the past three years, these tasks presumably have been done by members of the board or other volunteers. The people who have been carrying out this work are the best sources for finding out what the job involves and what kind of experience and skills are needed. Ask them to write short paragraphs describing what they do and how they do it. Put this information into one short paragraph that will become the job description. It may look something like this:

> The office manager is responsible for recording and managing the financial activities of the theater, maintaining a ticket reservation system, keeping a record of theater income and expenses according to accepted bookkeeping procedures, accepting and recording ticket reservations for all theater performances, maintaining a list of theater donors, and preparing solicitation letters for these donors during fundraising campaigns. The office manager is responsible for reporting theater activities, including expense reports, to foundations that provide support to the theater.

The skills and talents needed for this job probably include the following:

- **Attention to detail:** Keeping records of any kind requires close attention to getting things right and keeping them that way. Because this employee will spend most of her time making bookkeeping entries, maintaining mailing lists, and taking reservations, you'll want to find someone who's detail oriented.

- **Good written and oral communication skills:** The Appleton Community Theater office manager will be expected to answer the telephone and give information about upcoming performances. Although she will get direction from board members about fundraising letters and foundation reports, the final responsibility for preparing the letters and reports resides with her. Good spelling and grammar skills are essential.

- **Bookkeeping experience:** Although this position does not need to be filled by an accountant or even what's known as a full-charge bookkeeper, the job training will be much easier if the new employee understands the basic concepts of bookkeeping.

- **Computer skills:** Nearly all office work is done on computers these days. Although we think that keeping the financial records of a small organization is easier in a ledger than on a computer, easy-to-use accounting software is available. Word processing and database skills are necessary for preparing letters and maintaining lists.

> ✔ **Strong interpersonal skills:** These skills are essential for any employee, but they're critical for someone doing several different jobs as well as answering the telephone and working with members of the board. Although it's not an ideal situation, this office manager probably will answer to several managers, including the board president, the chair of the fundraising committee, and the volunteer theater house manager.

Special qualifications

The Appleton Theater office manager may not need a college degree, but other nonprofit jobs require various levels of formal education and special training. For example, if you're hiring someone to provide counseling services, that employee probably needs to meet certain education and licensing requirements in order to provide the services legally. Professional and business associations can provide helpful information about job qualifications. For example, if you need specifics about the qualifications that a speech pathologist should have, contact the American Speech-Language-Hearing Association (www.asha.org).

Some states have laws regarding background checks and/or fingerprinting for employees who work with children in certain situations. If you're not sure about the laws in your state, ask local childcare providers or school districts — they should have the information. If you're still not certain, consult your attorney.

You may want to specify that applicants have a certain amount of experience in doing the work you'll be asking them to do. If you do so, be prepared to pay a higher salary to fill the position.

You can't, of course, require that an applicant be of a particular ethnic background, race, age, creed, or sexual preference. You also can't refuse employment to a person with a disability as long as he can perform the job with reasonable accommodations.

Deciding salary levels

Deciding on a fair salary isn't easy. Compensation levels in nonprofits range from hardly anything to six-figure salaries. It's not unusual for executive directors of large-budget nonprofits to command substantial salaries. Keep in mind, however, that large nonprofit organizations represent only a small percentage of active nonprofits. Although exceptions always exist, the following list outlines some factors that determine salary levels:

✔ **Geographic location:** Salary levels differ from place to place due to the cost of living. If your nonprofit is in a major metropolitan area, expect to pay more to attract qualified staff than if you're located in a rural area.

✔ **Education and experience:** Someone with ten years of experience can command higher compensation than someone just beginning his career. Education levels also affect salary. Jobs requiring a master's degree or a PhD pay more than those that don't.

✔ **Job duties and responsibilities:** Employees who direct programs and supervise others typically earn more than employees who have fewer responsibilities.

✔ **Nonprofit type:** Compensation levels vary from one nonprofit to the next. Organizations providing health services, for example, typically have higher salary levels than arts organizations. To some extent, this difference is due to the specialized training needed by those who provide health-related services.

✔ **Organizational culture:** This category, which is harder to define, is connected to the organization's traditions and values. For instance, nonprofits with boards of directors filled with business and corporate members have higher salary levels than organizations with boards that don't have the corporate perspective.

A salary survey, which you can do by phone or mail, is a good way to assess the current salary levels in your area and for your nonprofit type. Telephone surveys probably should be done from board president to board president because most people are reluctant to reveal their own salaries. Mail surveys can be constructed so that respondents remain anonymous.

A simpler method is to look at job listings in the newspaper and on the Internet. Not all ads list salaries, but those that do can give you a general idea of what others are paying for similar work.

Using a search firm can be helpful, especially if the position requires a national search. Be prepared to pay a hefty fee, however. Fees are often based on a percentage of the first year's salary.

Some nonprofit management organizations conduct annual or biannual surveys of salary levels in the areas in which they work. More often than not, access to the surveys requires payment, but it's probably a good investment because these surveys tend to be the most complete and up-to-date.

Placing an ad

After you decide on the qualifications and skills needed for the job, advertise its availability. The cost of placing ads can add up quickly. Be sure to budget for this expense. Here's a list of ways to publicize your job opening:

- ✔ **Professional journals:** If you're hiring for a professional position, this is the place to advertise the job. Use your favorite Web search engine to track down the addresses of appropriate journals.

- ✔ **Classified ads:** Putting a classified ad in a newspaper is the usual way to seek applicants for a job. Frankly, we've never had much luck with ads in general publications, and ads can be expensive, especially in high-circulation dailies. Sometimes you get a better response from smaller neighborhood and ethnic weekly papers.

- ✔ **Bulletin boards:** Posting job announcements on bulletin boards at colleges, universities, other agencies, job centers, and even grocery stores is an inexpensive approach. In addition, you can put as many details as you want on a small poster at no extra cost.

- ✔ **Web sites:** The Internet has become a valuable marketplace for job seekers. Search for job listings in the occupation category you hope to fill. Also, look for local Web sites that carry job listings. Many Web sites charge a fee for posting a job opening. OpportunityNOCs (`www.opportunitynocs.org`), a project of The Management Center, is a good online site. It also has print versions in several U.S. cities.

- ✔ **Word of mouth:** This is a tried-and-true method. Spread the word to other nonprofits — especially those in your field — churches, and anywhere else people congregate.

 It's up to you whether to include the salary in the ad. We've seen ads with and without salary information. Generally, we think that stating the salary level is a good idea because doing so helps screen out applicants for whom the compensation may be too low.

Making the Hire

Now comes the time to make the big decision. Sifting through resumes, conducting interviews, and deciding on an employee can be a daunting task. Sometimes the right choice will jump out at you; other times, you'll have to choose between two or three candidates who have equal qualifications. That's when making up your mind gets hard.

Looking at resumes

Resumes and cover letters give you the first opportunity to evaluate candidates for the position. Respond quickly with a postcard or an e-mail to let applicants know that their materials have arrived. If possible, give a date by which they can expect to hear from you again. Doing so will reduce the number of phone calls you get asking whether you've received the resume and when you might make a decision. It's also the polite thing to do.

You'll probably reject at least half the resumes out of hand. We never cease to be amazed by how many people apply for jobs for which they don't have even the minimal qualifications. We understand that searching for a job is difficult and frustrating, but we also wonder whether applicants read our "position available" ads as closely as they should.

Separate your resumes into two piles — one for rejected applications and one for applications that needs closer scrutiny. Send the rejected candidates a letter thanking them for their interest. From the other pile, decide how many candidates you want to interview. One technique is to select the top three applicants for interviews. Reserve the other applicants for backup interviews if the first three aren't suitable or if they've already accepted other jobs.

Resumes come in various formats, and we don't really have an opinion as to which one is the best. Regardless of how the resume is laid out, here are the questions we ask ourselves when reviewing a resume:

- ✔ Is it well laid out and free of typographical errors and misspellings? One or two typos may be excused if everything else appears to be in order, but more than one or two errors implies that the candidate is likely to be careless in her job.

- ✔ Does the applicant have the right job experience, education, and licenses, if needed? We like to give a little slack on experience because sometimes experience is overrated. Nonprofit organizations often receive resumes from people who are changing careers. They may not have the exact experience you're looking for, but maybe what they've learned from their previous jobs will easily transfer to the position you're trying to fill.

- ✔ How often has the applicant changed jobs? You can never be guaranteed that an employee will stay as long as you think he should, but you have to ask yourself, "If I hire this person, will he pack up and move on even before he finishes job training?" But don't let higher-than-average job switching turn you off to an excellent candidate in all other respects. Maybe there's an explanation. Ask.

Cover letters also can be good clues to an individual's future job performance. For one thing, you get an idea of the applicant's writing abilities, and you may even get some insight into his personality. Some job announcements state that a cover letter should accompany the resume, and some even go so far as to ask the applicant to respond to questions such as "Why are you well suited to this job?" or "What do you think are the major issues facing so-and-so?" You don't have to ask applicants to address specific question in their cover letters, but if you want to do so, fine. It's up to you.

Keep in mind, however, that a well-written cover letter doesn't necessarily mean that the job candidate is a good writer. Good writers can be hired, even by job applicants. If good writing is a key skill needed for the job, ask for writing samples.

Digging deeper with references

We assume that no one would include a "bad" letter of recommendation in an application packet, so we don't pay that much attention to prewritten letters of recommendation. We do think that checking references by telephone or even in a personal meeting, if possible, is necessary.

But sometimes even talking to references doesn't provide much useful information. A job applicant wants to put her best face forward, so naturally she'll choose people with favorable opinions as references. Also, speaking to former employers yields little more than a confirmation that your applicant was employed between certain dates.

You can conduct formal background checks of education credentials, criminal history, and other information as long as you get the applicant's permission. If you feel that this type of research is necessary, we suggest hiring a reputable company that specializes in this sort of work.

Often, the grapevine is the best way to get information about a candidate. Using the grapevine is easier if the candidate has been working in your community, of course, but even if the applicant hails from another city, you can call other nonprofits to get information. You may be able to find people who have knowledge of the candidate's previous work. But be wary if you come across an informant who has a personal grudge against the applicant. It's not always easy to know whether this is the case, so don't depend on just one source. Talk to more than one person.

The degree to which you go to collect information about an applicant depends on the magnitude of the position. If you're hiring someone to lead a large and complex organization, you'll likely want to go deeper into a candidate's background than if you're hiring a data entry clerk. We do know of several instances when people were hired for big jobs after less-than-stellar performances in their previous positions. We're not suggesting that people shouldn't be given a second chance; we are saying, however, that you should know as much as possible about an individual's previous job performance before hiring her.

Interviewing the candidates

Now that you have chosen the top three or five or eight resumes, it's time to invite the applicants in for an interview. Interviewing job candidates is a formidable task. Big companies have human resource departments with trained interviewers who spend their days asking questions of prospective employees. We are neither human resource specialists nor trained interviewers, but here are some tricks we've learned over the years:

✔ Prepare a list of three or four standard questions that you ask all applicants. Doing so enables you to compare answers across applicants. The interview shouldn't be so formal as to make the candidate (and you) uncomfortable, but it's good to standardize it to some degree. Here's a short list of typical questions:

  • Why are you interested in this position?

  • What do you see as your strengths? As your weaknesses?

  • How would you use your previous work experience in this job?

  • What are your long-term goals?

✔ Try to have at least two people from your organization present at the interview. That way, you get more than one perspective; different people will notice different things about each applicant.

✔ Group interviews with three or more people can give interviewers good insight into how the applicant will perform in board and community meetings.

✔ If the job to be filled is for a director or supervisor position, arrange for each finalist to meet at least some of the staff he'll be supervising. Giving staff members a chance to meet their potential new boss is courteous, and their impressions are helpful in making the final selection.

You can't ask an applicant personal questions about his age, religious practice, medical history, marital status, sexual preference, or racial background. For good information about interviewing and other human resource matters, see HR ProOnline (www.hrproonline.com/ehome.htm).

Taking notes during the interview is acceptable, and you also may find it helpful to prepare a checklist on which you can rate the applicant in different areas. If you do so, try to do it discreetly. Job interviews are stressful enough without letting the applicant know that you rated him a 3 on a scale of 1 to 10.

It's your decision

We can't tell you how to make the final decision about whom to hire. You have to weigh qualifications, experience, poise, and desire. These decisions can be difficult, and frankly, you may not be certain that you've made the right choice until the new employee has performed on the job.

If possible, get more than one opinion. If qualifications and experience are equal, intangible factors come more into play. Will the candidate fit well into the organizational culture? Will the candidate's style of work fit with the organization's management style? Do the applicant's professional goals fit with the organization's goals?

Be cautious when making a personnel decision based on intangible factors. A candidate who's charming may be a treat to have around the office, but that doesn't always mean that the job will get done well. Making decisions based on race, appearance, age, and disability, can, of course, lead to charges of discrimination. Be sure that you document your reasons for making a personnel decision.

Bringing the New Hire Onboard

After the new employee accepts the position orally, it's common practice to send a letter to put the details in writing. Enclose a copy of the personnel policies (see the section "Developing Your Personnel Policies," later in this chapter) and place a signature line near the lower right-hand corner of the letter so the new hire can acknowledge receipt of the letter and the personnel policies. Ask the employee to return a copy of the signed letter to you, and keep the letter in the employee's personnel file.

The letter should include the employee's starting date, job title, and salary as well as other information that was agreed to in the pre-hire discussions held between the organization and the employee. For example, you might include a brief statement about the employee's responsibilities.

We put a sample hire letter on the CD so that you can get a better idea of what we're talking about.

In the United States, one of the first things a new employee must do is complete a W-4 form (for income tax withholding) and an I-9 form (to show proof of the employee's legal right to work in the country). These forms are required by law.

Getting someone started on the job

New employees don't begin producing at top form on the first day of work. Absorbing the details of the organization and learning the ins and outs of new job duties takes time. Here are some ways to ease an employee's transition to a new job:

✔ **Provide good working conditions.** You may think that listing the tools someone needs to perform his work is too basic, but we've heard about new employees who didn't even have a desk on their first day. Here are the basics:

- Desk and comfortable chair

- Computer (or easy access to one)

- Desk lamp

- Pen and paper, stapler, tape, paper clips, and calendar

- Telephone

✔ **Show the new person around.** Provide a tour of the office and the organization's programs on the first day. Introduce the new employee to other staff. If you're setting up a one-person office or if your nonprofit doesn't provide direct services, the tour may take less than five minutes. Oh yeah, don't forget to show the new employee where the bathroom is.

✔ **Give the employee information about the history of the organization.** Make available the organization's files and records. If you're hiring a new director, either for the first time or as a replacement, reading board minutes for the past year will give the new person insight into the board's activities. A new fundraiser also may find board minutes helpful, as well as past solicitation letters, donor records, and past grant proposals.

✔ **Answer questions.** Encourage new employees to ask questions, and provide the answers as soon as possible. This advice may seem obvious, but managers and board members often incorrectly assume that new employees can figure out everything on their own. Questions should be expected.

✔ **Offer special training.** A new employee may need special training — for example, about a computer software program or laws and regulations specific to your nonprofit — in order to perform her job. Sometimes the new employee can get the training by attending workshops; other times, someone in the organization can provide the training.

Paying employees

When an organization begins employing workers, establishing a payroll system is one of the first things to be done. The organization needs to decide how often paychecks will be distributed, for example. You can disburse paychecks on any schedule you choose — weekly, biweekly, semimonthly, or monthly. (*Biweekly* means every two weeks and results in 26 paychecks per year; *semimonthly* means twice a month and results in 24 paychecks per year.) In our experience, semimonthly is the most common schedule for payment, but the decision is up to the organization.

Although in-house staff can handle payroll, contracting with a payroll service is a better option. Most banks either provide payroll services or can recommend one. Payroll services are inexpensive — they're almost always cheaper than assigning a staff person the job of handling payroll. Payroll services make the proper withholding deductions based on income level, number of dependents, and state laws. They make tax deposits and maintain a record of vacation and sick leave.

If you decide to handle your own payroll, be sure to make tax deposits on time. Failure to pay federal and state payroll taxes is probably the quickest way to get your organization in serious trouble.

Typical deductions include the following, although state tax laws show much variation:

- ✔ Federal income tax withholding
- ✔ Social security tax (matched by the employer)
- ✔ State income tax withholding
- ✔ State unemployment and disability insurance

Kent Information Services provides links to information about tax laws and forms in each U.S. state at `www.kentis.com/siteseeker/taxusst.html`.

Benefits and perquisites

If your organization is new to hiring staff, you'll need to spend some time deciding on office hours, holidays, vacation time, sick days, and bereavement and maternity leave policies.

Health insurance is a benefit that your organization may or may not be able to provide. The cost of health insurance decreases based on the size of the group to which you belong. If your organization has only one employee, purchasing health insurance may be costly unless you can join a larger group. Check with state associations for nonprofit organizations or your local United Way office to see whether they have a health insurance program that will cover your employees. For more on insurance, see Chapter 11.

Employees must be given paid time off for jury duty and voting.

Paid vacation time is a benefit to both employees and employers. Taking a vacation from work is a way for employees to reenergize themselves. Employees will return to work rested and ready to give their best efforts to the organization. For this reason, people should be encouraged to take vacations during the year in which the vacation is earned.

Most organizations and businesses do not allow employees to accrue vacation time beyond a certain amount, often five days. This policy ensures that employees use vacations for the purpose for which they're intended. Such a policy also controls the amount of liability to make a cash payment for unused vacation time if the employee resigns or is terminated.

Using independent contractors

Maybe your organization isn't quite ready to take the leap into the employment waters. If work needs to be done that volunteers can't do, working with an independent contractor or consultant may be a way to accomplish some organizational goals.

For example, small organizations commonly contract with an accountant or bookkeeper to maintain financial records and prepare financial reports. Also, some nonprofits use independent contractors for grant writing and other types of fundraising. Organizations may engage businesses or individuals to do this work.

Although the practice isn't against the law, we don't recommend paying grant writers or fundraisers a percentage of what they raise. See Chapter 13 for more information about this question.

Independent contractors are almost always paid a flat fee or hourly rate for their work, ideally on a schedule that's set out in a contract that specifies the work to be done and the fee. Although you don't have to withhold federal and state payroll taxes, you need to file an IRS form 1099 that records the amount paid over a full year (usually a calendar year) and the contractor's Social Security number or federal tax ID number (EIN).

Proceed with caution, however, because there's often a thin line between an independent contractor and an employee. The IRS doesn't look kindly on trying to pass off employees as independent contractors. Here's a short list of factors that differentiate an independent contractor from an employee:

- ✔ Independent contractors are just that — independent. Although setting time parameters for the job is fine, contractors should be free to set their own schedules and work with little direction from the organization. They should provide their own offices and equipment.

- ✔ If you have to provide extensive training for the contractor to do the job, chances increase that the contractor may be considered an employee.

- ✔ If a contractor is working only for your organization and is putting in many hours each week, he may be considered an employee.

If you think that you may be pushing the envelope on this question, consult an attorney or tax specialist who can give you proper advice. Authorities are giving increasing scrutiny to the distinction between regular employees and independent contractors.

Managing your employees

Everyone needs a boss. The board assumes that role for the executive director, who, in turn, provides supervision to other employees, either directly or through a management team. The common way to visualize these relationships is through an *organizational chart,* a schematic drawing showing the hierarchical management relationships in an organization.

A chart such as the one in Figure 7-1 may be overkill for your nonprofit, especially if you're the only employee, but for larger organizations, charts help to delineate management responsibilities and who reports to whom.

Sample Organizational Chart

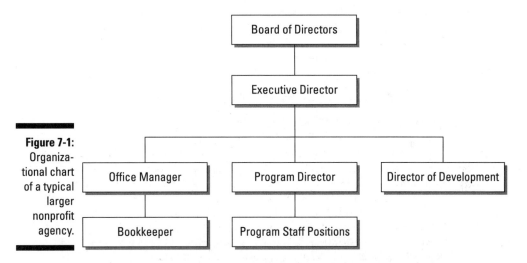

Figure 7-1:
Organizational chart of a typical larger nonprofit agency.

The responsibility of management to employees includes the following aspects:

- ✔ **Planning:** Planning happens at levels from the board of directors, who carry the responsibility for overall organizational planning, to the custodian, who plans how best to accomplish cleaning and maintenance tasks. It's best if managers work closely with those they're managing to develop department and individual goals.

- ✔ **Leading and motivating:** You may want to add inspiring to this category. We believe that good management grows out of respect and cooperation among managers and their employees. Be sure that staff members are familiar with the organization's goals and that they know how their work helps to achieve those goals.

✔ **Gathering tools and resources:** Don't ask someone to dig a hole without giving him a spade. In other words, you can't expect employees to do a good job if they don't have the means to do it. Time, equipment, proper training, and access to information are necessary.

✔ **Problem solving:** This is one of the most important aspects of good management. You can bet that problems will arise as you manage your organization and employees. Be understanding and creative in solving these problems. Ask for help in the form of ideas and suggestions from those you supervise. These are the steps to take in problem solving:

- Define the problem.

- Identify the cause of the problem.

- Develop strategies to eliminate the problem.

- Implement and monitor problem-solving strategies.

✔ **Evaluation:** Employees should receive formal evaluations once a year. Remember that evaluation begins with goal setting. If you work with subordinates, help them set clear goals and objectives.

Annual evaluations and probationary periods

Most organizations establish a period, usually three to six months, when new employees are "on probation." During this time, new employees learn their jobs, and managers can observe employees at their work. Although we don't especially like the term *probationary* because it conjures an image of misbehavior, this period is important for both the new staff person and her manager. Be honest with yourself and the employee. If it becomes apparent that the person can't do the job, making a personnel change during this period is easier than after she becomes a permanent employee.

Conduct a performance evaluation at the end of the probationary period. The evaluation should be written (and added to the employee's personnel file) and discussed in a meeting with the employee. Rating employees on a number scale on various aspects of the job was once the common format. Today, a narrative evaluation that addresses performance in achieving goals and objectives is much more helpful.

Developing Your Personnel Policies

Personnel policies and procedures outline how an organization relates to its employees. They're essential for both supervisors and employees because they provide guidelines about what's expected in the workplace and on the job. They ensure that all employees receive equal treatment, provide the steps necessary for disciplinary action if it's needed, and lay out expectations for employees.

Many start-up and small organizations that have only one or two employees give personnel policies a low priority. Frankly, you may have more important things to deal with, such as how to find the money to meet payroll next month. We suggest, however, that you begin early to formalize your rules in the form of an employee handbook. Doing so really doesn't take much time, and it can save you headaches down the road.

You must follow federal and state labor laws when establishing personnel policies. If you're uncertain about whether you can require certain behavior or work hours from your employees, consult an attorney.

Adding the essentials to your personnel policies

Begin with the easy stuff. Decide on your organization's office hours, holidays, and vacation policy. Most organizations follow the lead of others when setting holiday and vacation policy. Although you'll find a lot of variation, many nonprofits in the United States grant two weeks' vacation a year to new employees. Employees typically receive more vacation time after a longer period of service, such as three weeks after three years, and four weeks after five to eight years. The most common sick leave policy is ten days per year.

To help you determine your policies, consider reviewing the personnel policies of other nonprofit organizations in your area. A few telephone calls to other executive directors may help to answer questions that arise as you develop your policies. To get started, the Minnesota Council of Nonprofits has sample personnel policies on its Web site at www.mncn.org/sampers.htm.

In addition to vacations and holidays, you have other basics to cover in your policies:

- ✔ A statement that the board of directors may change the policies

- ✔ A statement of nondiscrimination in employment, usually presented as a policy established by the board of directors — especially important if your organization is seeking government grants or contracts

- ✔ A statement about parental leave and long-term disability policies

- ✔ A statement of hiring procedures and the probationary period

- ✔ A statement of employment termination policy, including a grievance procedure

Adding some bells and whistles

Be careful that you don't add too much extraneous material to the personnel policies and that the policies are clear and unambiguous. The following few items, however, will help new employees understand the organization:

- ✔ A statement of the organizational mission
- ✔ A statement outlining the history of the organization
- ✔ A statement of the values held by the organization

Communicating with Staff

We can't say enough about the importance of good communication between board and staff, as well as between managers and employees. If your non-profit has only one or two staff members, your job will be easier than if you need to communicate with 50 or more employees, but good communication is still important.

Communication is a two-way street. A good manager keeps an open ear and devises ways to ensure that his employees have a way to voice complaints, offer suggestions, and participate in setting goals and objectives.

Of course, confidentiality is important in some matters. For example, if the organization is contemplating major changes, such as a merger with another organization, some information needs to be withheld from the staff. On the other hand, letting rumors circulate about changes that may affect staff can create worse problems than being forthcoming about the details of potential change. Give people as much information as you can, and be sure that they have a chance to tell you how they feel.

People are resistant to change. It's human nature to prefer what we know over what we don't know. When change is necessary, you must help employees adjust to it. Doing so is often a difficult task, but when major changes are needed, don't delay in making them.

Staff meetings

Too many meetings can be a waste of time, but having regularly scheduled staff meetings is a good way to transmit information to employees and give them an opportunity to offer input and feedback and to keep everyone working toward the same goal. Keep these points in mind when arranging staff meetings:

- ✔ Try to schedule the meetings at a specific time on a regular basis. Hold meetings no more often than once a week and no less often than once a month, depending on the needs of the organization.

- ✔ All meetings should have an agenda. Nothing is worse than going to a meeting that has no point and no direction.

- ✔ Keep to a schedule. Unless you have big issues to talk about, one hour is usually long enough to cover everything you need to cover.

- ✔ Provide time on the agenda for feedback. Be sure that everyone has a chance to speak.

Memos to staff

Use memos to introduce new policies and other important information so that there are no misunderstandings. By putting the information in writing, you can clearly explain the situation. If the policy is controversial, distribute the memo shortly before a scheduled staff meeting so that employees have an opportunity to respond.

Some larger organizations create a staff newsletter that covers organizational programs and achievements. People sometimes work better if they receive recognition for their work. Stories about client successes, gains made by the organization, and announcements about staff comings and goings help to instill a feeling of accomplishment and organizational loyalty.

For very large organizations, a dedicated Web site or intranet that's accessible only to employees can transmit information and offer opportunities for staff to provide feedback and to communicate with one another.

Water cooler talk

Although formal written communication is important, nonprofit leaders also need to communicate informally by being accessible to staff in the hallways and around the water cooler. Some people are able to communicate concerns better in an informal setting than in a staff meeting. Managers who sit behind closed doors all the time often have a hard time relating with their staff.

Naturally, you don't want to gossip about other employees or reveal confidences. Being close friends with everyone isn't possible, and being a buddy to people whom you supervise is even harder. So don't force the camaraderie. Let it develop naturally. Being accessible for informal conversations is the best way to do so.

Staff retreats

From time to time, especially if the organization is facing big changes, you may want to arrange a half-day or full-day retreat to address issues, do department or organizational planning, or provide specialized training. A retreat needs an agenda that's flexible and developed with the help of participants. Every retreat should have an objective and be led by a competent group facilitator.

Chapter 8

Getting the Work Done with Volunteers

. . . .

In This Chapter

▶ Recognizing what motivates volunteers

▶ Getting a volunteer program off the ground

▶ Finding volunteers

▶ Helping volunteers to do their work

▶ Expressing your thanks to volunteers

. . . .

*V*olunteers are the lifeblood of the nonprofit sector. One survey suggests that more than 100 million people performed some volunteer work in the United States during 1999. That's a lot of people!

Of course, you may be sitting in your office asking, "Where are these volunteers?" This chapter offers suggestions to help you decide what kind of volunteers you need, how to find them, and how to keep them happy once they arrive.

Just about every nonprofit charitable organization uses volunteers in some capacity. In most cases, board members serve without compensation. Even if your organization employs paid staff, volunteers still provide a valuable service. And many larger nonprofits employ volunteer coordinators whose job is to recruit and organize volunteers.

Organizations depend on volunteers to staff telephone hotlines, lead scout troops, provide tutoring, coach youth sports teams, organize fundraising events, and stuff envelopes. So if you're going to manage a nonprofit organization, you need to know how to work with volunteers.

Understanding Why People Volunteer

The classic stereotype of a volunteer is someone who has lots of time to spare and is looking for something to do. Although this may have been true in the past when women tended to stay out of the workplace and give their energies to charity, the stereotype no longer fits. Women now make up a significant portion of the workforce, and everyone has many obligations outside of work — raising a family, taking care of aging parents, going to the gym, and keeping up with e-mail.

So why is it that people seem to be volunteering more than ever before? We think it's because more people have recognized the benefits of volunteering time to a favorite organization and because more people are being asked to volunteer.

Understanding why people volunteer makes it easier to find volunteers, organize their work, and recognize their contributions. Not everyone is motivated by the same factors. People volunteer for a variety of reasons, including their desire to

- ✔ **Help the community and others.** Helping others comes to mind when people think of volunteers. Sometimes these people are even called by the not-so-flattering name "do-gooders." But as you'll see as you read deeper in the list, their motives are not always this simple.

- ✔ **Increase self-esteem.** Volunteering makes people feel better about themselves. Giving a few hours a week, or even a month, to an organization creates good feelings.

- ✔ **Help out friends.** Friends are often the first people we turn to when we need help. You shouldn't abuse friendships, of course, but you can always ask for a hand. Be sure to reciprocate.

- ✔ **Make new friends.** Volunteering is usually a social activity. People use this opportunity to meet interesting people and develop new friendships.

- ✔ **Try out a job.** People considering a job in the nonprofit sector often discover that volunteering is a good way to get a peek at what happens on the inside.

- ✔ **Polish their resumes.** Adding volunteer experience to a resume shows a commitment to helping others.

- ✔ **Develop new skills.** A volunteer job often gives people an opportunity to learn how to do something they didn't know how to do.

Designing a Volunteer Program

Most start-up organizations depend on volunteers because money to pay staff is unavailable. And many more-established nonprofits are structured around the idea that volunteers always will do the organization's work without the help of paid staff.

Volunteers are desirable, of course, because they don't expect to be paid every two weeks. But that doesn't mean they come without costs. Recruiting, training, managing, retaining, and thanking volunteers require effort from someone in the organization.

Even if your organization is staffed completely by volunteers, we recommend assigning one of them the job of volunteer coordinator, a person responsible for overseeing or performing the following duties:

- **Appreciating:** Volunteers need to know that their work is valuable to the organization. You don't have to pass out plaques, but we do recommend some sort of regular acknowledgment. Saying thank you on a regular basis is essential.

- **Recruiting:** Volunteers don't grow on trees. Depending on how many volunteers you need and the turnover rate of current volunteers, recruiting may be a more or less continuous process.

- **Scheduling:** Volunteers need a schedule. Scheduling is even more important if your organization uses volunteers to staff an office or manage other tasks that require regular hours.

- **Training:** Volunteers don't come to work knowing everything they need to know. They can do any job for which they're qualified, but don't expect them to know the ropes until they're told what to do and how to do it.

Determining your need for volunteers

Look around your nonprofit organization and decide how many volunteers you need and what functions they should perform. We recommend creating a schedule of tasks to be completed — planning what needs to be done and how many people it will take to do the work. Table 8-1 lists the kinds of volunteer assignments you might jot down.

Table 8-1	Sample Volunteer Task List	
Task	*Number of People*	*Time*
Data entry - donor list	1 person	3 hours per week
Bulk mailing	4 people	5 hours per month
Lawn cleanup	1 person	2 hours per week
Childcare	2 people	3 hours on Saturdays
Filing	1 person	2 hours per week

It's possible to have too many volunteers. Almost nothing is worse than asking people to help and then finding out that there's nothing for them to do.

In the beginning, you may have to experiment before you know exactly how many volunteers you need for a particular job. For example, you'll eventually discover that a 2,000-piece mailing takes about five hours for four people to complete. You'll also find that hand-addressing envelopes takes longer than using labels, and preparing bulk mail takes longer than doing a first-class mailing.

Writing volunteer job descriptions

Just like paid staff, volunteers perform better if they know what they're supposed to do. Preparing job descriptions for volunteer positions helps you to supervise better and to know what skills you're looking for in volunteers. If you skipped Chapter 7 because your organization doesn't have paid staff, you may want to go back and look at the section on job descriptions.

If anything, volunteer job descriptions should be even more complete than paid-employee job descriptions. If you can break jobs into small tasks, all the better, because volunteers often share the same job. For example, a different person may answer the office telephone each day of the week. In that case, a job description that includes a list of telephone procedures, frequently used telephone numbers, and other important information near the telephone can bring consistency to the job.

Organizing volunteers

If your organization depends heavily (and solely) on volunteers, consider splitting responsibilities for different tasks among board members or more-experienced volunteers. You can also create committees to take responsibility for different jobs that need to be done.

Here's a fictitious example that gives you an idea of how to organize committees. A small nonprofit called the Sunshine and Health Project was organized to provide telephone referral and information sources for people seeking help with weight loss. It was started by three people who had successfully lost weight and decided to help others do the same. A board of directors of ten people provides governance for Sunshine and Health and undertakes key volunteer roles in the organization. The following committees were formed, each chaired by a board member but made up of individuals who provide volunteer services:

- ✔ **Telephone committee:** Sunshine and Health provides most of its services via telephone. The office receives about 60 calls each day from people seeking information about weight loss and referral to health clinics and counselors. The telephones are answered 12 hours a day, from 9 a.m. to 9 p.m., Monday through Friday. Two volunteers share responsibility for the phones in three-hour shifts. Forty volunteers are needed each week to answer phones and provide information. Backup volunteers also are needed in case volunteers are ill or can't make their shifts for some other reason.

- ✔ **Program committee:** This committee researches programs to which callers can be referred, maintains the database containing referral information, and provides training to telephone volunteers. Members of the committee include one physician and two registered nurses, all of whom provide professional oversight.

- ✔ **Publicity committee:** Sunshine and Health uses several methods to tell the public that its services are available. The publicity committee prepares and mails press releases and records and distributes public service announcements to radio stations. In addition, the committee operates a speakers' bureau of people who have benefited from Sunshine and Health's services. The committee also is working to develop a Web site that will offer basic information about weight loss and maintain a directory of services in various cities.

- ✔ **Administration committee:** Sunshine and Health receives individual donations from people who use its services, grants from foundations, and limited support from the health department in the city in which it's based. This committee is responsible for maintaining the organization's financial books, writing thank-you letters to donors, and maintaining a database of past donors.

You may be able to think of other tasks that can be assigned to a volunteer committee. The kinds of jobs that need to be done will vary, depending on the type of service your organization provides. The point to remember is that volunteer work needs to be organized (and supervised) in much the same way that paid work is organized.

In an all-volunteer organization, the responsibility for ensuring that the work gets done resides with the board of directors. The board must be committed to finding new volunteers and supervising their work. And board members must be ready to step in to do a job if no volunteers can be found.

Board members who also serve as program volunteers must remember to keep their roles as board members (governance and fiduciary) separate from their roles as program volunteers. In the latter case, the volunteers are operating like staff, not board members. There is a difference. Chapter 6 contains more information about separating the roles of board members and volunteer staff.

Hunting for Volunteers: The Great Search

Most organizations are always on the lookout for volunteers. Volunteers move away, get tired, lose interest, or take new jobs with new hours. If your organization depends on volunteers, you'll probably need to maintain a more or less ongoing recruitment process.

Here are a few tried-and-true methods for recruiting volunteers:

- **Announcements in the media:** Newspapers and radio and television stations often publish or air public service announcements for nonprofit organizations. Keep your press releases short — less than two pages if possible. See Chapter 19 for more information about writing and distributing press releases.

- **Posters:** Use your word processing program to design posters calling for volunteers and display them wherever you can. Grocery stores, drugstores, churches, schools, and civic buildings often have bulletin boards where you can post announcements.

- **Word of mouth:** Encourage your current volunteers to recruit others. People enjoy working with friends. Don't forget to post your posters in your own place of business and remind volunteers that more are needed.

- **Schools and churches:** Both institutions often look for ways for students and members of the congregation to get involved in community service. *Service learning* — the notion that students can learn by volunteering in their communities — is becoming a popular program at some schools. Don't forget to reach out to the young people in your area.

- **The Internet:** If you have a Web site and you're looking for volunteers, announce it on the site. You also can post your volunteer positions on some Web sites that exist just for that purpose. ServeNet (`www.servenet.org`), for example, provides a database of volunteer jobs. You can type in your zip code and find volunteer opportunities in your community. If your organization can use volunteers who are not physically located near your office, have a look at the Virtual Volunteering Project (`www.serviceleader.org/vv/`). Maybe you can use online volunteers to answer questions via e-mail, help write grants and press releases, or get consultation on designing your Web site.

Looking for volunteers at other nonprofits

No, we don't suggest that you steal volunteers from other nonprofits, but some organizations do exist to provide volunteer help. Volunteer centers, for example, make up a national network of organizations that recruit and place volunteers in nonprofits. You can find the volunteer center nearest you by following the links at the Points of Light Foundation Web site (www.pointsoflight.org/volunteercenters/volunteercenters.html).

Here's how some other organizations fill this need:

- ✔ Some United Way affiliates operate a loaned executive program.
- ✔ The Retired Senior Volunteer Project places retired people in volunteer positions.
- ✔ AmeriCorps (www.americorps.org) operates several programs, including VISTA volunteers.
- ✔ Some local court systems have community service programs for people working off parking fines.
- ✔ Corporations and businesses in some communities may be looking for volunteer opportunities for their employees.

Finding volunteers with special skills

If you're looking for volunteers with special training or experience, spend some time thinking about where you might find them. Save the public service announcements for the times when you're looking for people without specialized skills. Instead, target your recruitment efforts to places where you're more likely to find the people with the talents you need.

Suppose that your organization is seeking someone with accounting experience to help you maintain your books. Local accounting firms, corporate offices, and public school administration offices might be good recruiting ground for someone who can assist with bookkeeping.

Don't expect an accounting firm to provide a volunteer audit of your organization. An audit is a big job, and the accountant undertaking the task assumes responsibility for the findings. An audit is too much to ask from a volunteer.

When looking for people with special skills, don't forget other nonprofit organizations in your community. A more established nonprofit may have staff who are interested in your cause. You may be able to get some experienced help in setting up your fundraising plan, your computer network, or your publicity materials. Just because someone works at another nonprofit doesn't mean that she won't volunteer for you as well.

Using interns

Interns are specialized volunteers who come to you as a part of an education or training program. Sometimes internship programs require the nonprofit to pay a fee or to provide the intern with a modest stipend. Internship programs may require that you spend a specific amount of time providing training and perhaps mentoring.

As with employees and volunteers, you should provide the intern with clear expectations about job duties, attendance, and so on. If you decide to go this route, be ready to spend time supervising and evaluating the intern's job performance. Don't forget that the intern's experience is part of his grade.

Interviewing and Screening Volunteers

If volunteers are being placed in sensitive jobs, such as working with children or providing peer counseling, screen the applicants carefully. Screening, including a fingerprint check, sometimes is required by law, licensing requirements, or insurance carrier. Check with local authorities about the requirements in your area.

Treat all volunteer applicants the same. Don't pass up screening someone just because she is a personal friend.

We realize that screening can be a delicate issue. You're walking a tightrope between the rights of individual privacy and the rights of the organization to be sure that no harm will befall clients. Some potential volunteers may be offended by background checks. Explain to them that the procedures are not directed at them personally but are in place to ensure that clients are protected.

While the authorities do the fingerprinting and criminal background checks, you can do some screening of your own. Require volunteer applicants to fill out a job application just as if they were applying for paid work. Ask for references and check them. Review resumes and conduct formal interviews. (See Chapter 7 for information about job interviews.) Avoid paranoia, but don't discount your gut feelings, either.

If you're using volunteers in professional roles, such as accounting, or using pro bono consultants, check their qualifications just as you would check the qualifications of an applicant for a paid position. Again, it's possible that this process will offend potential volunteers, but it's far better to make sure the person can do the job, even if she's doing it for free.

A cheat sheet for the FAQs

Before you launch a volunteer recruitment drive, be prepared to answer questions when people call to volunteer. If you're already using volunteers to answer the telephone, prepare a list of common questions and their answers, and place that list near the telephone. On the Internet, lists of questions and answers are known as FAQs, which stands for Frequently Asked Questions. Here are some sample FAQs that the Sunshine and Health Project, a fictional nonprofit discussed in the section "Organizing volunteers," might need:

What are the hours I would be needed?

We answer the phones five days a week from 9 in the morning until 9 at night. We ask people to work a three-hour shift once a week.

How will I know what to say?

All volunteers receive one day of training. Training is offered once a month, almost always on Saturday.

What kind of advice can I give?

Our volunteers cannot give medical advice or advice on specific diets. We refer callers to existing services and professionals. We ask volunteers to be positive and to offer general support to all callers.

How do I know where to refer people?

We have a complete database of weight loss and related counseling services. It's a simple matter of looking through a loose-leaf notebook to find the appropriate phone numbers.

What if I get sick and can't cover my shift?

We have volunteers on standby to cover unexpected absences. If you aren't able to volunteer on a regular, weekly basis, you might consider being a backup volunteer.

Are we asked to do any other work?

Sometimes we ask volunteers to help with mailings between phone calls.

Will you pay my auto (or public transportation) expenses?

We're sorry, but our budget does not cover reimbursing volunteers for expenses. Some expenses may be deductible on your income tax, however. You should check with your tax specialist.

Can I deduct the value of my time from my income taxes?

No, the IRS does not allow tax deductions for volunteer time.

These questions and answers also can be printed in a brochure and mailed to potential volunteers who request more information. Also include background information about your organization.

Managing Your Volunteers

The degree and extent of training that volunteers need depend on the type of job they're being asked to do. Volunteers who answer telephones, for example, may need more training than those who work on the publicity committee.

If you need to provide a full day's training or training over a longer period, we suggest consulting with a professional trainer to either provide the training or help you to design the curriculum.

Training for a telephone referral service should include the following:

- ✔ **Background information about the program or service:** A phone volunteer for a weight-loss program, for instance, should understand and be able to clearly explain weight loss, including commonly accepted ways of losing weight and the dangers of medically unsafe methods. Other essentials include information about the organization, such as why it was organized, who the board members are, and what successes its programs have achieved.

- ✔ **Information about the types of services that are available:** Include possible costs and instructions for finding this information so that the volunteers can transmit the information to callers.

- ✔ **Practice answering telephones:** Who needs practice answering the telephone? Frankly, we all do. Friendliness and courtesy are essential. While in training, new volunteers should role-play different situations that they may confront when taking a telephone call.

- ✔ **Emergency procedures:** Volunteers need to know what to do if a caller appears to be endangering himself or others. Telephone hotlines and referral services receive calls from people who are depressed, for example. Teach volunteers how to handle these situations.

Putting it in writing

In addition to on-site training, volunteers should receive written materials that restate the information covered in the training. Also include attendance requirements, whom to telephone in case of illness, and other necessary information that volunteers may need to know when carrying out their tasks.

Larger organizations that use many volunteers sometimes create a volunteer handbook that reinforces information presented during training. A volunteer handbook doesn't need to be an elaborately printed document; it can be several typed pages stapled together. The more information you provide, the better your volunteers can perform.

Getting rid of bad volunteers

If you work with lots of volunteers, especially volunteers who perform complex and sensitive jobs, you may discover one or more volunteers who don't have the skills or personality to perform at an acceptable level. We hope you never face this situation, but if you do — for example, maybe someone is giving bad information or acting rudely — you shouldn't ignore the situation.

Discussing the situation with the volunteer is the first step. Treat this meeting as if you were counseling a paid employee whose job performance was below par. This is another reason why written job descriptions for volunteers and written standards for performance are important.

Exercise caution in these circumstances, especially if you don't have clearly written performances guidelines. Volunteers who were released have been known to sue the nonprofit agency. If you have concerns about this possibility, consult an attorney before you do anything.

Talking to someone, volunteer or not, about poor work is never pleasant. However, if someone working for your organization is being disruptive, giving bad information, or otherwise causing potential harm to your program, you have a responsibility to correct the problem.

Keeping good records

Keep records of your volunteers and how much time they spend doing work for your organization. You may be asked to provide a reference for a volunteer who's working to develop job skills or providing a service through an organized volunteer program.

If you use professional volunteers to perform tasks that you would otherwise have to pay for, include the value of the volunteer time as an in-kind contribution on your financial statement. See Chapter 10 for more information about financial statements.

Insuring your volunteers

Typically, nonprofit organizations carry liability and property insurance. Almost all states require that workers' compensation insurance be in place to cover on-the-job injuries to employees. Beyond this basic insurance, coverage depends on the type of services provided and the degree of risk involved. A nonprofit organization that provides medical or medically related services is wise to arrange for professional liability insurance. In other words, the organization should insure against its risks. We discuss insurance for nonprofits in Chapter 12.

Insuring volunteers is a subject of debate in the nonprofit sector. Some people take the position that insurance agents and brokers try to convince you to insure anything and everything. Others believe that liability insurance and, in some cases, workers' compensation insurance should be provided.

You have to do your own cost-benefit analysis. Keep in mind that volunteers usually are not liable for their actions as long as they work within the scope of the volunteer activity to which they have been assigned, perform as any reasonable person would perform, and don't engage in criminal activity. Unfortunately, people have become more eager to file lawsuits at the drop of a hat. If you or one of your volunteers is sued, you have to legally defend the case even if it's without merit. One advantage to liability insurance is that your insurance carrier will take on the responsibility of defending the suit.

Workers' compensation may or may not be available to volunteers in your state. States differ on whether volunteers can be included on workers' comp policies. If you can include volunteers under your state law, consider doing so, because a workers' comp claim usually precludes the volunteer from filing a suit for damages against your organization.

As is the case with all insurance questions, evaluate your risks and decide whether the cost of insuring against risks is a good investment. This process is called risk management. To find information about risk management for nonprofit organizations, contact the Nonprofit Risk Management Center at www.nonprofitrisk.org.

Saying Thank You to Volunteers

Volunteers give their time and, in many cases, expertise to help your organization succeed. It's only right that you thank them and thank them often. Saying thank you is easy when you see someone in the hallway after they've completed their work for the day, but formally recognizing their contributions also is important. Here are some standard ways of recognizing volunteers:

- ✔ **Annual recognition event:** This is the most formal (and probably the most expensive) way of thanking volunteers. Some organizations have a sit-down dinner once a year to say thanks to those who have volunteered. Awards are often given to longtime volunteers or those who have made extraordinary contributions.

- ✔ **Wine and cheese reception:** For smaller organizations with smaller budgets, this type of event can serve just as well as a sit-down dinner.

- ✔ **Gifts:** Although some nonprofits give small gifts to volunteers, we recommend caution when using this approach. Don't spend lots of money buying presents for volunteers because you can bet that some of them will be offended and will ask why you're spending scarce nonprofit money on something that isn't necessary. If you can get a local business to donate gift certificates or other items, that's a better way to go.

✔ **Admission to performances or events:** If your organization presents plays, musical performances, lectures, or readings, consider offering free admission to some events as a thank-you gift.

✔ **Public acknowledgment:** If you have a newsletter, you can mention the names of your volunteers. A larger-budget alternative is an annual newspaper ad that lists the names of your volunteers.

✔ **Thank-you letters:** Don't underestimate the power of a simple thank-you note. Unless you have hundreds of volunteers, a handwritten note is appreciated more than a typewritten form letter.

In addition to thank-you letters and recognition events, you can increase volunteer satisfaction (and retention) by treating volunteers well on a day-to-day basis. Here are some easy tips to keep volunteer satisfaction high:

✔ Don't make volunteers work in isolation if you can avoid it. Many volunteers give their time because they enjoy socializing with others.

✔ Unless a volunteer is performing a specialized task that only he can do, vary the job to avoid boredom. You may need help cleaning the storeroom or hand-addressing 1,000 envelopes, but try to assign jobs that offer more mental stimulation as well.

✔ Pay attention to the work done by your volunteers. Your interest in what they're doing adds value to their work.

✔ Help volunteers understand your nonprofit's work. If they've been answering the telephones in the front office, give them a chance to observe or participate in other activities of the organization. Give them a behind-the-scenes tour.

✔ Bring in pizza or doughnuts once in a while as an impromptu thank you.

✔ Give gifts to volunteers during the holidays if you can do so without spending lots of money. Avoid using the organization's money for this purpose. Dip into your own pocket.

✔ Talk to your volunteers. Don't treat them like hired hands. Get to know them.

Chapter 9

Planning: Why and How Nonprofits Make Plans

● ●

In This Chapter

▶ Why organizations plan

▶ Getting ready to plan

▶ Converting plans into actions

▶ Making program plans

▶ Scorecard: Comparing plans to results

● ●

The word *planning* can be intimidating. It brings up images of daylong meetings in stuffy conference rooms with outside experts wielding marker pens. Of course, not all planning takes that sort of effort — perfectly good plans can be made with a pencil on the back of an envelope, or written in your head. People make plans all the time, from organizing a vacation to deciding how to get all the errands done on a Saturday afternoon.

Organization planning, however, requires more effort. It's a group project that calls for research, brainstorming, discussion, and, in the end, agreement on a goal and the strategies and tactics needed to reach that goal. Simply put, organizational planning is deciding where to go and how to get there. The planning process helps to ensure that everyone is headed in the same direction.

In this chapter, we cover planning for nonprofit organizations in all its forms, from work plans to strategic plans to program plans. Plan to join us!

Planning to Reach the Bottom Line

Think of a plan as a blueprint or scheme describing what needs to be done to accomplish an end. In an ideal world, if your organization completes every step of its plan, you should achieve your goals.

A nonprofit organization undertakes planning for the following reasons:

- ✔ To create a structure that guides its activities in pursuit of its mission.
- ✔ To allocate organizational resources in the most effective way.
- ✔ To create a framework against which the organization's performance can be evaluated.
- ✔ To reach agreement among board, staff, and supporters on desirable goals for the organization.

No organization has unlimited funds. Even the largest, wealthiest nonprofit needs to decide how to allocate its resources effectively. Planning helps you make decisions about how to spend your organization's money by answering questions such as "Is now the best time to invest in a new program?" and "Is it better to hire another staff person for the fundraising department, or should we hire a consultant?"

The *act* of planning is equally important as the final plan itself because, in theory, the planning group's decision-making process ensures that everyone understands what needs to be done and agrees that it's worth doing.

For convenience, planning can be divided into three levels: organizational, unit/department, and individual. Table 9-1 breaks down these levels. Keep them in mind as you read this chapter.

Table 9-1	Levels of Planning	
Planning Level	*Type of Planning Required*	*Who Should Do It*
Organizational	Long-range/Strategic	Board members, staff, clients, other stakeholders
Unit/Departmental	Action plans/Goals and objectives	Department heads, staff
Individual	Work plans and schedules	Individual/Supervisor

Making the Organizational Plan

Organizational planning is what people usually think about when they think about planning. Many funders, for example, ask whether you have a long-range or strategic plan, and some ask you to include it with your proposals. Having a document to pass around is important; the process may be more meaningful than the written plan itself.

An organizational plan, usually covering a three- to five-year period, sets goals for the organization and describes the objectives that must be accomplished to achieve those goals.

The steps for successful organizational planning are as follows:

1. **Decide whether it's the right time to plan.**
2. **Assess the external and internal situation.**
3. **Hear from stakeholders.**
4. **Look at your mission.**
5. **Make decisions.**
6. **Write the plan.**

Getting ready

Make no mistake: A full-bore, all-out organizational planning effort requires considerable time, energy, and commitment from everyone involved. Some nonprofits spend a year or more developing an organizational plan.

Don't jump into the process without understanding that it will add to your workload and complicate your life for a period of time. Also, you can't plan by yourself. If you're the executive director of a nonprofit organization who thinks that planning is needed, but the board of directors doesn't agree with your assessment, don't try to start the process on your own. Take a couple of steps backward and begin the work of persuading board members that planning is worth the effort.

Don't start the planning process if your nonprofit is in a crisis mode. It's tempting, for example, to launch a strategic planning effort if you just lost a major source of funding. But you have more immediate concerns to deal with in that situation. Delay planning until you see a period of smooth sailing.

If you have the support and foreclosure isn't hanging over your agency's head, the best way to get started is to form a planning committee. This small group of board members, staff, and one or two outside people can take on the role of guiding the planning process and, in the beginning, pull together the facts and observations that you'll need to make your planning decisions.

Working from your organization's mission

Reviewing the organization's mission statement is one of the first tasks facing an organization beginning the long-range planning process. (Chapter 3 covers mission statements.) Ask yourself these questions:

✔ Is the problem we set out to solve still a problem?

✔ Can we fine-tune the mission statement to make it more specific, or is the mission statement too specific?

✔ Does the mission statement contain enough flexibility to allow the organization to grow?

Keep your mission statement in mind throughout the planning process. At every turn, ask yourself: "If we do this, will we be true to our mission?" "Will this new program we're considering help us accomplish what we want to do?"

Assessing the external situation

One of the first things to do in long-range planning is to collect information about external factors that influence the nonprofit's operation. Someone, or a subcommittee of the planning committee, should find the answers to the following questions and distribute them to everyone on the committee before the formal planning meetings begin.

✔ Are other nonprofits providing similar services in the community? If so, how are our services different?

✔ What are the demographic trends in our area? Will they have an impact on the number of people who may need or use our services?

✔ What are the trends in the professional area in which our nonprofit operates? Are new methods being developed? Will there be a shortage of professionally trained staff?

✔ How stable are the funding sources on which we depend? What about changes in government funding? Are there new potential sources of funding?

The decisions you make are only as good as the information on which you base them. Therefore, it's important to find the best and most up-to-date data available that may have an impact on your organization and its programs.

You may want to collect information from the general public or a particular constituency of your nonprofit. Questionnaires and focus groups are two ways to get input from the public. Before you undertake either of these techniques, however, spend some time thinking about what you want to find out. Write a list of questions for which you want answers.

If possible, consult with someone experienced in preparing surveys, because the phrasing of questions affects the answers you get. Look for expertise in this area at local colleges and universities. If you can't get expert help in this area, consider doing a series of one-on-one interviews with fewer people.

Bad information leads to bad decisions. Or, put another way, garbage in, garbage out. So, when gathering background information to guide planning decisions, take the time to get the most accurate, up-to-date facts available.

Assessing the internal situation

In addition to surveying the environment in which the organization operates, you need to expend some effort assessing the organization itself. Consider the following factors when doing an internal analysis:

- ✔ Is the board of directors fully engaged with organization? Are there weaknesses on the board that should be filled? Is the board engaged in fundraising?

- ✔ What are the capabilities of the staff? Does the organization have enough staff to implement changes in how it operates? Is staff training needed?

- ✔ What are the organization's major accomplishments? What are its milestones?

- ✔ Has the organization operated within its budget? Is financial reporting adequate? Are appropriate financial controls in place?

- ✔ Does the organization have adequate technology? What are its future equipment needs?

- ✔ Are funding sources stable? What is the ratio of earned income to contributed income?

Hearing from all your stakeholders

Unless you have a very small organization, you probably can't include every single person in the planning process. You do need to include all stakeholder groups, however. A *stakeholder* is someone who has a reason for the organization to succeed. Paid employees and, presumably, members of the board certainly qualify. But although these two groups may be the most closely connected to the nonprofit, they're by no means the only people who have a stake in the organization's success.

In our view, you should include all the following groups in planning:

- ✔ Board of directors
- ✔ Staff
- ✔ Users of services

- ✔ Volunteers
- ✔ Donors
- ✔ Community leaders

Some organizations make the mistake of leaving planning only to the board of directors. Although the board does hold the final responsibility for guiding a nonprofit, the staff, clients, and donors have different perspectives on the nonprofit's operation that should be included when considering the organization's future.

If you don't have a client representative on the board (and you probably should), organize a client advisory committee and empower the members to appoint one or two people to the planning committee. The same holds true for staff. Although we don't recommend that paid staff members serve on the board of the nonprofit that employs them, they should be involved in the planning process. Staff members often have information about the organization and the environment in which it operates that's crucial to the making of a good plan.

One purpose of organizational planning is to bring stakeholders together in pursuit of a common goal. People will work harder to achieve the goals if they've been asked to help set the goals.

Studying your organization's pros and cons

Be objective when looking at the pros and cons of your organization. It's tempting, for example, to put the best face on the activities of the board of directors. They are volunteers, after all. How much time do they really have to govern the organization? But if you don't identify important deficiencies because you don't want to hurt someone's feelings, your planning efforts will be handicapped by bad information.

The same advice holds true when evaluating staff strengths and weaknesses, and when assessing of your external situation. For example, pointing out that the executive director may need more training in staff supervision may not be easy, but if you aren't honest, you won't identify problems, and positive change won't occur.

Guard against bias. Sometimes people get so close to the situation they're evaluating that they can't see the true picture with an objective eye. Include outside people who have no history with the organization and have no personal stake in the outcome.

Also, don't assume that all the people you interview know what they're talking about. Accepting statements without verification can lead to bad decisions. For example, if someone says that getting a grant to pay the costs of a program start-up will be a piece of cake, check with potential funders before you agree that it's an easy task.

Yes, honesty can create conflict. Be prepared for it. Set some rules when going into planning meetings. Make sure that all the participants have a chance to state their case. Demand that all the participants show respect for one another. Arguments can be productive if they don't disintegrate into shouting matches. Always place the emphasis on the organization, not on personalities.

Planning is an ongoing activity. A formal effort to develop a long-range or strategic plan may occur only once every three to five years, but planning for the purposes of accomplishing objectives, creating a budget, and developing fundraising programs goes on all the time.

Calling in the SWOT team

One common way to analyze the information you've collected is to perform a SWOT analysis. SWOT is an acronym for Strengths-Weaknesses-Opportunities-Threats. SWOT analysis is usually done in a facilitated meeting in which the participants have agreed upon ground rules. If you prefer, however, stakeholders can complete their version of the analysis individually and then come together to discuss the results as a group.

The results of a SWOT analysis for an organization providing counseling services to families may look something like the following:

Strengths

- ✔ The program staff is highly qualified and committed.
- ✔ Clients rate the program services as high quality.
- ✔ The organization has a surplus equal to approximately three months of operating expenses.
- ✔ Program costs are largely funded by government grants.

Weaknesses

- ✔ The cost per client is higher than in similar programs.
- ✔ Most revenues are from government sources; contributed income is low.
- ✔ The programs are not well known in the general public.

Opportunities

- ✔ Population trend predictions indicate that the client base will increase over the next ten years.
- ✔ Review of news coverage suggests that the media is showing increasing interest in covering issues important to nonprofit organizations.
- ✔ The organization has cash reserves to invest in growth.

Threats

- ✔ Local government (the primary funding source) will face a budget deficit during the next fiscal year.
- ✔ Over the past five years, program costs have increased at a rate of 6 percent a year.

A review of this SWOT analysis reveals an organization that has been successful in providing quality services and getting those services funded by government contracts. However, the responses also make it clear that the program's future may be in jeopardy if organizational change doesn't take place. Depending on a single source of income for most costs is troublesome, especially because the funding government entity apparently needs to make budget cuts in the next few years. Even if the program continues to be funded by government, cost-of-living increases may cease because of tight financial needs. Over time, as program costs increase and funding remains stagnant, the organization runs a risk of not being able to get reimbursed for the full costs of its programs.

On the positive side, this organization has time and resources to begin to diversify revenues. Little effort has been made to interest donors in supporting the organization's work; in fact, the programs are more or less invisible in the community. One strategy to increase revenue would be to develop an annual campaign led by the board of directors and, at the same time, to work toward getting coverage of the nonprofit's programs in the local media.

As this example shows, one or more items often can be listed as both a strength and a weakness. Here, for instance, the fact that programs are largely funded by the government is seen as a strength, but it's also a weakness because it has created a situation in which the organization relies on a single source of funding.

Pulling it all together

After the research, analysis, and discussion, it's time to determine future directions and put the results into a final plan. Ideally, the plans of the organization will become apparent after sifting through and discussing the material assembled. If the planning group can't reach consensus, more discussion (and perhaps more data) is needed.

We recommend using a professional meeting facilitator. A facilitator brings a neutral viewpoint to the proceedings and can be very effective in helping a group arrive at a consensus about organizational goals.

Organization goals should be specific, measurable, and attainable. Don't set a goal like "In five years, the XYZ Tutoring Project will be the best tutoring program west of the Mississippi." You have no way to evaluate whether the organization is the best tutoring program west of the Mississippi, and even if you could determine the "best" program, the goal is so general and vague that there's no way to set objectives to achieve it.

Instead, an organizational goal for this program might be something like, "In five years, the XYZ Tutoring Project will provide tutoring services that are recognized by classroom teachers as effective in improving student performance." This goal can be measured. It's also attainable through implementing a series of strategies that may include better training for tutors, improved communication with classroom teachers to determine student needs, acquisition of computers to aid in tutoring sessions, and so on.

Itemizing the parts

When consensus is reached, assemble a written plan. The components of the plan include

- ✔ An executive summary
- ✔ A statement of the organizational mission (and vision and values statements if you have them)
- ✔ A description of the planning process, including the groups represented
- ✔ Organizational goals
- ✔ Strategies to achieve those goals
- ✔ Appendixes that contain summaries of the background material used to determine the plan

Assign the task of drafting the document to your best writer. When the draft is finished, the planning committee should review it to ensure that the plan is stated clearly. Submit the final draft to the full board for approval.

Clear and simple language is your friend

A common failing of planning documents (and grant proposals, for that matter) is the use of jargon and vague language. An organizational plan that uses such wording and lacks clarity does nothing to increase your credibility with your constituents or your funders. You don't want readers to ask, "What is it that they're going to do?"

If you have a choice between a five-syllable word and a one-syllable word, choose the latter. Don't try to impress people with your vocabulary.

Simple language is better than complex language.

Monitor your use of jargon. People working in a particular field or area develop special meanings for words that their colleagues understand. In a way, this is a sort of shorthand that makes communication easier and faster. But avoid using these "professional" terms when writing a document for general consumption. If you have no other alternative, be sure to define all terms.

Don't chisel your plan in stone

Although having a plan is important, flexibility in its implementation is just as important. Things change. Reviewing your plan should be an ongoing activity; probably once a year, you should submit your organizational plan to a formal review by the stakeholders who developed it.

Your plan should be flexible. For example, suppose that your organization has decided through the planning process to begin offering after-school tutoring services but later discovers that another agency plans to do the same thing. In that case, don't move ahead until you consider the consequences of entering into competition with another nonprofit. If you face this situation, we recommend talking with the other nonprofit to find a common solution. Maybe a joint program is called for, or maybe you'll find that the other group is in a better position to offer the program. Don't force your decisions. If circumstances change, change your plans.

Putting Plans into Action

Unfortunately, too many organizational plans end up in a drawer or on a bookshelf. Participants may have expended great effort to create the plans, and board and staff may have formed close bonds during the planning process. But if the decisions made during that wonderful board/staff retreat at the charming lakeside inn aren't translated into goals, objectives, and outcomes, what's the point besides camaraderie?

Defining goals, strategies, objectives, and outcomes

If planning is moving from the general to the specific, working out the goals and objectives is the middle point of the process. Goals and objectives have been a part of planning for many years. Only in the past ten years or so have planning specialists put more emphasis on outcomes.

Here are brief definitions of the four terms:

- ✔ *Goals* are things your organization hopes to achieve. Goals can be set at the organizational level, the program level, or the individual employee level. If you return to the road map analogy, a goal is traveling from Chicago to New York.

- ✔ *Strategies* are approaches or ways to achieve goals. Usually, more than one option exists. You can travel to New York by several methods: plane, train, automobile, or foot. After considering the costs, your schedule, and your hiking ability, you decide to travel by car.

- ✔ *Objectives* are smaller steps that one must accomplish to reach a goal, and they're always stated in a way that can be measured. So on a trip from Chicago to New York, an objective may be to drive 325 miles on the first day. When you pull into the motel parking lot, you can check your odometer to see whether you have achieved your objective for the day.

- ✔ *Outcomes* describe the result of reaching a goal. In the example of driving from Chicago to New York, the outcome is clear — you're in New York, not Chicago. Like objectives, outcomes should be measurable or in some way testable. In New York, you look out the hotel window and see the Chrysler Building. Yep, you're in New York.

To see how all four terms come into play, look at the example of a plan in Table 9-2. Reading from top to bottom, you have the whole plan, from organizational goal to outcome.

Table 9-2	Organizational Goal to Outcome
What We Call It	*What It Is*
Organizational goal	Diversify income
Strategy	Increase individual contributed income
Strategic goal	Develop annual campaign
Objective 1	Compile prospect list

(continued)

Table 9-2 *(continued)*	
What We Call It	*What It Is*
Objective 2	Create appeal letter
Objective 3	Mail appeal
Outcome	Organization is less dependent on a single funder

Don't get bogged down in terms. How you label the different steps in the planning process doesn't really matter all that much. The important thing is to understand that goals, strategies, objectives, and outcomes are a good way of talking about what you're trying to accomplish and how you're going to do it.

Creating an action plan

You can see in Table 9-2 that the objectives are still general. You can add a way of measuring them by stating how many prospects you want to acquire, how much the appeal will cost to produce, and how many appeal letters you will mail. But each objective in Table 9-2 requires several steps. This is where action plans come into play.

Action plans grow out of organizational and program goals and are the nuts and bolts of planning. They're also called work plans. They contain specific objectives associated with a deadline for completion and a notation as to who is responsible for completing the task. Sometimes grant proposals, especially proposals for government funds, require specific objectives described in an action plan.

Individual employees also can develop action or work plans, either at their supervisor's request or simply as an exercise to help the employees organize their work. Action plans also are used to deal with an organizational crisis or rapid organizational change.

Think of an action plan as a blueprint for work. It provides a way to keep on top of what has to be done and when it needs to be completed. Action plans also can be used as management tools.

An action plan contains the answers to the following questions for each objective:

✔ What is the end result?

   If possible, quantify the results. For example, three grant proposals will be submitted.

✔ How long will it take to do the job?

✔ Who will be responsible for doing the job?

✔ What resources are needed?

A typical action plan may look like Table 9-3.

Table 9-3			Sample Action Plan	
Objective	*By When*	*By Whom*	*Resources Needed*	*Date Completed*
Research three potential foundation funders	April 30, 20__	Allen	Foundation directory	April 28, 20__
Prepare three grant proposals	July 30, 20__	Allen	Program objectives, budgets	July 21, 20__
Follow up on proposals	September 15, 20__	Allen	None	September 10, 20__

Action plans require that a job be broken down into smaller tasks. In Table 9-3, for example, the three objectives could be split into even smaller tasks. The objective to complete three grant proposals could be divided into the individual steps for writing a grant (covered in Chapter 17):

✔ Assembling background information and support materials

✔ Developing the budget

✔ Writing the first draft

✔ Revising and rewriting

✔ Proofing and assembling the proposal

✔ Submitting the proposal by the deadline

REMEMBER

Of course, you can take the creation of an action plan to a point of absurdity. For example, you could split the job of submitting a proposal into even smaller steps, such as finding the envelope, affixing proper postage, walking to the post office, and dropping the envelope in the mail slot. You see what we mean. Don't make action plans so detailed and specific that writing the plan takes more time than doing the work the plan specifies.

Planning for Programs

Program planning is such an important part of nonprofit work that we think it needs its own section. Nearly all nonprofit organizations provide a service of one sort or another. The organization provides services through programs. A small nonprofit may have only one. Larger nonprofits may have dozens. No matter how many programs you have, you may be thinking of adding a new one or changing the ones you have.

Assessing needs

A needs assessment is an important part of this exercise. If you're thinking of starting a new program, for example, a needs assessment to determine whether the program is necessary should probably be the first step you take.

A needs assessment is more or less a research project. You don't necessarily need to hold to the strict requirements of scientific inquiry, but just as you do when collecting information to help guide organizational planning, you should do everything possible to ensure that the information is accurate and free of bias.

Determining the questions to be answered

You probably already have a general idea of what you need to find out in your needs assessment. The most basic question is, is the program needed? But in order to answer that question, a needs assessment should evaluate the answers to the following questions:

- **Are other programs providing the same service?** Obviously, you don't want to duplicate services if another organization is already doing the job. If you believe that your competition isn't doing a good job, that's another question. Jump to the second point.

- **How many people might use the service?** Getting a good estimate of the numbers of people the new program will serve is important. Doing so helps you justify establishing the program and helps you to plan for staff needs.

- **Can and will people pay for the service?** If so, how much? This gets to the question of how to fund the program. Can you expect 25 percent of your clients to pay the full fees for the service; 25 percent to pay 75 percent; 25 percent to pay 50 percent; and 25 percent to need full subsidies?

- **Are there any special requirements for providing the program?** Does it need to be near good public transportation? Is parking important? Will people come to the neighborhood where the services are provided?

> ✔ **What are the trends?** Will the number of people using the service increase or decrease in the future? Is the population in your community increasing, decreasing, or staying the same? If you begin with 25 clients, how many clients do you expect to have in three years?

Finding the right data

Just as when you collect information for organizational planning, your goal is to get the most accurate, unbiased data available. Don't depend on only one source of information. Here are some ways to get it:

> ✔ **Talk to colleagues in your community.** Ideally, you have relationships with the people and organizations that provide similar services. Ask their opinions about your ideas for new programming.

> ✔ **Look at census data.** There probably is no better source for population information than the numbers collected through a census (`www.census.gov`). Some municipal and regional planning groups also publish population growth projections. These are estimates, but census data doesn't represent an absolutely accurate count of the people in your community, either. Get all the numbers you can get.

> ✔ **Get information from potential users of the service by distributing questionnaires and holding focus groups.** The questions you ask in large part determine the answers you get. If possible, find someone who has experience in preparing survey questions to give you a hand.

> ✔ **Look at similar programs in other communities.** Although you can't always depend on the experience of others fitting exactly with your particular situation, examining what others have done is always wise.

Some people say that they don't want to share an idea with others because they're afraid someone may steal it. Although you can't rule out the chances of this happening, we believe that it's a rare occurrence. In almost all cases, being open about your plans is a good idea.

Going beyond the needs assessment

Just because a new program is needed doesn't necessarily mean that your organization should be the one to start it. You need to take other factors into account before taking the leap into starting a new program. Consider the factors in the following sections when assessing your ability to start a new program.

Expanding the Elmwood Tutoring project

Consider the case of the imaginary Elmwood Saturday Morning Tutoring Project, a five-year-old volunteer tutoring program serving 50 children ages 8 to 14. Volunteers tutor children in 30-minute sessions. Supervised activities and refreshments are available from 9 until noon on Saturdays during the school year. The program has one paid staff person: a volunteer coordinator and trainer who sometimes writes grant proposals. A board member does the bookkeeping. Eight members of the 12-member board also volunteer as tutors. No fees are charged to families. The $75,000 annual budget covers the costs of the single staff person's pay, supplies and refreshments, and insurance. Elmwood receives grants of $25,000 a year from the school district and $30,000 from the city. The remaining $20,000 is raised from small foundation grants and contributions from board members, volunteers, and parents. The program takes place in the Methodist church basement, the use of which is donated to the program.

The Elmwood board of directors is considering expanding its programs to offer after-school tutoring one afternoon a week from 3:30 to 5:30 p.m. The directors decide that the following questions need to be answered:

✓ Do parents express interest in additional tutoring and activities for their children? If so, how many? Are parents able and willing to provide transportation to and from the tutoring program on a weekday afternoon? Is there a preferred day of the week?

✓ What are the enrollment trends of the school district? Is the number of students increasing or decreasing? If so, at what rate?

✓ Are other organizations, or is the school district itself, considering establishing an after-school tutoring program?

✓ Will volunteer tutors be willing to increase their time commitment to provide tutoring in the afternoon program? Are other members of the community willing to become tutors?

✓ Will the church basement be available during this time?

✓ How much additional administrative work will the new program require?

✓ Will funders support the program's expansion by increasing their financial support?

Not all of these questions require a needs assessment, of course. For example, discovering whether the church basement is available is probably a simple matter of a single phone call. The Elmwood board president can speak to the school district and city government about the chances of increased funding. Additional scheduling and volunteer training will be needed. Elmwood determines that enough additional work will be created to warrant the hiring of one half-time assistant for the volunteer coordinator and trainer. Hiring an additional staff person will slightly increase the bookkeeping needed.

The other questions, however, should be addressed by completing a needs assessment. Elmwood decides to go it about this way:

✓ Elmwood receives permission from the school district to mail a questionnaire to parents of third through seventh graders. The questionnaire begins with a short description of the proposed program and questions about interest, time, and transportation. Questionnaires are also passed out to parents whose children are enrolled in the Saturday program. Elmwood board members who serve as tutors discuss the proposed program with parents who use the Saturday morning program.

✔ Population trend projections for the next ten years for the community are acquired from the city government. School district projections are secured from the principal's office.

✔ Elmwood board members make contacts with social service agencies in the community to determine whether a similar program is being considered.

✔ Tutors are polled about their interest and availability for an afternoon program.

Through these activities, Elmwood discovers that parents are interested in the program. By comparing the results of the returned questionnaires and discussions with parents, it's estimated that an average of 30 children may be enrolled in a program on Tuesday afternoons. Parents can provide transportation to and from the program, and the church basement is available. Both the school district and the city indicate that additional funding is a possibility, and the school population is projected to increase slowly but steadily over the next ten years. No other agencies are planning to start tutoring programs.

So far, so good. Parents and the school district appear to be interested. Increased funding is a definite possibility, and space is available.

There is one problem, however. Only two volunteer tutors are available on Tuesday afternoons from 3:30 to 5:30. Other volunteers have either work or family commitments that don't allow them to add time to their volunteer activities.

Elmwood needs to secure more tutors before the program can proceed. Before Elmwood commits to the program, it has a local radio station air public service announcements calling for volunteer tutors. A short feature article about Elmwood appears in the local newspaper. It also sends out a call for more volunteers. Within a week, Elmwood has received 20 phone calls from people expressing interest in volunteering for the project. Elmwood assumes that if half these people actually become tutors, it will have sufficient volunteers to carry out the new program.

Voilà! The pieces have fallen into place. Perhaps a bit too neatly for the real world, but you get the idea.

Paying attention to the budget

A new program is almost always going to add expenses to your organizational budget. If we thought about it long enough, we could think of an example in which increased program costs are not a factor, but we don't have all year. To be sure that you don't get yourself into a financial hole, carefully project the additional costs you will have from additional staff, increased space, equipment, and insurance.

After you have solid expense projections, you have to project where you'll find the additional revenue needed to pay these costs. If you're sitting on a surplus, be careful about tapping into this money for new program expenses. Program expenses recur every year; your surplus funds may not be there in a year's time.

Evaluating organizational and staff capability

Does your organization have the knowledge and expertise to provide the program services? This may not be a concern if the proposed program is merely an extension of what you've been doing. If your organization is branching out into new areas, however, be sure that you or someone in the organization has the credentials to provide a quality program.

Also pay attention to hidden staff costs. For example, consider whether your current program director will have sufficient time to provide adequate supervision for the new program.

Remembering special requirements

Check whether you'll need additional licensing or accreditation to provide the program. This issue is especially important for human service programs. For example, if you've been working with teenagers and want to expand to elementary and preschool children, find out whether your program space must meet additional code requirements in order to serve a younger client group.

Arts organizations also should be aware that adding new programs can create problems with building codes. For example, suppose you have a visual arts gallery that typically serves no more than ten people at a time. If you decide to hold poetry readings every Tuesday night and expect audiences of 50 or more, your building may not have enough exits.

Fitting it into the mission

From time to time, we're all tempted by the idea of doing something new. Gee, wouldn't it be nice if we could sell goldfish in the front lobby? But you have to ask yourself what selling goldfish has to do with your organization's mission. If you go too far afield, you'll be exploring unknown territory.

Missions can be changed, of course, but you shouldn't do so without considerable thought. Altering a mission statement just to justify a new program probably isn't reason enough to do so.

Thinking long term

An idea that looks good today may not look good next year or the year after. To a great extent, you can address questions about a program's long-term value and stability in the needs assessment by looking at population trends and projecting future developments in technology.

Don't forget, however, that costs will rise year after year. Your staff will appreciate raises occasionally, and the overall costs of doing business will increase. Try to imagine where the program will be five and ten years into the future.

Program planning as a team

As with organizational planning, program planning should be done as a group exercise. It doesn't have to be as extensive as the organizational planning process, but you'll get more acceptance of the new program and guard against omitting important details if you work with others to develop new programs.

TIP

To explain your program, take a tip from the business sector

If you were starting a new business and looking for investors, one of the first things you would do would be to create a business plan. Nonprofits are wise to follow this model when developing a new program. A business model is useful in explaining the program and can form the basics of grant proposals when you seek funding.

Business plans should include the following information:

✔ An executive summary that covers the main points of the plan.

✔ An explanation of the need for the program and who will use it. (This is comparable to the market analysis in a for-profit business plan.)

✔ A description of the program and your strategies for implementing it.

✔ Resumes and background information about the persons who will provide and manage the program services.

✔ Three-year projections of income and expenses for the project. Include an organizational budget for the current year.

You certainly want to include members of the board of directors in your planning, and if your board has a program committee, that's a good place to seek input on your ideas. Also, if you're fortunate enough to work in a nonprofit that has a program director, consult her from the beginning to the end of the process. Also include any staff members who will be working in the new program. Don't forget to include potential users of the service, too.

Hindsight: Evaluating How You Did

Planning is a way to move toward the future in an orderly fashion, but the goals and objectives that result from the planning process also permit a nonprofit organization to look backward and evaluate its performance and (we hope!) its successes.

Evaluation is particularly important to nonprofit organizations because, unlike for-profit businesses, nonprofits can't evaluate their performance on showing a profit at the end of the year or on the value of their stock. Foundations almost always require that grant-funded projects be evaluated, and of course, you yourself may want to know how you're doing.

Evaluations come in many varieties. Sometimes they're as simple as documenting that the program did what it was supposed to do; more in-depth evaluations may test whether some anticipated change occurred as a result of the project. Elaborate and complex evaluations often require an outside professional evaluator.

Selecting the right kind of evaluation

Nonprofit organizations are concerned with three basic types of evaluation:

✔ **Process evaluation:** Did the project do what it was supposed to do? Often, this is no more than simple counting. "This series of school concerts will have a combined audience of 1,500 children." To complete the evaluation of this statement, all you need to do is to keep audience attendance figures.

✔ **Goal-based evaluation:** Did the project reach its goals? Depending on the goal being evaluated, this type of evaluation can be either simple or complex: "Establish an AIDS awareness program in the southeastern quadrant of the city that reaches 500 individuals during its first year." Determining whether a program was established is simple; figuring out how many people the program actually reached is a little more difficult. This depends, of course, on what method the project is using to reach people. In other words, you must define what you mean by "reach" before you start the program.

✔ **Outcome evaluation:** Did the project have the desired outcome? For example, if you oversee an AIDS awareness program, a desired outcome may be a reduced risk of contracting HIV. Evaluating such an outcome would require an in-depth study of the population in that section of the city to determine whether behavior changed in a way that reduced the chances of HIV exposure. The evaluator would need to collect or have access to baseline data about HIV exposure before the program began in order to evaluate this outcome adequately.

Sometimes more than one type of evaluation is used on a project. Combining process- and goal-based evaluation is very common, for example.

Planning for evaluation

Setting up an evaluation framework after a project has started isn't impossible, but is certainly more difficult. Under the best circumstances, you should determine what you're going to evaluate and how you're going to evaluate it up front during the program design.

Many, if not most, evaluations require that data be collected during the life of the project. So if the plan is to ask clients to evaluate the services they receive, you should be ready to hand over a questionnaire to the first person who walks in the door.

Planning for evaluation also helps you to set programs goals and objectives. Just ask yourself: Can it be measured? Here are some other questions to ask yourself when planning for evaluation:

✔ For what purpose is the evaluation being done?

✔ Which of the following people will read the evaluation?

- Foundation program officers

- Board of directors

- Managers and supervisors

- Yourself

- The public

✔ What is the method of evaluation? Evaluations can be done in several ways. Decide which of the following methods or combination of methods is best for your purposes:

- Questionnaires and surveys

- Review of project documentation

- Interviews/focus groups with users of the program

- Program observations

- Pretesting and post-testing

Selecting evaluators: Inside or outside?

Some projects require an outside evaluator — someone who is familiar with the program area, has experience as an evaluator, and is not associated with your organization. In other words, you're looking for a person who has nothing at stake in the results of the evaluation. Projects that need this in-depth analysis are usually large and complex. If a funding agency requests an outside evaluator, expect the agency to pay for the evaluation as part of project expenses.

Most evaluations are done by internal staff members. Though not as expensive as hiring a consultant, even an internal evaluation involves costs. Project budgets should reflect the staff and materials costs that result from evaluations.

Telling the truth

Honesty and forthrightness are important in evaluations. You may be tempted to fudge the results of attendance figures or the number of clients the program has served, but in more cases than not, the truth will come out in the end. An organization can damage its reputation among its peers and funders if evaluations are discovered to have been falsified.

Programs do fall short of their goals. We wish this didn't happen, but it does. Remember, you're evaluating against a set of goals and objectives that were projections, maybe as long as three years earlier. The best approach is to provide honest numbers and explain why or how the results were different than those you expected at the beginning of the project.

Chapter 10

Showing the Money: Budgets and Financial Reports

. . . .

In This Chapter

▶ Anticipating typical expenses

▶ Constructing a budget

▶ Managing cash flow

▶ Tracking income and expense during the year

▶ Making ends meet

. . . .

*N*onprofit organizations are expected to spend cautiously and honor the trust placed in them by their donors. As a result, they need to be especially good at budgeting and living within their means.

Designing budgets is a critical part of program planning, grant writing, and evaluation. Maintaining a financially stable organization is one of management's most important tasks. And asking the right questions about financial reports is one of the board's key responsibilities.

M-O-N-E-Y . . . frankly, there's no getting away from it. No money, no program.

A Budget Is a Plan

Because a budget is composed of numbers and because most of us were taught to imagine mathematics as an exact science, you may panic when faced with making a budget. What if you don't get it absolutely right?

Relax. Making a budget is yet another form of organizational planning (the topic of Chapter 9). Often it's done hand-in-hand with other types of planning. It estimates how you intend to gather and disperse money on behalf of your organization's mission. In the course of a year, the cost of utilities or postage may rise, and the cost of airline flights and computer equipment may fall. You're not expected to employ extrasensory perception in making a budget, just to be reasonable and thoughtful.

You may ask why a budget is important. If your organization does not spend more than it takes in and if it holds onto a little emergency money at the bank, why does it need a budget? We have two answers — closely related to one another:

✔ A budget that is constructed carefully and used well helps you save money. Have you ever tried the diet technique of writing down every single item of food you eat every day? We've had good luck with it. The discipline makes you pause before biting into that "little" candy bar or a second sliver of cheesecake. Similarly, once you've written your budget, you'll be writing down all the income and expenses that relate to the expenditures you planned. It's a discipline that makes you watchful.

✔ A budget provides a road map for your organization, helping you anticipate income and expenses ahead of the present moment. You may have enough to pay five salaries in January, but do you still have enough to pay them in May? You may not be able to afford a new computer system in July, but maybe you'll have the money by September.

Although budgets have built-in flexibility, another kind of financial document — a financial statement — is designed to be precise. If your finances are complicated and you must prepare a financial statement, you'll probably need to get help from an accountant with experience in nonprofit organizations.

Beginning with zero

Zero is a hard place to start when you're making a budget. An easier approach is to look at your records for a previous year and ask yourself what kinds of changes you expect of the future, based on past experiences. But at some point all organizations must start with the knotty moment of zero money in the bank, in the hand, or in the bush, and make a budget.

A budget has two key sections — income and expenses. (See Figure 10-1 for typical line items.) We suggest that you begin with income. Chapter 13 has more information about anticipating sources of income. Here are some common questions to ask yourself as you begin the budget process:

✔ Are the founders and board of your organization able to contribute some start-up funds?

✔ Is your organization likely to receive a grant or grants?

✔ Are you capable of sponsoring a fundraising event?

✔ Could you charge membership fees to people who want to become involved in your cause?

✔ Will you offer services for which you'll charge money? How many services and how often?

It's common to separate your income statement into two general categories, "earned" and "contributed" (sometimes called "revenues" and "donations," respectively).

Anatomy of a basic budget

INCOME
Earned Income
      Government contracts
      Product sales
      Memberships
      Interest from investments
         Subtotal
Contributed Income
      Government grants
      Foundation grants
      Corporate contributions
      Individual gifts
      Special events (net income)
         Subtotal
         TOTAL INCOME

EXPENSES
Personnel Expenses
      Salaries
      Benefits @ _% of salaries
      Independent contractors
         Subtotal personnel
Non-personnel Expenses
      Rent
      Utilities & Telephone
      Insurance
      Office supplies
      Program materials
      Local travel
      Printing
         Subtotal non-personnel
         TOTAL Expenses
         Balance (the difference between total income and total expenses)

Figure 10-1:
Showing how income and expense items usually are named.

In anticipating expenses, start with anything concerning salaries for personnel or types of payments to other people. That list may include the following:

- **Salaries for employees, both full-time and part-time:** On your budget, list each position by title and identify the full-time salary and the percent of full time that person will be working for you.

- **Benefits for salaried employees:** In most states, at a minimum, you will need to pay approximately 12.5 percent of salaries to cover legally required benefits such as employment taxes. Your organization may also provide optional benefits — such as health insurance or a retirement plan — to its employees. If so, you will want to compute those costs as percentages of your total salaries and include them in your budget immediately after your salary expenses.

- **Fees for services to consultants or service agencies:** You may hire a publicist, grant writer, evaluator, or other consultant to handle important tasks. Such consultants are responsible for paying their own tax and insurance costs. Fees paid to consultants should be shown directly after salaries and benefits in your budget.

    At this point, compute a subtotal for all your personnel costs.

Consultants should bring independent expertise and equipment to the job. They work with salaried personnel in an advisory capacity or contribute a specific kind of skill or knowledge. You may encounter trouble with tax authorities if you hire as independent contractors persons who ought to be regular employees — who consistently will be trained or supervised by your staff or board of directors.

Next, identify all the non-personnel expenses, beginning with ongoing operating costs that allow your organization to offer programs. These may include the following:

- Rent
- Utilities
- Telephone and Internet expenses
- Office supplies
- Printing
- Insurance

If you're working with a new organization, you may have special start-up costs for the first year. These may include such purchases as desks and chairs, computers, a telephone system, a postage machine, a photocopier, signs, shelving, office cubicles, and even playground equipment.

Finally, do you have costs associated with the specific nature of the work of your organization? These will range widely but could include: diagnostic tests, carpentry tools, classroom supplies, and printed materials.

As much as possible, keep notes about your basis of computation on a worksheet in your budget files. For instance, if you are planning to print a catalogue or book, indicate the quantity and dimensions and note whether it is printed in color. Thinking through such details helps you draft a more accurate budget, and keeping your budget worksheet will help you to remember your assumptions and follow your budget when it comes time to place your order with a printer.

Three different organization budgets are presented on the CD with this book. Two of the examples show how organizations compare budgets to actual costs.

Figure 10-1 shows you some very common line-item titles in a budget.

What's a good budget?

This may seem too obvious to say, but a budget is supposed to balance. The income and expenses should be equal to one another, you should have somewhat more income than expenses, or you should have a clear plan for how you'll make up the difference if you're short of income. Planning for a deficit is discouraged.

Organizations' budgets vary widely, and there is no one right way to create a budget. As a general rule, however, your budget looks healthy if you show multiple sources of income and a combination of contributed income and earned revenues. Why? Wouldn't it be easier to keep track of one or two major grants and contracts? Or one annual special event?

The reason is based on the adage "Don't put all of your eggs in one basket." What if there's a power outage on the night of your gala? What if one of your major granting or contract sources changes its guidelines? Your programs could be jeopardized.

Another sound concept is "saving for a rainy day." Many organizations slowly develop a *cash reserve,* money put aside in case unexpected expenses arise. If they need to use their cash reserves, they take care to replace them as soon as possible.

Onward and upward (or downward)

As your first year of operating passes and your organization develops programs, it also will develop a financial track record. Once you have some kind of financial history, anticipating the future can be easier. You'll need to analyze every assumption you make, but at least you have a baseline of costs from the first year.

Here are some questions to consider in drafting future years' budgets:

- How many of your current year's grants or contracts may be renewed and at what levels?

- How likely are you to increase individual giving or special events revenues in the coming year?

- What are your earned income trends? Are they likely to continue or change? Do you face any new competition or opportunities?

- How does your personnel policy affect your budget? Do you offer benefits that kick in after an employee has worked with you for three months or six months or five years? If so, don't forget to include these costs.

- What is the duration of all employees' employment periods? Anticipate the scheduling of possible annual raises.

- When does your lease obligate you to pay for rent increases or taxes?

- Have rate increases been scheduled for utilities, postage, or other services?

What do you show if you don't have to pay for it?

Some nonprofit organizations benefit from donated goods and services rather than or in addition to contributed and earned cash. Suppose, for instance, that a local business provides office space for your organization so that you don't have to pay rent, 50 volunteers each contribute five hours of labor to your organization each week, and a major advertising firm has contributed a campaign to promote its work.

These "non-cash" gifts of goods and services are called "in-kind" contributions. How should you show these valuable forms of income in your organization's budget?

First, we encourage you to make the effort. If you don't show these contributions, you don't truly represent the scope of your agency in your budget. In addition, Financial Accounting Standards Board (FASB) guidelines for financial statements call for inclusion of donated professional services that you would otherwise have to pay for. On the other hand, we don't favor mixing up the contributions of materials and services with the cash. It makes following and managing your budget confusing.

So what's the solution? We prefer that you create in-kind subheadings within the budget or that you summarize all the in-kind contributions at the end of the cash budget in a separate section.

No matter which approach you take to accounting for your in-kind contributions, consider two things: 1) In showing the value of a volunteer's time, identify the value of the time spent completing the volunteer task. In other words, if a surgeon volunteers to drive a bus for you, the value of that time is at the rate of a bus driver's salary, not a surgeon's. 2) If you show in-kind contributions in the income section of your budget, also include them in the expense section. Forgetting to do this is a common mistake and makes your budget look as if you have much more income than expenses.

Making Budgets for Programs or Departments

Many nonprofit organizations manage several programs or departments. Each of these programs has a budget that must fit within the overall organizational budget. Often in applying for a grant, you will be asked for a project budget and an organizational budget, and the funding source will analyze how the two documents fit together.

Suppose that when your nonprofit organization begins, you offer only one program — an after-school center that provides tutoring and homework assistance for low-income children. The program really clicks, and more and more children begin showing up after school — some because they need tutors but others because their parents are at work and the kids need a safe place to go. To serve these new needs, you add art classes and a sports program.

So now, rather than one program, you have three. Each program has its own special budgetary needs. A volunteer coordinator trains and recruits the tutors and purchases books, notebooks, and school supplies. The art program requires an artist's time, supplies, space for art making, and access to a kiln. To offer a sports program, your agency rents the nearby gym, hires four coaches, uses the volunteer coordinator to recruit parents and other assistant coaches, and purchases equipment.

The specific costs of a program — books, art supplies, coaches — are called its *direct* costs.

But each of your three programs also depends on materials and services provided by other people, such as the full-time executive director of your agency, the part-time development director, and the bookkeeper. Those people work on behalf of all programs. Each of the three after-school programs also depends on the agency offices, utilities, telephones, and printed materials that advance the entire organization's purpose.

The costs that are shared by various programs — such as the executive director's salary, office expenses, and telephone bills — are called *indirect* costs. You can think of these shared costs as the glue that holds the agency together.

Dealing with indirect costs — the "sticky" part

Direct costs are pretty straightforward. For example, you know what you have to pay your tutors per hour, and you know how many hours they work. But indirect costs can be sticky, and we don't mean because they are the organizational glue. They're sticky to deal with because indirect costs are always percentages and portions of this and that. To show you what we mean, take a look at Table 10-1 — all the indirect costs for the after-school center.

Table 10-1	Indirect Costs: After-School Center
Expense and Rate of Computation	*Cost*
PERSONNEL	
Salaries and benefits	
Executive director, ($45,000) @ 100%	$45,000
Development director ($40,000) @ 50%	20,000
Benefits @ 20%	13,000
Subtotal: salaries and benefits	$78,000
Independent contractors	
Bookkeeper @ $400/month	$4,800
Graphic designer @ $250/quarterly brochure	1,000
Subtotal: independent contractors	$5,800
Total personnel	$83,800
NON-PERSONNEL	
Rent @ $1,200/month	$14,400
Utilities @ $250/month	3,000
Telephones and Internet @ $333/month	4,000
Printed materials @ $900/quarterly brochure	3,600
Subtotal: non-personnel	$25,000
Total expenses	$108,800

As you can see, total indirect cost of the entire after-school program is $108,800. But what is the *direct* cost of this service? Good question, and Table 10-2 shows you the details.

Table 10-2	Direct Project Costs: Tutoring Program
Expense and Computation	*Amount*
PERSONNEL	
Salaries and benefits	
Coordinator of volunteers @ 75% ($40,000)	$30,000
Benefits @ 20%	6,000
Subtotal: personnel	$36,000
NON-PERSONNEL	
Volunteer and student appreciation events	$4,000
Textbooks and reference books	1,000
Computer maintenance and repair	3,500
School supplies	1,500
Subtotal: non-personnel	$10,000
Total expenses	$46,000

So, the bottom line of direct costs for the tutoring program is $46,000.

Maybe you're looking back at the indirect cost total — $108,800 — and wondering whether it's a tad heavy compared to the actual cost of delivering service to kids. Sure it is, but be patient: We're building the example this way to show how indirect costs will be allocated as the after-school program expands.

A year after the tutoring program launches, the after-school center adds the art program and the athletic program. Here are the direct costs for all three programs:

Tutoring program	$46,000	30% of total direct costs
Art program	$43,000	28% of total direct costs
Athletic program	$64,000	42% of total direct costs
Total direct costs	$153,000	100% of total direct costs

Allocating indirect costs

Budgets at the after-school center become just slightly more complicated when the program expands beyond one program. The question is how to allocate indirect costs to each program. An easy way is to divide the $108,800 in indirect costs among programs based on the proportion of total direct costs that each program represents. In this example, the tutoring program represents 30 percent of total direct costs, so it makes sense to charge 30 percent of the total indirect costs to it. The math looks like this:

$$\$108,800 \times 30\% = \$32,640$$

If you add that number in one lump to the tutoring program budget, the result looks like Table 10-3.

Table 10-3	Total Project Costs: Tutoring Program (Version 1)
Expense and Computation	*Amount*
PERSONNEL	
Salaries and benefits	
Volunteer coordinator @ 75% ($40,000)	$30,000
Benefits @ 20%	6,000
Subtotal: personnel	$36,000
NON-PERSONNEL	
Volunteer and student appreciation events	$4,000
Textbooks and reference books	1,000
Computer maintenance and repair	3,500
School supplies	1,500
Subtotal: non-personnel	$10,000
Total direct costs	$46,000
Indirect costs	$32,640
Total costs	$78,640

Some funding sources balk at paying for indirect costs when they're shown as a lump sum. They want to know what actual expenses contribute to those indirect costs. To respond to this potential complaint, you need to integrate the indirect costs alongside the direct costs, as shown in Table 10-4. You're showing the same information, and your overall figures are the same, but the form of presentation is different.

Table 10-4	Total Project Costs: Tutoring Program (Version 2)
Expense and Computation	**Amount**
PERSONNEL	
Salaries and benefits	
Executive director @ 30% time ($45,000)	$13,500
Development director @ 15% time ($40,000)	6,000
Coordinator of volunteers @ 75% time ($40,000)	30,000
Benefits @ 20%	9,900
Subtotal: salaries and benefits	$59,400
Independent contractors	
Bookkeeper @ 30% ($4,800/an)	$1,440
Graphic artist @ 30% ($1,000/an)	300
Subtotal: independent contractors	1,740
Subtotal: personnel	$61,140
NON-PERSONNEL	
Volunteer and student appreciation events	$4,000
Textbooks and reference books	1,000
Computer maintenance and repair	3,500
School supplies	1,500
Office space rental @ 30% of annual rent ($14,400)	4,320
Utilities @ 30% of annual cost ($3,000)	900
Telephone @ 30% of annual cost ($4,000)	1,200
Printed materials @ 30% of total ($3,600)	1,080
Subtotal: non-personnel	$17,500
Total costs	$78,640

See how the indirect costs have been woven into the direct costs? The development director's line, for example, is right above the line for coordinator of tutorial center volunteers.

Another common and slightly different method is to assign a portion of the shared overhead (indirect costs) to the administration/management category and a portion of shared fundraising costs to the development category. These costs are not divided among your various projects. This approach assumes that some of the work of the executive director, development director, bookkeeper, and so on is purely administrative (or development) work and that some of it contributes to projects. In a condensed example, the tutoring center's budget may look like the one shown in Table 10-5.

Table 10-5		Tutoring Center Budget by Cost Centers		
Tutoring	**Arts**	**Sports**	**Administration**	**Fundraising**
$59,500	$55,600	$82,900	$35,000	$28,800

Some people believe in thresholds or standards limiting the costs for administration and fundraising. Most donors like to see their money going toward the cause rather than paying for overhead. We can't blame them. But frankly, setting a clear standard for reasonable overhead can be hard. "Reasonable" depends a great deal on the organization's age, mission, and point of development as well as on its primary sources of income. Piloting a new activity often is more expensive than sustaining it once you've worked out the kinks. Maintaining a historic site can be unusually costly. In fundraising, writing a grant proposal is likely to cost less than producing a costume ball or conducting a direct mail campaign.

Sometimes other indirect cost formulas than the ones we describe may make more sense for your organization. Once we directed a nonprofit organization managing four primary programs within a single building. Most of the organization's shared indirect costs were based on the expenses for renting and maintaining the building. Our indirect cost formula was based on the percentage of the total square footage that each program used.

A foundation or corporation program officer reviewing an organization's budget often looks at your indirect costs in a different way: as a percentage of your total costs. If your budget shows more than 33 percent of total project costs going to indirect costs, that proposal reviewer may be alarmed. Be prepared to explain why your indirect cost rates may be higher than this 33 percent level.

Projecting Cash Flow

A cash flow projection is a subdocument of your budget. Although grant-making organizations and major donors are likely to want to see your budget, your cash flow projection generally is a document for you, your board, and, possibly, a loan source.

If you think of a budget as the spine of an organization — supporting all of its limbs — the cash flow statement is its heart and lungs. A good cash flow statement is in constant movement, anticipating and following your every move.

You can map out a cash flow statement at various levels of detail. Some create quarterly charts, some monthly, some weekly. Our personal preference is to tie cash flow planning to the frequency with which you pay employees. Most often this is every two weeks.

You always want to be on top of meeting your payroll obligations.

Constructing your cash flow projection

To set up a cash flow projection, begin with a copy of your budget and add details to the names of all of the various categories. For instance, under "Foundation Grants," write down the names of every foundation from whom you now receive money and of any from whom you anticipate receiving a grant. Add the same kinds of details for your expense categories. For example, under "Utilities," add separate lines for water, electricity, gas, sewer service, and any other such services.

We recommend that you project forward by going backwards. Sounds contradictory, doesn't it? Create columns for the most recently completed quarter. Go through your records and fill any income received into the appropriate periods and spread all your expenses into the right categories and time periods. If you've forgotten any categories, this is a chance to add them. Having these actual figures for the recent past helps you see patterns of income and expense and to be realistic about your expectations.

Now, go back to each line item and write down the estimated amount that will be due during each two-week period. Begin with the "easy" items — like the rent that is a constant amount due on a certain day each month or the employer's share of federal payroll taxes.

Next, look at the consistent bills that change a little bit over time. If your utility bills are high during winter months because your agency is using the furnace more, don't forget to project that increase. If you hold a phone-a-thon twice a year that causes unusually high usage rates, figure that in.

As you get into the flow of making predictions, it's easy to become too optimistic about your anticipated income. If you've applied for a grant that you're just not sure about, don't put it into your cash flow projection. If your annual fundraising event has raised between $25,000 and $32,000 each year, project $25,000 in income. The reason? You probably won't have any problem knowing what to do when you have more money than anticipated, but you may have a problem making up a shortfall! Your cash flow projection is supposed to help keep you from falling short, not to boost your expectations.

You're almost finished now. As a next step, look back at your financial records to see how much money you had at the beginning of the first two-week period on your cash flow projection. Place this figure as "Balance Forward," and make it the first income item at the top of your first two-week period. Compute the balance for the first two-week period and insert that "Balance Forward" at the top line of the income for the *next* two-week period. And so on. And so on. The balance from the bottom is carried over to the top.

Table 10-6 shows a highly simplified sample of a cash flow projection:

Table 10-6	Simple Cash Flow Projection		
Income	*1/1–1/14*	*1/15–1/28*	*1/29–2/11*
Balance Forward	$21,603	$14,684	$53,242
Government Contract		50,000	
Williams Grant	$5,700		
Power Company			2,500
Board Giving	2,000	750	
Total income	$29,303	$65,434	$55,742
Expenses	*1/1–1/14*	*1/15–1/28*	*1/29–2/11*
Payroll	$11,197	$11,197	$11,197
Health Benefits	447		447
Payroll Taxes			
Rent	2,500		2,500
Electric Company	475		475
Telephone			875
Office supplies		120	120
Travel and Transportation			8,700
Total expenses	$14,619	$12,639	$23,439
Balance:	$14,684	$53,242	$32,303

ON THE CD

See the CD accompanying this book for a detailed sample cash flow projection and for a blank form you may use to begin your own cash flow statement.

What if there isn't enough?

You probably won't have more income than expenses in every single two-week period throughout the year. During some periods, you'll get ahead, and at other times, you'll fall behind. Your goal is to sustain a generally positive balance over the course of time and to be able to cover your most critical bills — payroll, taxes, insurance, and utilities — in a timely manner.

Some grants are paid as reimbursements for expenses you already have incurred. You may need to prepare for cash flow problems while waiting to be reimbursed.

We wish that we could promise that you'll always have enough resources to sustain your organization's good work. But some times will be lean. Then what?

First, your cash flow projection should help you to anticipate when you may fall short. That part of your budget enables you to plan ahead and solicit board members who have not yet made a gift this year, send letters to past donors, and cut costs.

We also recommend being proactive about contacting your creditors. If you think you can't pay a bill on time, call and ask for an extension or explain that you're forced to make a partial payment now with the balance coming in a few weeks. Your ability to do business depends upon your earning and sustaining other people's trust. If you can't have perfect credit, being honest and forthright is the next best thing. This is hard to do, but important.

Don't "hide" behind your bills, thinking that if you don't say anything, nobody will notice. If you're facing a period of debt, call anyone to whom you owe money and explain the situation and your timeline for paying your bills. Among other things, your honesty will help them with *their* cash flow.

When you must put off paying creditors, don't forget to include federal, state, and local tax agencies on the list of organizations to notify. Just because they're distant and bureaucratic doesn't mean that you shouldn't make personal contact. Fees and interest on unpaid taxes add up quickly. Setting up a payment plan, both over the phone and in writing, can prevent your assets (or a board member's) from being frozen.

Small businesses, other nonprofit organizations, and independent contractors are creditors who are the least likely to hassle you about late bill payments or to charge you interest. They also are in the weakest position to absorb late payments and bad debts. Don't overlook their needs and potential vulnerability.

Borrowing to make ends meet

Another route to managing cash shortfalls is to borrow the money you need to cover your bills. Your cash flow statement, if constructed carefully, can help you plan the size and duration of the loan you need. Here are some of your options if you need to borrow money:

- Ask a board member for assistance. If the board member can help, you can probably secure the loan quickly and at a reasonable interest rate (or no interest rate).

- Ask local foundations whether they know of a loan fund for nonprofit organizations. Some associations of grantmakers offer such loans at low interest to their grantees who face cash flow problems. Such a program is likely to be more sympathetic to your needs than a commercial lending institution might be.

- Apply for a small business loan at your bank. Foundations sometimes make this easier by guaranteeing bank loans of nonprofits.

- Check to see whether you qualify for a line of credit from your bank. A *line of credit* allows you to borrow up to a certain sum for a certain period of time. When the borrowed amount is repaid, the organization may not borrow from its line of credit again for a month or two. Your organization may wish to apply for a line of credit even if it doesn't expect immediate cash flow problems. Doing so can provide a safety net for emergencies.

- As a last resort, borrow the money from a staff member's (or an organizational) credit card. Do this only if you're positive that the loan will be repaid quickly and that interest can be covered.

Some nonprofit directors have taken out second mortgages on their homes to cover their organizations' debts, but we don't recommend doing so. Dedication is worthy, but drastic steps can lead to resentment and job burnout, which may be more destructive to an organization than owing money.

Borrowing money rarely occurs without financial or emotional costs. Borrowing from a board member may erode the board's confidence in the organization and trust in its leadership. Borrowing from a foundation-supported loan fund draws potential funders' attention to your organization's cash flow problems. Borrowing from banks may involve paying high interest rates. Credit card borrowing is fast, but the interest charged is high.

In an ideal situation, your organization can anticipate potential financial stresses and put aside a cash reserve fund. You can spend these emergency funds as needed and replenish them as soon as possible. Some boards set goals for the size of a cash reserve as part of the annual budget review process.

Living, breathing documents

Your budget and cash flow statement will not be capable of getting up and walking out of the room, but they should be "active documents." If you simply create these documents once a year to keep in a file folder and submit with grant proposals, they won't do you much good. A good budget is crumpled, coffee-stained, and much scrutinized. A good budget guides and predicts.

Numbers in budgets and statements are meant to be compared. You can compare such things as income to expenses, budget to actual costs, and contributed to earned income. Such comparison exercises bring your budget and cash flow projections to life (and give them those oh-so-valuable coffee stains).

The CD accompanying this book demonstrates two ways of tracking actual income and expenses in comparison to budgeted income and expenses.

Other useful exercises for your "living/breathing" budget are:

- ✔ Keep your cash flow projection up-to-date by inserting "actual" income and expenses as they're received or spent.

- ✔ If your organization's situation changes, prepare and adopt a formal budget revision. We recommend this step only if the change is significant, because budget revisions are time consuming. On the other hand, don't try to proceed with a budget that doesn't reflect the size and scope of your organization. You don't want to try to find your way through Colorado with a map of Utah.

- ✔ Provide copies monthly or quarterly to your entire board or board finance committee. Encourage your board treasurer to summarize the organization's financial situation and invite questions and discussion at each meeting.

- ✔ Keep notes with the budget about changes you recommend in years ahead. Another important way to give life to your budget is involving key staff and board members in its development and refinement. Just as all members of a family need to learn to live within a household budget, everyone in your organization needs to live within means.

- ✔ Involve your staff (paid and volunteer) in the early stages of drafting the coming year's budget. Include their ideas. When you can't afford all their dreams, involve them in setting priorities.

- ✔ Meet with a small committee of board members to review and refine a budget draft after you've met with your staff. Present the draft with options and recommendations to the entire board for discussion and formal approval.

Preparing Financial Statements

If a budget is a futurist document, a financial statement is history. Nonprofit organizations prepare a financial statement at least once a year, at the end of the fiscal year. Many organizations also prepare monthly or quarterly "in progress" versions of their annual financial statement.

Preparing and interpreting financial statements is a special area of expertise that goes beyond the scope of this book. Many nonprofits in fact seek outside professional help for this essential task. If hiring such assistance is beyond your organization's means, we recommend that you become acquainted with *Accounting for Dummies, 2nd edition* (Hungry Minds, Inc.). If you do choose to prepare your own financial statements, you may want to hire an accountant at year's end to review them for accuracy.

The information in your yearly financial statement closely resembles the Form 990 financial report that your organization must submit to the IRS if it has received $25,000 or more in the past year. You'll also be including this document in your board orientation packets and with requests for funding. Some organizations publish it in an "Annual Report" of activities.

You can find a copy of Form 990 on the CD.

Some of your funders, such as foundations that award you grants, may require that your financial statements and internal financial control systems be examined by an independent outside auditor. Or your board may decide that it's a good idea to have the books examined by an outside auditor.

Although your organization can learn a great deal from an audit, the practice is not appropriate or necessary for every nonprofit. (As of the late 1990s, only about 5 percent of the nonprofits in California had an outside audit.) The process is expensive and time consuming. If there's any question about whether an audit is necessary or appropriate, consult an attorney who is familiar with the management of nonprofit organizations.

Many nonprofits wonder whether they should seek pro bono audits from large accounting firms. Although we're big fans of contributed services, a pro bono audit is a bad idea. An auditor is supposed to be neutral about your organization: An audit, to have value, should be prepared independently of the organization's staff and board. It loses its value as the voice of outside validation when provided as a gift.

Managing Financial Systems

Even in a small organization, you'll want to establish careful practices about how you handle money and financial documents. If you have a one-person office, creating all of the following controls may be impossible, but you should try to implement them as far as possible:

- Store checkbooks, savings passbooks, blank checks, financial records, and cash in a locked, secure place.

- Regularly back up financial records that are kept on computers and store a copy off-site in a safe location.

- Assign to different people the separate functions of writing checks, signing checks, reconciling bank accounts, and checking the canceled checks that return from the bank. If you can arrange for three different people to perform these tasks, great. If not, maybe a board member can double-check canceled checks. Look for accuracy and for anything that looks fishy, such as checks made out to vendors you don't recognize, checks canceled by people or businesses other than those to whom they're written, or canceled checks that are missing from bank statements. Embezzlement is rare but possible, and taking these steps is a way to detect it. Trust us, we've discovered such a case!

- Require two signatures on checks or bank transfers over a certain amount, often $1,000. (You can adopt this requirement as an internal policy, and your bank often will monitor larger transactions to make sure that the policy is followed.)

- Retain in organized files all paperwork that backs up your banking documents. These may include personnel time sheets, box office or other records for tickets sold, receipts, and invoices.

Chapter 11

Creating a Home for Your Nonprofit and Insuring It

....

In This Chapter
▶ Selecting the right location
▶ Determining what you can spend on a facility
▶ Protecting your enterprise with the right insurance

....

Some nonprofits can travel light. The service they provide can be managed out of a spare bedroom or small commercial office. Others need specialized, technically sophisticated facilities.

Some nonprofits fit easily into a wide variety of locations. Others can fulfill their missions only if they're located in specific neighborhoods or geographic regions.

Some nonprofits pay nothing (or a symbolic $1 per year) for their space: A church, a school, or a public agency gives them shelter. In some parts of the country where real estate is becoming prohibitively expensive for nonprofits, a few philanthropic foundations are buying property for their own offices and offering space to their grantees at reasonable rates as a form of subsidy.

Lots of options, lots of decisions. This chapter explores the ins and outs of finding a suitable home base for a nonprofit organization, and of protecting the entire enterprise — furniture, fixtures, real estate, staff, volunteers, and board — against the risks of everyday life.

Finding a Place to Do Your Work

For some nonprofit organizations, their physical presence is critical to their identities. When people think of them, they envision specific buildings or natural settings. . . . Other nonprofits adapt easily to a wide variety of places.

If your organization is grappling with a move to a new (or to its first) building, you're facing some critically important decisions about how and when and where to go. You'll want to think through some critical questions up front, and you'll probably have to be somewhat flexible about matching your needs to available properties. This effort is likely to have three phases:

- ✔ Planning for your needs
- ✔ Identifying possible locations
- ✔ Analyzing the feasibility of the locations you find

Planning for your needs

In making your facility plans, ask yourself the following critical questions:

- ✔ Will you own, lease, or take something free?
- ✔ How much space do you need and of what type?
- ✔ How important is a specific location to fulfilling your mission? What are the parameters of that location?
- ✔ How much can you afford to invest in the space you find?

Owning, leasing, or taking a free ride

Because of the tax benefits of private home ownership, many people automatically assume that it's best for a nonprofit organization to own its own building. Although a nonprofit's building can be a valuable asset remember that a nonprofit is already exempt from paying most business taxes, so any interest it may pay on a mortgage or building loan is not a deductible expense — it's just an expense.

The major disadvantages of building ownership for nonprofits are that it increases workload and requires a continuing investment. If the organization buys a building that is larger than what it needs for its own programs, it may become a landlord to others. It must then be prepared to advertise the property, negotiate leases, provide a professional level of building maintenance, and respond to needs for repairs. Whether or not it has tenants, it becomes responsible for taking care of the building.

If your nonprofit organization buys its own building, it should set aside a cash reserve as a building maintenance fund. Otherwise, if a boiler explodes or the roof leaks, you may need to suspend operations for an extended period of time.

Here are two major advantages of building ownership:

- ✔ It stabilizes costs. If your organization is based in a real estate market where rents and leases are increasing rapidly, purchasing a building may be a way of controlling and stabilizing monthly operating costs and preventing an untimely eviction.

- ✔ It improves the public image of your organization. Organizations owning their own buildings appear in the public eye to be more permanent institutions. This perception can help them to raise money.

Taking a free ride through the donation of public or private space to your nonprofit sounds wonderful, doesn't it? Indeed, it can help to contain your organization's operating costs and allow you to use more of your resources for programs. But you must be willing to look a gift horse in the mouth. A free building is a worthwhile asset only if it is in the right location, is the right size, and serves your organization's needs. It's very difficult to do effective work in inappropriate space. Ask yourself, if it wasn't free, would we have picked it for our nonprofit?

Possible disadvantages to accepting free space include the following:

- ✔ **Inappropriate connections:** Making use of free space belonging to another public or private entity identifies your organization with the building's history and other uses. Often this is fine, but if the partnering agency is unpopular or unstable, that perception can reflect badly on your organization.

- ✔ **Perception of lack of need:** You may find that your organization is at a disadvantage in raising money because funding sources know that one of your major costs has been covered. You may be seen as having less need than other worthy agencies.

- ✔ **Loss of control:** If someone provides something free to you, you're put in a weak bargaining position. You may not have a lease, ensuring your use of the space for a prescribed period of time. You may not be able to control who your neighbors are, and incompatible uses may be combined under the same roof. You may not feel that you can complain if building maintenance is sloppy or repairs are postponed.

In considering whether to lease, own, or accept free space, first be confident that the building and its location are right for your organization. On the heels of that question is a second query: Can you create a long-term, stable, and affordable relationship with the building?

You must weigh the value of ownership against the labor and responsibility involved. Also important are the duration and terms of your lease and your relationship to your landlord. All these factors are further shaped by particulars of your community: How volatile is the real estate market? Are values rising or falling? Are interest rates rising or falling? How well are tenants' rights protected by law?

How much space and of what kind?

Before you go out to seek a location for your organization, make a list of your organization's specific needs. If you've ever shopped for an apartment or house, you know that some features are critically important and some are desired but not essential. Often it helps to break down your space needs by function and then include a list of general requirements. The following table shows the space needs of a community counseling center.

La Raza Counseling Center Space Needs

Space Use	Size	Accommodating/Features
Reception area	200 square feet	Space for desk, bookshelves, 2 small sofas
Office	600 square feet	Three workstations with electrical outlets, good light,
Conference room and library	400 square feet	Large conference table and chairs, good light
Six counseling rooms	400 square feet	Desks and chairs
Overall center	1500–1800 square feet	Natural light, street level location, good heat and air conditioning

Many nonprofits have highly specialized building needs. Dance studios, for instance, need large rooms without internal, supporting pillars; high ceilings; specifically designed "sprung" floors; dressing rooms; and excellent light.

In choosing a building, consider whether your organization will be changing the building's use and function. Different building codes are enforced according to a building's use. When more people use the building at the same time, for example, fire codes become more stringent, and more bathrooms are required. When looking at real estate, consult with an architect, a trusted realtor, or your town's planning department to find out about any building codes you may be required to meet.

To help you anticipate and specify all of your organization's facility needs, look for the "Facilities Requirement Worksheet" on the CD.

Tales of misplaced nonprofits

You may think that you've found the perfect location for your organization, but wait. Ask the people who will work there and use the organization's services. Three true stories note relocation errors made by nonprofit organizations:

✔ A youth development organization working with former and current gang members moves four blocks north into a larger, more comfortable building. Although not far, the move places the organization in a new gang's territory. Its clients are afraid to go to the new building.

✔ A parenting support group based in a public school in a low-income neighborhood moves into its own office for the first time. Although still in the same neighborhood, the new office requires the organization's bus-riding constituents to transfer from one bus line to another. The transfer doesn't take much time, but it does make the commute more complicated and forces parents to wait at an isolated bus stop in all kinds of weather. Parent attendance erodes.

✔ A Chicano theater company in a neighborhood where many recent immigrants live gains a strong critical reputation. As a matter of pride and seeking equity, it builds a new, larger theater in the city's downtown theater district. This places it close to major hotels and to commercial theaters frequented by tourists and more affluent local residents. Two years later, it can barely keep its doors open. Its loyal neighborhood following has eroded, and it can't invest enough in marketing to compete with commercial theaters and attract tourist audiences.

Location, location, location

A popular saying in the real estate field is that the three things that matter most in choosing a building are location, location, and location. Because many nonprofit organizations are designed to serve specific constituents, they're unlikely to fill their missions if they're not placed where those constituents can easily get to them.

Many nonprofit organizations have learned the hard way that having a beautiful new facility doesn't necessarily mean that their students, patients, or audiences will go there. We suggest that an organization conduct a simple marketing test of the location to see whether the people they serve can find it and would choose to go there. This "test" may take the form of a written survey, interviews, or an open house/walk-through at the proposed site followed by discussion groups.

Another assumption to test is whether *more* people will go there. Many organizations "build up" to larger facilities because their programs have grown too large for their current sites. And many nonprofits discover that offering more seats, classes, therapy sessions, or other resources doesn't necessarily mean that they will be used. Is there clear evidence of interest in your organization's services that exceeds its current capacity? If so, test your intended future location among these potential clients. Will they go there?

Just because your organization has been in the same neighborhood since it began doesn't necessarily mean that the location is its only or even its best possible site. Demographic characteristics of neighborhoods change over time, and your constituents may have moved. Stay alert to the best locations for fulfilling your organization's mission.

Figuring how much you can spend on facilities

You may want to read this part of the chapter alongside Chapter 18, which addresses capital campaigns and feasibility studies in greater detail. The question is how much you can afford to invest in moving, leasing, and possibly renovating or constructing a building. There's no magic formula for size and scale. Generally, large organizations with significant resources can succeed with grander capital projects. However, small organizations with the right board and campaign leadership can accomplish a lot. So can organizations whose projects are happening at the right place and at the right time — such as those qualifying for redevelopment agency funds or for low-interest bank loans for community development.

You can find leads to community loan and development funds for nonprofits on two helpful Web sites: www.communitycapital.org/cdfi_locator and www.socialinvest.org/Areas/SRIGuide/loan.htm.

Some organizations, such as community development or low-income housing corporations, focus their work exclusively on managing capital projects. You may find opportunities to work in partnership with them. For instance, La Raza Counseling Center, discussed earlier in this chapter, may share in a capital project with a nonprofit housing development corporation that is building new housing in a predominantly Spanish-speaking neighborhood. The tutoring center may provide services on the building's main floor, providing easy access to residents living upstairs, and the La Raza group may make its teaching rooms available after hours to a group of parents living in the building and running an informal tutoring program.

The primary reason to take on a renovation project is to create a facility that supports and advances your organization's work. If you operate a counseling center and are moving into a building that used to be a drugstore, you'll need to rearrange the internal space.

You may be faced with choosing between a relatively inexpensive, unfinished space and a more expensive building with lots of amenities. Consider your financial options. In the first case, the organization must conduct a capital campaign to raise renovation funds, but once the renovation is complete, monthly expenses will be affordable. In the second case, the nonprofit can begin offering services immediately without investing time and attention into a capital campaign, but monthly operating expenses will be higher. Which expenses — renovation or ongoing rent — is your organization in a better position to cover?

You may be wondering why the organization is responsible for the renovation costs. If it doesn't own the building, shouldn't the landlord pay for them? Depending on the rental market in your community, you may be able to convince the building owner to cover all or part of the costs of renovation, usually called the "build-out." If you do this, however, be prepared to pay higher rent. Build-out expenses are almost always prorated back into your rental agreement.

Also, your organization may have specialized space needs or require building upgrades to meet code requirements based on your use of the building. Does your landlord care about this? It depends on the office rental market in your community. If space is readily available, the landlord will be more accommodating; if space is tight, probably not.

Estimating costs

This section describes various costs you may encounter. Those with simple moving projects can stop reading near the top of the list. If your project is more complex, however, read through all the categories. A more detailed outline of capital costs — including the costs of raising money — is included in Chapter 18.

✔ Moving costs

- Moving van rental or moving service

- Boxes and shipping containers (a substantial cost for archives, museums, and historical societies)

- Transfer of utilities (garbage, water, and power) and services (phone, cable, and computer lines)

- Public notices about your move (printing, mailing, press releases, and e-mail announcements)

- Revision of basic printed materials (reprinting brochures, stationery, and other publications)

✔ Interior alterations

- Gutting the existing space and removing the rubble

- Constructing new workspaces, service spaces, and shelving

- Moving electrical outlets and adding phone and computer lines

- Buying furniture and fixtures

- ✔ Renovation or new construction
    - Architectural drawings
    - Engineering fees
    - Building permits
    - Site preparation and demolition
    - Foundation and structural repairs
    - Interior finishes, partitions, doors, and glazing
    - Accessibility — ramps, railings, elevators, and lifts
    - Plumbing systems
    - Heating, ventilation, and air conditioning systems
    - Power and communications systems
    - Fire protection systems
    - Exterior paving and landscaping
    - Contractor's fees
    - Contingency (15 percent of construction estimate)
    - Temporary storage costs
- ✔ Capital needs
    - Cash reserve for maintenance and repairs
    - Endowment restricted to building maintenance costs
- ✔ Other costs
    - Capital campaign expenses
    - Financing costs (if money is borrowed)
    - Loss of income if your agency needs to be closed for a period of time during the construction and move

See the CD for samples of two capital campaign budgets — one for a modest project and one for a large, budget-building project.

You must estimate the cost of improvements to be made in a chosen space — and test the feasibility of raising the needed money before purchasing a building or signing a lease agreement. An architect or contractor who's friendly to your organization should be willing to look at the space, point out major anticipated changes you'd want to make, and offer some very rough cost estimates. The second step in this process is called a "feasibility study" — a process most often led by a consultant who interviews key stakeholders in your organization and other supporters whose grants and gifts are essential to its success, to estimate how much you are likely to raise with a capital campaign.

Making it new?

Many nonprofits are based in older, restored, or renovated buildings. These organizations choose such buildings for a variety of reasons. Affordable (even forgivable) loans are available for restoring abandoned buildings in some locations. By moving into an existing building, nonprofits often can maintain staff and programs while also conducting capital campaigns and managing building improvements. Since the 1970s, the concept of creating "site-specific" work has been very strong in the arts. Taking over an old building and restoring it — responding to its architecture and original uses — aligned capital projects with ways of making art. Two wonderful examples are The Mattress Factory's restored buildings in Pittsburgh, Pennsylvania, and the Headlands Center for the Arts restored army buildings in Marin County,

California. And a kind of mystique has been associated with lofts — known as "creative spaces" — which often are placed in old factory and warehouse buildings.

Times are changing, however. New technology is changing the needs of working spaces, and in some parts of the nation, building code requirements are becoming more stringent, making many types of renovation projects very costly. Many nonprofits are discovering the pleasures of building new facilities to suit their specific needs. Such new construction may be cheaper and more efficient than reuse of existing buildings.

We're not suggesting that a new building is always the best course, but neither should you automatically rule out new construction.

On the CD accompanying this book, you can find an outline and a sample interview script for a feasibility study as well as the Nonprofit Finance Fund's "Organization Capacity Worksheet," which helps you to informally assess whether your organization is ready to undertake a capital campaign.

These interviews both test the likelihood that the project will succeed and begin the process of cultivating future project donors. A paid consultant is most often used because interview subjects are more likely to be candid when talking to someone not directly affiliated with the nonprofit agency.

The money needed for a capital project generally comes from a variety of sources:

- ✔ Large gifts from individuals, including trustees
- ✔ Medium-sized grants from foundations and corporations
- ✔ Small grants and gifts from businesses and individuals

The costs of renovating a building are likely to increase (at a rate of some 10 percent per year), and major donors may pledge a contribution but wait a year or longer before sending a check. For those reasons, borrowing money to complete construction (if reasonable interest rates are available) can help to contain costs while a capital campaign is being conducted and construction gets started. In some areas, community or private foundations may consider granting low-interest loans — often called "program related investments." Community development and economic development corporations may do the same, as may banks that see such loans as an important form of philanthropy.

Insuring Against What Can Go Wrong

Many people who start a nonprofit hope to improve conditions in the world, and they conduct their work with modest resources. They're not naïve, but they may have little time to dwell on the things that possibly can go wrong. (Okay, okay, we're making a generalization. There are some serious worriers out there in the nonprofit arena.)

But inevitably, things do go wrong. That's why nonprofits need insurance like everyone else. For the eternal optimists and for worriers alike, we highly recommend finding a good insurance broker as a guide to making appropriate choices of insurance and finding the most reasonable rates. We also recommend practicing risk management.

Managing your risks

Risk management means identifying and analyzing the risks your organization faces in carrying out its daily business. If you're a smart manager, you'll eliminate as many of these risks as possible (within reason). You'll be financially rewarded for pursuing this course: The more risks you can eliminate, the lower your insurance premiums will be.

Here's a simple example to illustrate risk management: The sidewalk in front of the entrance to your office is beginning to crack in two places. The concrete is uneven and may cause someone to trip and fall. Repairing the sidewalk is better than risking the chances of injury to a visitor.

Adding smoke alarms, sprinkler systems, and emergency lighting is another way to practice risk management. Those safety features are wise investments and probably will lower your property insurance. Although no one can think of everything that may go wrong, try to eliminate as many risks as possible. Insurance agents and brokers can be helpful in this exercise. You can find more information about risk management at the Nonprofit Risk Management Center (www.nonprofitrisk.org).

You must be honest on insurance applications, fully stating your agency's risks. If falsehoods are uncovered, your coverage will not protect you.

Determining your insurance needs

A nonprofit's insurance needs will vary according to the following:

- ✔ Whether it has employees
- ✔ Whether it makes use of volunteers
- ✔ Whether it has direct contact with clients, students, patients, or audiences and the nature of that direct contact
- ✔ Whether it offers services within its own (or a rented) piece of property

Providing health insurance

Beyond the employee benefits required by law, you will want to provide health coverage for your employees if at all possible so that they can afford medical attention if they're sick or injured. Offering this benefit also helps you recruit better-qualified employees.

In most cases, an organization can secure group health insurance for its employees at a more reasonable cost than what employees would have to pay if they bought it on their own. Generally health insurance becomes more affordable as your organization grows and the group for which you're buying it becomes larger. For small organizations and those just beginning to consider providing health insurance for employees, here are some ways to get started:

- ✔ Begin with insurance that covers only major health catastrophes. If you can't afford a full coverage, you may want to begin with insurance that covers major, very expensive medical problems. Usually such insurance is less costly because a major crisis occurs less frequently. If such medical problems do arise, they can destroy your employee's family, home, and stability. You can add insurance for more routine medical attention later, just as you can add dental and vision care.

- ✔ Begin with a higher deductible amount. Again, your employees' personal and professional stability is more threatened by expensive medical costs than by routine check-ups and an occasional flu shot. Most insurance doesn't begin to cover costs until the employee has paid a certain amount up front, the amount that is referred to as *deductible*. Sometimes you can secure comprehensive health coverage for your employees if the deductible amount is relatively high — say, $1,000 rather than $200. Then, as you can afford it, you can improve their coverage by getting insurance with a lower deductible.

- ✔ Try to join with a group. Many nonprofit service organizations offer their members the benefit of joining a group health insurance plan. In selecting your insurance options, don't forget to contact your local United

Way office, your statewide or province-wide association of nonprofit organizations, or service organizations specializing in the type of work your nonprofit provides.

Statewide nonprofit associations — some of which help with group insurance plans — can be found through the National Council of Nonprofit Associations (). Also check with your local United Way office.

✔ If you're a new entity and using a fiscal sponsor, check on whether it can help. It may provide access to health and other types of insurance as a service to sponsored projects.

You can find more about employee health insurance in Chapter 7.

Insuring against workplace injuries

If an employee is injured in the course of performing duties for your nonprofit, workers' compensation insurance covers the cost of medical treatment and — in some cases — the cost of retraining the employee for a different profession.

For example, in this age of frequent computer use, some employees experience carpal tunnel (or repetitive stress) syndrome in their hands and arms. In mild cases, they may recover through rest, special exercises, and the rearrangement of their desks, chairs, and equipment. In serious cases, they may never again be able to type or may be able to type only for short periods of time. Workers' compensation insurance should cover the costs of their therapy and retraining.

The cost of your workers' compensation insurance is calculated according to your number of employees, the number of hours they spend on the job, and the nature of the work they do. Rates for office clerks are considerably lower than rates for lion tamers and trapeze artists.

In most states, workers' compensation insurance is not an option like health insurance. It is required by law. As a nonprofit manager, therefore, you don't make a choice about whether to buy it, but simply attend to the details of how your choice is exercised. Here are two examples of information you should be analyzing:

✔ Do you use docents or other consistent volunteers? We highly recommend including them in your workers' compensation insurance coverage. We have witnessed two instances in which volunteers were seriously hurt in the course of assisting nonprofit organizations but weren't covered by workers' compensation insurance. The results were nearly catastrophic for the agencies.

✔ If your organization's staff size or the nature of the work your employees do changes during the course of the year, contact your workers' compensation insurance carrier and change your coverage accordingly. Do you have an annual "work day" in which everyone pitches in to clean and repair your building? Do you have a large annual benefit for which lots of employees are working on ladders, stringing lights and garlands? If you plan ahead to change the definition of the type of work they perform, you can be confident that they're covered.

Workers' compensation insurance is a specialized field of law. If you encounter a legal problem about your coverage, seek assistance from an attorney with experience in this field.

Some nonprofit organizations require volunteers to sign waivers that release the nonprofits from responsibility for insuring them. However, waivers may not stand up in a court of law.

Purchasing liability insurance

Someone carelessly stretches an electrical cord across a hallway, and a client trips and falls. A shingle falls from the roof and hits a visitor on the head. Sigmund Freud might have said that there are no accidents, but liability insurance is based on the oops and ouches of daily life and human error. No matter how minor it may seem, if you make a mistake while performing your organization's duties and someone is injured as a result, you can be sued.

By purchasing liability insurance, you have access to a source of revenue for settling a lawsuit should you be sued for this kind of mistake. Your insurance company also may provide legal defense, if it's needed. Most businesses purchase liability insurance as a matter of course. You may get by without it for a time, but be required to get it if you meet any of the following conditions:

✔ You accept a contract or grant from a government source.

✔ You rent offices or other facilities (whether for a short time or a long term).

✔ You seek a city or county permit to use public property.

✔ You seek an operating or construction permit.

You need to purchase specialized kinds of liability insurance if your organization has significant direct client contact that involves a potential risk. Health clinics and therapy programs need such insurance to protect them should a client be hurt or handled inappropriately. So do programs offering activities with possible physical dangers, such as rock climbing, sailboating, or horseback riding.

If your organization occasionally produces events or conducts work in locations other than its central office or building, double-check to make sure that you're covered for these off-site events. You may want to purchase a rider to your regular liability insurance policy to cover such situations.

Protecting directors and officers from lawsuits

Although corporate laws vary by state and nation, in most contexts, the personal assets of directors and officers of nonprofit organizations are protected from legal proceedings against those nonprofits if the directors are providing reasonable oversight and governance to the organization. Nevertheless, just to make sure, you can purchase directors and officers liability insurance.

Board members usually are well protected in lawsuits against nonprofits if they attend meetings, ask questions, and keep well informed about the organization — in other words, if they're doing reasonably good jobs of being a board members. If they're not doing their job, they may be considered personally negligent and become vulnerable.

For example, board members' personal assets can be liable if the nonprofit organization isn't paying its federal employee taxes. However, even in this dire situation, if the nonprofit has contacted the Internal Revenue Service and worked out a payment plan, board members are unlikely to be affected.

So why would you want to pay for directors and officers insurance? The biggest advantage is that it covers the cost of your organization's legal defense against lawsuits. It also may be reassuring to board members and potential board members. Some people refuse to serve on a board if the organization doesn't have director and officers insurance. And, as an organization's visibility and assets grow, such insurance becomes more important. Here are some examples of situations in which it is highly recommended:

- ✔ If your organization has to lay off or fire employees, directors and officers insurance may be worthwhile. The most common type of lawsuit brought against nonprofit organizations is for "wrongful discharge."

- ✔ Your organization's work is controversial, making it a potential target for lawsuits.

- ✔ Your organization is a hospital, health clinic, or another kind of entity that — because of the intense, professional service it provides — also is more liable to malpractice and other kinds of liability lawsuits.

- ✔ Your organization has weathered a severe financial crisis. In attracting new board members, you want to firmly reassure them that this financial crisis will not come back to haunt them personally.

✔ Your organization has grown and thrived. It has a large endowment and cash reserves, increasing the likelihood of being a target for lawsuits.

✔ You have the good fortune to have wealthy and influential board members. Although their assets should be protected if they are attentive board members, they're natural targets for nuisance lawsuits.

Protecting property and vehicles

If you own a home and your own car, you undoubtedly value those possessions enough to insure them in case of damage, loss, or theft. You need to protect your nonprofit's building and vehicles in the same way.

Suppose that the big bad wolf comes by and huffs and puffs and blows your nonprofit down. Say that a tornado swoops past, taking with it more than you and your little dog Toto. You need property insurance including — if you're lucky enough to find it — coverage against malicious animals and tornados.

Each part of the world has its own set of anticipated natural disasters. You may need to anticipate earthquakes (we do here in California), hurricanes, tornadoes, tsunamis, monsoons, firestorms, blizzards, or hail the size of golf balls.

The cost of your property insurance varies according to the size and value of your property and how the buildings are constructed. In many places, insuring a house of straw generally is more expensive than insuring a house of bricks. A terrible irony is that the disaster that you're most likely to face is the one for which your insurance will be most expensive. Sometimes you simply can't get insurance for your likeliest disaster.

So, unlike health insurance, for which the most inexpensive plans cover only large-scale catastrophes, if you want to add coverage to your property insurance policy for floods, hail, earthquakes, or whatever goes wrong in your part of the world, your property insurance may become prohibitively expensive. Ideally, you want your property insurance to cover your organization for damage repairs — both to the building and its holdings — and provide business interruption insurance covering your losses of income if you are forced by a disaster to be closed for a period of time. In some instances you won't be able to find property insurance that includes coverage for a likely disaster and you will have to purchase a separate policy for protection from that potential crisis or do without that protection. Day-to-day drips and clogs, creaks, and rips are both likelier to happen and more affordable to cover with property insurance. And the higher the deductible, the lower the cost of your insurance.

Most property insurance policies cover the contents of a facility in addition to the building itself. Your policy may place a limit on the amount it would pay toward replacing those contents should something go wrong. Make sure that the coverage is adequate to cover the replacement cost of your organization's furniture, fixtures, and equipment.

If your organization owns its building and has tenants, you need a particularly comprehensive and flexible property insurance policy. Insist that your tenants have their own insurance: You can include this condition in the terms of their leases.

Your organization may own or dream of owning a company car, van, bus, truck, or other vehicle. So, of course, vehicle insurance is necessary. If you can't limit the use of this vehicle to one or two drivers, such insurance is prohibitively expensive.

Maybe your organization doesn't own a building or vehicle. You still need insurance that protects your property. Buy theft insurance to protect your equipment and furniture, and renters' insurance to cover the cost of repairing accidental damage to the property caused by you or others at your organization.

Getting even deeper into insurance

Property and liability insurance are the two primary types of insurance that an organization should consider, but they're by no means the only types. Here are a few more:

- ✔ **Employee dishonesty insurance or fidelity bonds:** Insurance of this type protects the organization against employee theft or embezzlement.

- ✔ **Umbrella insurance:** This policy covers some types of extraordinary losses. For example, if you have a general liability policy that pays for losses up to $500,000, you may want to get an umbrella policy that kicks in if a settlement is higher than $500,000. Umbrella policies also set an upper limit on coverage but tend to be less expensive than basic liability policies.

- ✔ **Long-term disability insurance:** Although the cost may be prohibitive for small organizations, offering long-term disability insurance is an excellent employee benefit.

- ✔ **Sexual misconduct or abuse insurance:** Insurance to guard against charges of employee sexual misconduct may be important for programs that serve clients and, in particular, children.

Chapter 12

Finding Outside Help
When You Need It

. . . .

In This Chapter

▶ Finding consultants and working with them

▶ Getting help from other nonprofits

▶ Going to school

▶ Finding help online

. . . .

*E*veryone needs a helping hand from time to time. Fortunately, nonprofit managers and volunteers can travel a number of avenues to get assistance and advice.

Many experienced consultants specialize in working with nonprofit organizations. They help with everything from board training to fundraising. In fact, many nonprofit organizations exist to provide consulting services and training classes to other nonprofits! If you decide you want to go back to school to get a degree in nonprofit management, many opportunities await you. And the advent of the Web has brought advice, examples, forms, regulations, and discussion groups to your home or office with the click of a mouse.

This chapter guides you through all these different sources of assistance and points you in the right direction.

Bringing In a Hired Gun — a Consultant

Well, maybe *hired gun* is a little extreme. We don't want to give the impression that consultants are gunslingers from the Old West. Consultants are just like everyone else, except they have more experience and knowledge in selected topics and have more time to worry about these topics than you do.

We can think of three reasons why you may want to bring in a consultant:

- To apply expertise that no one on your staff or board has to a problem or project
- To undertake a task that you don't have time for
- To bring a fresh, outside perspective to a situation that is causing problems for your organization

You may be able to come up with other reasons, but we think these are the primary motivations for seeking outside help.

Consultants can help you with just about any aspect of your organization, from personnel matters to hooking up a computer network. But nonprofits most commonly bring in a consultant to help out with

- **Fundraising.** Fundraising consultants help with grant writing, planning for fundraising, and major gift and capital campaigns, among other methods of raising funds.
- **Organizational development.** Organization development consultants work to advance your organization and build its capacity by guiding board and staff through a planning process or by facilitating better communications between staff members and the board of directors, to name a few examples. The possibilities for organizational improvement are endless.

Have a clear idea of what you want to accomplish before you seek help. Sometimes you won't know exactly what you're aiming to accomplish, but you should still try to articulate as clearly as possible what your aim is in hiring a consultant before you go looking for one.

Consultants can't solve all of your problems; they don't carry magic beans in their pockets. They make recommendations, but quite likely it's going to be up to you to carry them out. Consultants should be seen as a tool to help your organization perform better, but in the end it comes down to what you and your associates do to push your agency forward.

Finding a consultant: Best way, ask around

There's no single best way to find consultants. You can certainly look in your local yellow pages or search the Web for nonprofit consultants who work in your area, but we think that the best way is to use word of mouth, if possible. A few calls to other nearby nonprofits may be necessary to get some leads, but that's time well spent. You also may be able to find a consultant through a *nonprofit support organization,* which we talk more about later in this chapter.

Grant writers won't do it all for you

Don't expect a hired grant writer to solve all your funding problems. Hiring grant writers is fine, but understand that they need to work with your programs, financial statements, brochures, and so on. Grant proposals are really a group production; they depend on input from program and management staff, among others. And while a well-written grant proposal is important, writing alone won't nail down the grant. You'll need to have a solid program or project, a well-thought out argument for why it deserves funding, and a solid financial plan.

If another nonprofit recommends a consultant to you, you'll have a head start in deciding if he or she is the right person for your organization. You want to find out, of course, if the consultant's last project was successful. Getting some perspective on a consultant's working style is also helpful. Will his or her personality fit with your needs and your workplace?

We prefer consultants who have more than one way of doing things. Not all nonprofits are alike, and what works for one may not work for another. Some consultants have either accepted a particular school of thought or have developed their own tried and true methods. Be cautious when a consultant tells you that there is only one way to do something.

Some consultants work as sole practitioners; others work in consulting companies. Working with a company or consulting group may give you access to more varied expertise. On the other hand, consultants working alone tend to have lower overhead expenses so their fees may (and we stress *may*) be lower.

Interviewing consultants

Interviewing a consultant is similar to interviewing a regular job applicant. You want to review the resume carefully to see if the candidate's experience and expertise match your needs.

Don't be intimidated just because the person sitting across the table from you has more experience than you do. He or she will be working for you. Ask any questions that you feel are necessary so that you can be sure that you've chosen the right person.

You may have the opportunity to use a volunteer consultant provided by a program that provides free or low-cost assistance to nonprofits. Interview these individuals just as you would a paid consultant. Remember that it's still your decision and your organization.

Overcoming the fear factor

Staff, and sometimes board members, can feel threatened by a consultant, especially if the consultant is coming in to solve a problem or to recommend changes in the organization. Change, even the threat of change, is difficult for all of us.

Handle the situation by encouraging open communication among the people who potentially are affected by the consultant's recommendations. People need to talk and be reassured, when possible.

Ask interviewees to describe their method or approach to the problem or project that you're seeking to solve or complete. Don't expect them to give you a full-blown plan in the interview, but they should be able to give you a good picture of how they will approach the issue.

Don't expect a consultant to solve your problem before you enter into a contract. Although learning whether the consultant has the ability to do the job is important, expecting him or her to give you all the answers before you agree to pay for the work is unreasonable. Speaking from a consultant's point of view, we've learned the hard way not to suggest solutions before we're hired. Doing so is called giving away the store.

Interview more than one person before you make your decision. As with interviewing for staff positions, having more than one person present at the interview is important because it lets you see how the prospective consultant interacts with a small group and gives you multiple perspectives on the consultant.

Signing the contract

You should have a signed contract with every consultant with whom you work. These points should be clearly stated in the contract:

- ✔ **Fees, of course.** Some consultants charge an hourly rate plus expenses; others charge a flat rate that may or may not include expenses per project. The contract should state that you must approve expenses over a certain amount. Or you can write into the agreement that expenses will be limited to a certain sum each month. Consultant fees vary, just like salaries, from one geographic area to another and depend on the type of work to be done and the experience of the consultant.

We don't recommend paying fundraising consultants a percentage of money raised. Although some consultants, grant writers, and, in particular, telemarketers work under this arrangement, percentage payment is not considered good practice by most fundraisers and nonprofit

managers. See the Association of Fundraising Professional's Code of
Ethics for more information about this issue www.nsfre.org/ethics.

✔ **The schedule of when you will pay the fees.** Some consultants who
work on an hourly basis may send you an invoice at the end of month.
Consultants working on a flat-fee basis may require advance payment on
a portion of the fee. This is fine. It's protection for the consultant who
probably has as many cash-flow problems as you do. The final payment
should not come before the project is completed.

✔ **Special contingencies.** What if the consultant gets sick? What if your
organization faces an unforeseen crisis and you don't have time to work
with the consultant? What if you've chosen the wrong consultant? So
you should include a mutually agreed-upon way to end the contract
before the project is completed. A 30-day cancellation notice is common.

✔ **A timetable for completing the work.** You and the consultant need to
negotiate the timetable. Have you ever had remodeling work done on
your house? You know that contractors can get distracted by other
work, right? That's why having a schedule is so important.

✔ **What the organization's role will be in the project.** If the consultant
needs access to background materials, records, volunteers, board members, or staff, you must provide this access in a timely manner so that
the consultant can complete the job.

✔ **What work is to be done and what results are expected.** This will be
more or less detailed depending on the type of project the consultant is
performing. If the consultant is being hired to facilitate a one-day retreat
for your board of directors, be sure that the contract includes the preparation time needed. Also, will the consultant be writing a report following the retreat? Try to touch on as many details as possible. The more
specific, the better.

We think having the consultant prepare the contract is a good idea. It's the
final chance to make sure that he or she understands what it is you want
done. You may suggest changes when you see the first draft.

Getting Help from Other Nonprofits

Some nonprofits have the mission of helping other nonprofits do their jobs
better. They are known as *nonprofit support organizations* or *technical assistance providers.* These organizations are funded by fees for their services and
by grants from foundations and corporations interested in *nonprofit capacity
building,* the jargon for helping a nonprofit develop infrastructure and management techniques so that it can do its job more effectively.

Nonprofit support organizations often have consultants on staff who do the
same work as private consultants and consulting companies. They also may

provide training workshops in a variety of topics ranging from building your board of directors to personnel matters. Most nonprofit support organizations charge a fee for both consulting and training workshops, but the fees often are based on a sliding scale keyed to the size of your annual budget.

If you live in major metropolitan area, there is a good chance that you have one or more of these organizations near you. The Alliance for Nonprofit Management (www.allianceonline.org) has a search function on its Web site that lets you find the nearest support organization in your area.

You can also visit the Web sites of CompassPoint Nonprofit Services (www.compasspoint.org), a support organization in the San Francisco area, and MAP for Nonprofits (www.mapnp.org/services-home.html), a support organization in the Minneapolis/St. Paul area, for more information on how support organizations function.

Seeking informal help from colleagues

You can certainly ask staff and board members at other nonprofit organizations for advice and help. In fact, maintaining a network of contacts with other nonprofit managers and board members is a good idea. Informal support networks can be very helpful for exchanging ideas, passing on tips, or just offering and accepting moral support in a profession that sometimes can be frustrating.

In some areas, nonprofit managers have organized support groups that meet on a regular basis, like a monthly brown-bag luncheon, for instance.

 If you're new to nonprofits, try to find a mentor whom you can go to for advice. A mentor is someone who has more experience than you and is willing to give you some time on a semi-regular basis to pass on advice and to act as a sounding board for ideas.

Professional associations

Check to find out if there is an umbrella group for organizations doing similar work as yours. Ask a colleague at a similar organization, or go on the Web. For example, if you're running a local symphony orchestra, you could join the American Symphony Orchestra League (www.symphony.org). These umbrella groups, essentially trade associations for nonprofits, often provide technical support and training to member organizations. You'll probably need to pay an annual membership fee, but it's money well spent.

 The American Society of Association Executives (www.asaenet.org/main) is a large organization providing support to nonprofit managers, mostly of large organizations.

In the United States, there are 39 different state associations for nonprofits. It doesn't matter what sort of service you're providing. If one of these organizations is present in your state, your nonprofit can join and take advantage of association benefits that may include training sessions, publications, group insurance programs, and consulting services. You can find out if your state has a state association by visiting the National Council of Nonprofit Association's Web site (`www.ncna.org/states.htm`).

Going Back to School

After you get involved with a nonprofit organization, you may find that you want or need formal training. In the last decade, an explosion in graduate degree programs for nonprofit managers has occurred. At last count, 180 colleges and universities offered such programs. Researchers at Seton Hall University have compiled a list of programs that you can see by visiting `pirate.shu.edu/~mirabero/Kellogg.html`.

As the nonprofit sector grows, more and more nonprofit managers hold graduate degrees, either in some aspect of nonprofit management or generic degrees such as MBAs or Masters of Public Administration. Many colleges and universities also offer non-degree programs, often through continuing education departments, that lead to certification. Many programs schedule evening and weekend classes for the convenience of working students.

For training in fundraising we can recommend one book and two long-standing programs. The book is *Grant Writing For Dummies* (Hungry Minds, Inc.). The programs, both of which offer workshops throughout the United States, are

- ✔ The Grantmanship Center (`www.tgci.com`). The Grantsmanship Center's classes are, as you might guess from the name, focused on preparing grant proposals.
- ✔ The Fund Raising School (`www.philanthropy.iupui.edu/fundschool.htm`). This school is associated with the Center on Philanthropy at Indiana University. Its classes cover everything from fundraising for small nonprofits to running capital campaigns.

These programs require registration fees and tuition. We know that finding the resources (and the time) to sign up can be challenging. You may be able to obtain scholarships to attend some of the programs, and colleges and universities have financial aid and loan programs available. Also, your organization may be able to get a small grant to pay for all or part of your tuition.

The Foundation Center (`fdncenter.org`) offers free introductory workshops on grant seeking and grant writing at its libraries in New York, Atlanta, Cleveland, San Francisco, and Washington, D.C.

Much closer to home, you can dip into Chapter 16 of this book for easy reference on seeking and winning grants.

Going Online

Online resources for nonprofit organizations are becoming more abundant every day. You can find everything from IRS forms to discussion forums and listservs. We think that the amount of resources available on the Web will continue to grow and that more people will turn to the Web for information to help them run their nonprofit organizations.

All of the resources listed earlier in this chapter have Web sites and many even allow you to register for courses online. But you still have to get in a car or climb on a bus to get to the classes. Some formal programs in grant writing and nonprofit management are now being taught exclusively on the Web. This means, of course, that you can sit at home or in your office and learn at your leisure.

Getting to the information

Going on the Web for the first time, or even the 10th time, can be a scary experience. It can be like going into a library that doesn't have a card catalog.

Here's a quick overview of different types of online tools and destinations.

Search engines.

Search engines maintain a database of Web pages. You type one or more keywords into the search window, click the search button, and a list of Web pages containing the keywords you entered, ranked for possible relevance, pops up on your screen. Different search engines use different formulas for searching pages, so it's rare that two search engines will return the same order of pages.

In using most search engine searches, you get thousands of possible pages returned. We find that usually only the first ten or twenty or so are worth taking the time to check out. After that, you're likely to end up at the Ukrainian Water Treatment Plant home page.

One of our favorite search engines is Google (google.com), but many other search engines are out there. Your online service provider may have a search engine that you typically use.

Some search engines are set up to search other search engines. They are called *metasearch engines*. Dogpile (www.dogpile.com) is an example. It returns results from several different search engines.

Directories

Directories are sometimes confused with search engines. At a directory, Web sites are organized by human editors into categories. When you go to the home page, you see a listing of broad categories. When you click on one of the categories, Business and Economy, for instance, another page opens with more defined categories, and so on and so on.

Other directories include Looksmart (`www.looksmart.com`) and the Open Directory Project (`dmoz.org`). Links for the Open Directory Project are compiled by volunteer editors.

Nonprofit Directories

Nonprofit directories are Web sites that provide links to online materials of interest to nonprofits. We don't want to toot our own horn too much, but one coauthor of this book (Stan) runs the About site for nonprofit charitable organizations (`nonprofit.about.com`). The site has a lot of original articles, as well as links to other materials about every aspect of nonprofit management and fundraising. After you check out Stan's About site, here are some other nonprofit directories you may want to visit:

- `www.mapnp.org/library`. The Nonprofit Management Library has many links and a lot of information about management issues.
- `www.guidestar.com`. GuideStar maintains a database of charitable organizations in the United States.
- `helping.org`. A project of the AOL foundation, Helping.org provides free information and a free online donation service.
- `www.techsoup.org`. This site refers to itself as "The technology place for nonprofits" and has volumes of helpful information.
- `www.benton.org`. Another site with helpful information to help your nonprofit solve its technology issues.

We could go on and on. The point is that resources on the Web can help you do everything from plan for your computer needs to construct a business plan.

Listservs and Web-based discussion forums

If you don't find what you're looking for on a Web page, you can ask someone online. Although online discussions about nonprofits will never surpass sports talk or attempts at romance, you can find people who like to talk (that is, type) about nonprofit organizations and are happy to answer your questions.

A *listserv,* by the way, is an e-mail list. You subscribe to a listserv and wait until the e-mail starts to arrive. Many listservs maintain digests of past conversations, so catching up if you're just starting out is easy. *Web-based forums* are similar to listservs in terms of the discussions, but you must go to the Web site and sign in with your login ID and password to read online conversations (called *threads*) about various nonprofit topics. When you join in the conversation or ask a question, it's called *posting*.

The Charity Channel listservs (`CharityChannel.com/forums`) generate much conversation. You can sign up for over 30 different topics and discuss everything from fundraising in Canada or the United Kingdom to ethical issues faced by nonprofits and their staff and board members.

If you want a more structured discussion around particular topics and if you're looking for information about fundraising, FundClass (`www.fundraiser-software.com/fundclass.html`) may be the ticket. It's a listserv but it focuses on one fundraising topic at a time by bringing in volunteer experts who give online tutorials and answer questions about raising money.

Helping.org (`www.helping.org/nonprofit/forums`) also provides targeted online discussions, mostly about technical issues and using the Internet. This isn't a listserv that sends e-mail messages to your computer; it's a Web-based discussion forum. You use your browser to read messages people have posted to the topic thread.

A few words about online etiquette

Before you jump in start posting on listservs and forums, holding back and just listening (that is, reading) for a few days is a good idea. You'll learn the habits and the manners of each particular group. This knowledge eases your entrance into the ongoing discussions. In others listservs or forums, holding back for a few days helps you avoid making a fool of yourself by posting off topic or repeating what others have said.

Nonprofit listservs and discussion forums are, by and large, polite places where heated arguments occur infrequently. Still, they do happen. Take a little time to see the lay of the land before jumping in. And if you don't feel like joining the discussion, you can still learn a lot by reading what others say.

A few other pointers about online discussions:

✔ Always identify yourself and your organization when you participate in an online discussion. Doing so lets people know who you are and where you're coming from.

✔ Write in short paragraphs. Reading on a computer screen can be tedious, and reading a solid block of text can be almost impossible. Spread things out.

Getting a formal education online

Remember correspondence courses? *Distance learning* is the new name for the old concept, and the Internet has changed the means by which remote teaching is offered. If you want to do your homework in your pajamas, distance learning may be for you.

You can earn a certificate in nonprofit management and continuing education credits, for example, by signing up with the Learning Institute's (www.learningstream.com) certification program. It consists of eight modules that cover subjects such as planning, raising funds, and marketing.

When looking into online courses, always be sure to assess their legitimacy. Ask if you can be in touch with former students so that you get a first-hand account of their experiences.

Part III
Raising Money and Visibility

The 5th Wave — By Rich Tennant

"And here's our returning champion, spinning for next year's operating budget of the Take a Chance Foundation."

In this part . . .

We lead you into the realm of financial grants and annual fund drives, galas and golf tournaments, revealing the mindset of people who receive your requests for funds, including charitable foundations, private corporations, individuals, and the government. And we help you to understand the language of fundraising. In case a fund drive or building project is part of your plans, we give special attention to capital campaigns.

Almost any organization can better fulfill its goals — and raise more money — if the public is well informed about its work. So Part III also covers marketing and public relations. These combined efforts — fundraising and marketing — invite others to share in your nonprofit's mission.

Chapter 13

Crafting a Fundraising Plan

*I*f an organization is going to provide a public service, it needs money. Plain and simple. It may be run by volunteers and need just a little money, or it may need lots of money to pay for employees, office space, and so on.

Any nonprofit — whatever its purpose — grows out of someone's idea, someone's passion (maybe yours!) to make the world better. Raising money is inviting others to share in that belief, in that passion.

Different kinds of causes appeal to different people or institutions. Your organization could get most of its money from the government, or from grantmaking foundations, or from businesses, or from individuals. Successful fundraising is based on a plan, and a good plan is based on understanding an organization's likeliest sources of funding. A good plan is also balanced. No organization should put all of its eggs in one basket, or — in this case — imagine its entire omelet coming from one chicken.

In this chapter, we show you how to gather your funding eggs from a number of nests.

Making Your Plan in Five Steps

Making a fundraising plan is a lot easier when you have a guide to follow. And here's your guide! If you follow the steps carefully, you should end up with a truly useful funding plan.

1. **Create a document that provides a brief overview of the previous year's sources of contributions.**

   Indicate which ones the agency can anticipate receiving funds from again and which are unlikely sources for the coming year.

2. **Next, outline the agency's likely amounts of earned revenues.**

   These revenues can be from something like the sale of tickets to a workshop or they can come from interest earned on an endowment, if your organization is lucky enough to have one.

3. **Next, map out the organization's goals for different types of contributions.**

   The plan is likely to include goals for some (maybe all!) of the following categories:

   - Government grants or contracts
   - Foundation grants
   - Corporate contributions
   - Individual contributions
   - Annual fund
   - Major gifts
   - Memberships
   - Special events

4. **For each of the above revenue areas, indicate who will work on raising the money, how many prospective sources you'll need to meet your goal, and outline a general timeframe for how long it will take.**

   This step is the one that's most often overlooked. Having goals is great, but what actions will you take to achieve them? The agency should take a second look at the information you gather for this step. Is the plan piling much too much work onto one person? Are all the major deadlines falling in February? Perhaps it should reschedule and reassign work to adjust and balance these pressures.

5. **Figure out the cost of achieving each fundraising goal.**

   It's a good idea to create a cash-flow plan that estimates when income will be received and when major expenses will need to be met.

6. **Put the fruits of your labor together in one document, and you have your funding plan!**

   Just make sure that you read the rest of this chapter before you get started.

Many agencies create an optimum plan and a bare-bones plan — one based on their hopes and one based on what they must secure to survive. During the course of the year they rebalance and adjust their plan.

The overall goal is to achieve a healthy balance among your nonprofit's mission, goals, and resources.

The CD accompanying this book includes two sample fundraising plans and budgets, one for a small school music organization and another for a slightly larger neighborhood park improvement organization.

Naming Your Sources of Funds

We need to introduce some of the terms that we use in this chapter to describe the different kinds of contributions an organization might seek or different ways of raising money.

- ✔ **Grants.** Grants are formal contributions made to an organization by foundations, corporations, or government agencies, most often to help the nonprofit address defined goals or manage specific programs. Some grants (called *project* or *program* grants) are for trying out new ideas or enhancing existing programs. Others (called *general operating* grants) support the overall work of an organization.

  Contracts that are awarded to nonprofits may seem like grants, but there's a distinction. Contracts are payments made to organizations in exchange for a specific service. Most often contracts are awarded by government agencies. Contract applications may resemble grant proposals, but usually the terms of a contract are more clearly and specifically defined by the agency that awards it. (The government has defined what needs to be done and the applicant is trying to prove that it is the best organization to complete the job.) The most important distinction may be that a contract awarded to a nonprofit is considered earned income rather than a contribution.

- ✔ **Corporate contributions.** Some corporations create their own foundations (which award grants) and some award contributions directly — most often out of their public affairs, community relations, or marketing departments. Many corporations give *in-kind* gifts, which are contributions of goods and services rather than or in addition to cash contributions.

✔ **Individual contributions.** Gifts to organizations from private individuals may be given in support of specific programs or may be for any of a nonprofit's costs. Common types of individual contributions include

- **Annual gifts.** A contribution (often for a modest amount) written once a year to a charity is, appropriately enough, called an annual gift. The consistency of such gifts makes them of great value to the recipient.

- **Major gifts.** As suggested in the name, a major gift is a large amount of money. *Large* is a deliberately vague word here: Each organization has its own idea of what a large amount of money is. For some organizations it may be $100, and for others it may be $500,000.

- **Memberships.** Similar in some ways to an annual gift, a membership is a contribution made in exchange for some benefit or service from the nonprofit organization. Some nonprofits are structured so that their members play a role in their governance. Many provide modest gifts to their members or special opportunities, such as previews of new programs, private viewings of art exhibitions, or advance notice of special events.

Some people consider memberships to be earned income rather than contributions because members are, to an extent, purchasing a service. The nonprofit organization just has to let donors know the value of any gifts or benefits they receive in return for a membership.

- **Planned giving/bequests.** These are contributions that donors make to nonprofit organizations through their wills or other legal documents regulating what happens to their money and property after they die. Generally, the donor works with a trust officer at a bank or law firm to design his or her planned giving. Large organizations often have staff who specialize in providing technical assistance in this area to donors.

- **Special Events.** From marathons to chicken dinners to celebrity concerts, income generated by fundraising events supports organizations. Contributors can deduct from their taxes the portion of their event ticket that is above and beyond the cost of producing the event. Individuals, corporations, and small businesses are the likeliest supporters of special events. We talk about special events at greater length in Chapter 15.

- **Endowment.** If a donor of any kind designates a gift to a nonprofit as being for the endowment, the nonprofit must invest the money so that earnings from the investment can, in the future, be used to support the work of the nonprofit. Some foundations make endowment grants. Individuals (sometimes through bequests) also make endowment gifts.

Tracing Money to the Source

Surveys indicate that nonprofits' money comes from the following sources and in the following percentages:

> 39 percent from dues, fees, and charges (money that you earn)
>
> 31 percent from government sources
>
> 18 percent from private sources (foundations, corporations, and individuals)
>
> 7 percent from other sources
>
> 5 percent from endowments (income you earn from money you have invested)

Within this big picture, the primary sources of income change dramatically depending on the type of nonprofit organization. Some things to consider, depending on your type of organization:

- **Social service organization:** About 50 percent of your income is likely to come from the government and 20 percent from private contributions.

- **Health services organization:** About 48 percent of your income is likely to come from dues, fees, and charges, and 41 percent from the government.

- **Education or research organization:** About 7 percent of your income is likely to come from dues, fees, and charges, and 20 percent from the government.

- **Arts or cultural organization:** About 40 percent of your income is likely to come from private contributions and 24 percent from dues, fees, and charges.

- **Religious organization:** About 95 percent of your income is likely to come from private contributions.

Recognizing where your organization fits within this broad outline helps as you start to shape the broad outline of a funding plan.

Just because the average agency of a given type earns X percent of its income from individuals or Y percent of its income from government contracts doesn't mean that there's anything wrong with a nonprofit that has a different pattern. An organization's fundraising may be quite vital but not at all like the average. Also, the figures that we give are national. Sources and opportunities are different in different parts of the country.

The above figures show that the government is an important source of money and a critical part of the funding plan for most kinds of agencies. But when thinking about fundraising, most nonprofits think about asking for private contributions. So, let's take apart that important category. These percentages shift slightly from year to year, but the averages are

- ✔ Corporations and company-sponsored foundations account for 9 percent of private contributions.
- ✔ Bequests (gifts made through individuals' wills) account for 8 percent of private contributions.
- ✔ Individuals responding to letters, personal visits, special events, and many other forms of asking account for 77 percent of private contributions.

While many of us dream of securing big grant, individual donors give more by far to nonprofit causes than other kinds of private contributors. When you consider bequests and other kinds of gifts, individuals represent 85 percent of private giving. If these numbers don't jive with your organization's numbers, don't worry about it. Individuals represent such a high percentage of total private giving because the average figures include those from religious organizations.

Analyzing Your Potential

You have to be both ambitious and realistic when you make a fundraising plan. As you try to figure out how much money you can glean from each possible funding source, keep the following questions in mind.

How far do your services reach?

Do lots of people understand, care about, and benefit from your organization's cause? Do you focus on a small geographic area or work at a national or international scale? The answer to this question tells whether the nonprofit should be casting its net close to home or all over the country or world.

Are you one of a kind or do other nonprofits do the same work?

If you're unique, you may have a harder time explaining to potential donors who you are and what you do. But you may have an advantage when you appeal to foundations that like *model* — unusual programs that can be replicated in other places.

How popular is your cause?

We all know that important social and political ideas gain and lose popularity. One year everyone is talking about healthcare, another year public education, and still another year it's pollution or farm subsidies. Regardless of what's happening politically, the focus of your organization's work will go through times of gaining and losing media attention and broad-based donor support.

Does your cause elicit strong feelings?

Even if it's not a cause that's backed by large numbers of people, a hot topic that a small number of people believe in strongly can often attract large gifts. Research is important for all types of fundraising, but it's particularly important if your cause elicits strong feelings. You want to focus in on the right people, right corporations, or right foundations that share those strong feelings.

Where are you on the controversy scale?

This is closely aligned with the hot-topic question. If an organization focuses on something that is potentially controversial — like abortion, use of pesticides, or incarceration of juveniles — it may find that corporations and businesses are uncomfortable with having their names associated with the cause.

How well known and highly regarded are your leaders?

Most of us feel better about supporting an organization if we believe in its leaders. If an agency is conducting medical research and the doctors with whom it is working are well regarded, widely published, and nationally known, it may be in a strong position to secure government grants or contracts. Your organization's leaders also are important in private fundraising.

How well known is your organization?

If your organization is a theatre group, are its performances often reviewed by critics? If it's dedicated to helping young mothers, are its services often featured in news stories? Or is it the type of agency that works quietly behind the scenes? If it is the behind-the-scenes type, it may be wise to focus on sources — the government, foundations, or corporations — that know your organization's field well and will understand the quality of its work and the key role that it plays.

A behind-the-scenes organization doesn't do as well with trying to raise money from large numbers of individual donors: Educating donors about who it is and what it does is just too expensive. Individual donors may be attracted to the organization later, as its reputation grows.

What can you give back to a donor?

Maybe your organization produces sumptuous musical concerts and can offer contributors the best seats in the house, print their names in the programs, and give them special access. Maybe the organization is based in an attractive building where a corporate donor's banner could be displayed.

Individuals have a wide variety of preferences when it comes to receiving personal recognition for gifts. Some want to give anonymously. Others want to have buildings named after them (known as *the edifice complex*). Corporations (particularly when they give directly out of their marketing budgets, more about this later) often want their gifts to be visible to the public.

Do you need money right now or can you wait for slower-growing sources to bear fruit?

In general, government money takes the most time to secure. Individuals are the best source of fast money. If an agency needs a fast start, it should try low-cost special events and have its leaders solicit people whom they know. We're talking about the pancake breakfast, the rummage sale, or the cocktail party in someone's lovely home.

Then it may move on to pursue the often-larger amounts of money that come from government and foundation grants.

Why the sun never sets on some nonprofits

We all know that small businesses come and go. Most nonprofit organizations are not founded with the idea of going out of business, but they come and go too. Although it may sound harsh, in some cases it is just fine. An experimental arts organization associated with a particular movement may not be needed when the next movement has come along. A medical research group may make the key discoveries it was seeking and close.

But some nonprofit organizations are created with a vision of institutional perpetuity. Organizations like museums that hold important historical documents, major symphonies, hospitals, and universities. Not all of them survive, but their intention to do so helps them when it comes to raising money for endowments and bequests (which often go into their endowments).

Do you have the money you need to cover fundraising costs?

Special events and *direct mail* — fundraising letters sent to large numbers of people — are expensive forms of fundraising. Grant writing takes time, but its cost is relatively low. If you're writing grants, corporations often respond more quickly than independent or community foundations, and all three of these types respond more quickly than the government.

Do you have expertise?

Specialized consultants or professional staff members may be useful in all aspects of fundraising, but trained experts are particularly important in the area of planned giving (seeking bequests) because they know about the legal issues and estate taxes. Also, experts are often used for help with direct-mail fundraising, telemarketing, and special events.

Applying the Principles

So, how good are you at coming up with a funding strategy? See what you think about the options that we choose for the two fictional nonprofits that you meet next.

Saving sea creatures

For years, a prominent North American organization has had the mission of rescuing injured marine mammals. It is managed by well-regarded scientists and has received international awards for its contributions to animal welfare and the environment. Recent news stories have drawn public attention to the effect of pollution in the oceans and improper fishing practices that endanger animals. The organization maintains several facilities where animals can recover before being released back into the ocean and school groups visit these sites. Staff members do most of the organization's fundraising. It has put aside some money to work with consultants.

The fundraising plan for this organization may include:

- Government grants for protection of coastal watershed areas, preservation of endangered species, and research.

- National foundation grants for publication of research that might assist similar centers in other parts of the United States.

- Grants from local foundations and corporations for

  - Paid internships for teenagers who are thinking about careers in marine biology.

  - School field trips.

  - A summer institute for local teachers who want new ideas about how to teach biology and ecology to their classes.

  - Building new tanks and facilities to care for rescued animals.

- Personal visits to high-profile individual donors conducted by the well-known scientists leading its staff.

- Personalized fundraising letters to families who have visited its facilities.

- Fundraising letters to individuals with photographs of rescued animals and dramatic stories about how they were saved. These letters might be mailed to people who live along the coastal area that the organization serves, to those to give to other animal rescue causes, or to people who subscribe to science and wildlife magazines. The paid consultants probably will design this campaign, test sample letters, and choose the most appropriate mailing lists.

Drug treatment center, inner city

The center is a brand-new organization that provides drug treatment services in a low-income inner city neighborhood. It does not have past experience in this field, but its founders have lived in the neighborhood for a long time, watched it decline, and believe that drug addiction is a major problem and the root of other problems. It plans to hire a professional staff, but as it is just starting, it has no money to pay them.

Fundraising considerations for this nonprofit include the following:

✔ The major asset is the many years its founders have spent living in the neighborhood. People know and trust them. Therefore, these leaders should begin fundraising by contacting neighbors and local businesses and asking for their support because of a shared concern for the area. These gifts may be modest, but they will help to cover basic, beginning costs. They are important because they can be won easier than many other kinds of contributions.

✔ Once the nonprofit has an address, letterhead, and a modest program, the founders could go to the businesses in the neighborhood that are branches of large corporations — banks, insurance companies, clothing stores, and fast-food restaurants. Through the local branches they can approach the parent corporations for larger contributions and grants.

✔ In the meantime, the founders have conducted research into city, state, and federal drug treatment program funding sources. The applications are long and complicated, and the responses are often slow, but the amounts may be generous and could be given year after year if the quality of services is maintained.

✔ Once the agency is up and running, it probably will charge modest fees for the use of its services. Doing so will alleviate some of the fundraising pressure.

Casting the Cold Eye of Realism on Your Plan

After you've looked at the broad outline of how you can expect to raise money and you've analyzed your fundraising strengths and weaknesses, it's time for one more set of questions and one more reality check.

✔ **What was raised last year?** If the agency raised any money, where did it come from? Are those sources likely to give again? What can be learned about them and their usual levels of giving? Does it seem as if they may give more this time?

Are there kinds of fundraising that might help the agency that have not been tried in the past? Does the staff have the knowledge and resources to pursue them?

✔ **How do similar organizations do?** Yes, other nonprofits offering similar services are the competition, and that's precisely why it may be useful to look at their annual reports. What were their primary sources of support? How does one organization's chances stack up against another's? Maybe one is better known, but the other offers more services or has a more influential board.

And yes, development directors (the fancy term for fund raisers) spend more time at the symphony reading the donor list than the biography of the composer, memorize donor walls in lobbies of major buildings, and clip stories from the newspaper about leaders of local businesses that are doing well.

✔ **Who does the agency know?** The nonprofit's contacts are important to its ability to raise money, especially when seeking funds from individuals. Knowing somebody who may write a big check to an organization is great, but knowing a lot of people who may write small checks is just as good.

✔ **Who knows how to do it?** Maybe the nonprofit's director has extensive experience writing and securing government grants. The organization may be likely to continue to succeed in that area of fundraising, but if it wants to branch out and enact a broader fundraising plan, do other staff members or board members have experience with other methods of raising money? If not, they may want to enroll in a training program or class.

If a nonprofit's staff is undergoing training in a new area of fundraising, a board member should try to take the class also. Not only does this ensure that the knowledge will stay with the organization if the staff members leave, it builds a greater understanding of development and commitment to it within the board.

Budgeting for Fundraising

We've said before that raising money costs money. And no organization receives every grant or gift that it seeks. It needs to be sure up front that it can afford its potential fundraising costs and that the costs are appropriate in relationship to the possible return for the nonprofit. A normal range for fundraising costs is 8 percent to 25 percent of an organization's budget, but when an organization is starting up or when it is launching a major new fundraising effort, those percentages may be even higher. It almost always costs more to recruit a new donor than to secure a second gift from a past supporter.

From the beginning, the nonprofit will want a system allowing it to keep timely records on all of its donors. This may be a handwritten card file or it may be a complex database. It is important, for instance, that nonprofits remember when they receive grants, how much money they receive, when reports are due, and what kind of reporting is required.

Nonprofits also need to keep information up to date about individual donors: who in the organization knows or knew them, how and why they gave their gifts, and whether any special recognition or invitations were promised to them when they gave. Because nonprofits hope to talk to or keep in touch with these people over time, recording their spouse and children's names, their interests, their business affiliations, and any other pertinent personal information is important.

So the first investment in fundraising may be to acquire a record keeping system. You may also have to budget for the time it takes to keep the system up to date. A great resource, the nonprofit software index, (www.npinfotech. org/tnopsi) provides analysis of software for nonprofits and can guide you in selecting a database program. One good, inexpensive option is eBase (www. eBase.org), a free program that runs on FileMaker Pro. You don't need FileMaker unless you want to customize eBase. Specialized fundraising software is terrific, but it can be quite costly. We recommend investing in it when your fundraising depends on large numbers of grants, corporate gifts, and contributions, and when your annual operating budget is $1 million or more. Some other fundraising activities and their costs include:

- ✔ **Grants and contracts:** Most of the cost of securing grants and contracts are labor costs for planning and writing the grant proposal. Some proposals, particularly in the arts, may require videotapes, audiotapes, or slides of past work, which cost additional money. If numerous copies are required, that too is an expense, as is shipping the proposal. Sometimes the applicant organization's representative may want to travel to meet in person with the agency awarding the money, so that's another expense to consider.

  Nonprofits need to pay attention to a grantmaker's requirements for reporting the results of a project and make sure that they can afford to do the report. Some grants require collection and analysis extensive data. Some require a particular kind of audited financial statement.

- ✔ **Individual contributions:** Costs related to securing individual contributions stem from time spent by staff or volunteers compiling lists of possible donors and time spent developing a script for soliciting a gift and rehearsing that script before making personal visits. If the nonprofit is organizing a personal visit, the representative will want to take along a *case statement* (which is like a simple grant proposal that includes some attractive photographs, charts, or other compelling information about your agency). If the agency is sending a letter and following up with phone calls, bringing together everyone who is making the calls to train them, feed them, and build their "team spirit" is a good idea. Direct mail is another common technique for reaching individual donors and a relatively costly form of fundraising. Expenses may include a consultant to write the mailed materials and select appropriate lists, and certainly include printing and postage.

✔ **Special events:** Having special events can be one of the most expensive ways to raise funds. Spending 50 or 60 percent of the income from an event to pay for costs isn't unusual. Printing, advertising, food, and entertainment all cost money. Also, special events are labor intensive. An agency will want to have an experienced volunteer group or an excellent paid staff. In spite of the costs, special events can be an important part of a fundraising plan because they are a good way to focus attention on your organization and attract new donors. Also, they may be a relatively quick way to raise money.

✔ **Planned giving:** If a nonprofit is not familiar with tax laws regarding wills and estates, it will want to employ or hire on contract (or attract as a board member) a planned giving expert. Bringing this person on board can be expensive in the short term but doing so can yield important long-term support for the agency.

Planned giving works best for organizations that have been around for a long time and show good prospects for continuity. Universities, museums, and churches come to mind. Small, new groups have a hard time attracting bequests.

Two sample fundraising plans and budgets are on the CD.

Chapter 14

Raising Money from Individuals

. . . .

In This Chapter

▶ Writing a case statement

▶ Tracking down possible donors

▶ Asking for contributions

▶ Soliciting donations via direct mail and the telephone

▶ Fundraising on the Web

. . . .

*E*veryone has had some experience with asking for money. Maybe you sold cookies for a scout troop when you were a child. Maybe you sold ads for the high school newspaper. Maybe you once had to call Mom and Dad when you were stranded at a bus station in Toledo and couldn't get home for Thanksgiving.

These moments can be awkward, but asking for money for yourself and asking for money for an organization or cause you believe in are very different. Organizational fundraising can feel good because it enables you to do something important for a cause you care deeply about. The hard part is finding the right words to say, the means for conveying those words, and the audience who will be receptive to those words.

Responding to the right cause, the right message, and the right person, individual donors give to many kinds of organizations. In fact, they represent the largest portion of private giving in the United States. This chapter shows you how to flex your own fundraising muscles and convince individual donors to give to your organization.

Writing a Case Statement

A *case statement* is a short document that presents a case for giving to a non-profit — a positive story about the organization. The document can be a brochure, a one-page information sheet, or a glossy folder filled with information sheets presented alongside photographs, budgets, or charts. It should be professional, factual, and short enough that readers will read it all the way through.

A good case statement is a flexible tool that can be used in many ways in fundraising:

- After talking about the agency with a potential donor, you leave behind a copy of your case statement for him or her to consider.

- If you need to phone a potential donor, you keep the case statement close at hand as a reminder of the key points to make about the agency.

- If you send a fundraising letter, you might borrow wording from the case statement to write that letter or include a copy of the case statement with the letter.

Instructions for writing a case statement resemble a recipe for stew or soup. A few basic ingredients make any version of this dish delicious, and the cook can spice it up with whatever other quality ingredients are available.

You begin by writing down notes about the following subjects. Be selective; allot no more than 100 words to any of these items.

- The history of the organization

- The services it offers

- The organization's key accomplishments

- Affidavits, reviews, or quotes from enthusiasts who have benefited from the organization's work

Then you toss in no more than 50 words on each of these topics:

- The organization's philosophy or approach to providing service

- If appropriate, how the organization relates to or works with other organizations — locally, nationally, or internationally

It's time to sprinkle on top whatever else is you have on hand. These garnishes can include

- Compelling photographs of the organization's work.

- Charts or maps demonstrating growth — for example, increasing numbers of clients the organization serves or increasing geographic area it serves.

- An overview of the organization's budget and finances, particularly if the budget is balanced and the finances are healthy. For example, maybe the nonprofit has achieved steady growth or has been in the black for 14 consecutive years.

- Anything else that's compelling about the agency: publications completed, awards received, testimony given, and so on.

Finally, what giving opportunities does the nonprofit offer? In your case statement, the giving options must be clear and not too complicated.

Sometimes opportunities are linked to the cost of providing services, such as the following:

- The cost of immunizing one child against a deadly disease

- The cost of replacing one chair in a symphony hall

- The cost of rescuing and rehabilitating one injured wild burro

- The cost of college tuition for one year for one student (or the gap between tuition and the true cost of educating one student)

- The cost of planting one tree in a reforestation area

Sometimes opportunities are linked to premiums or gifts the donor will receive in return. For example:

- For a gift of up to $50, the donor will receive a coffee mug as a token of thanks. A larger gift will be acknowledged with a tote bag.

- For a gift of several hundred dollars, the donor's name will appear on a brass plate on the chair the gift has paid to refurbish.

- For a gift of $1,000, the donor will receive quarterly progress reports from the scientist whose research the gift is supporting.

- For a gift of several thousand dollars, the donor's name will be etched on a tile in the lobby of the new building that the gift has helped to fund.

- For a gift of several million dollars, the lobby will be named after the donor.

Sometimes opportunities are more abstract, and the giver is identified in a public document — a newsletter or performance program — as a Supporter, Patron, Guarantor, or Chief Mucky Muck depending on the size of his contribution. A donor who gives $100 or less would be listed as a Supporter; someone who gives between $101 and $250 would see her name in the Patron category; and so on. You get to choose the donor category names and contribution amounts. In choosing how to recognize your donors, you'll want to consider the cost of that recognition, the nature of the activity supported, and how donor recognition advances (or doesn't suit) your organization's purpose and mission. A simple, printed list of names is dignified and inexpensive. While donor gifts cost money, having your organization's name printed on T-shirts, coffee mugs, bumper stickers, and tote bags that are then used or worn by your donors and distributed throughout a community may be an effective way of promoting your work. Some of your donors may increase their contributions because of the value of the gift they receive in return. This proves to be particularly effective with most fundraising for buildings:

Offering donors opportunities to have their names featured in or on buildings they have supported can inspire larger gifts. The appeal is strong but not universal: If yours is a building for that important neighborhood drug treatment program we described in Chapter 13, "naming opportunities" may not be appropriate.

You need not follow the exact order in which the elements are listed here. Lead with the strongest points and leave out the items that seem less compelling.

When producing the case statement for distribution, make sure to match its look to your nonprofit and its intended audience. Different causes suggest different tones. For example, if your nonprofit is a modest, grassroots organization, your case statement should be simple, direct, and not at all flashy — maybe printed on newsprint and featuring political cartoons rather than photographs. If it's an environmental organization, you want to produce the case statement on recycled or forest-free paper. If it's an internationally known opera company, your case statement should look dramatic and elegant.

Identifying Possible Donors

Your doorbell rings, and you open it to greet an adorable child you've never met before. The child is selling candy bars to raise funds for band instruments at school. You played in a band when you were young, so you buy a candy bar, wishing the little fundraiser success.

A few minutes later, the doorbell rings again, and you open it to greet a second adorable child. You know this child because he lives next door. You remember when his mother brought him home as a newborn, and you watched him ride his first bicycle down the sidewalk. He's selling the same candy bars to benefit the soccer team at his school: They need equipment and uniforms. You buy *five* candy bars.

Rich or poor, most of us have strong personal feelings about money, and making gifts to charitable organizations reflects our values. Even more important when we make charitable giving decisions is our comfort in contributing our money to people we know, either directly or indirectly. Mapping the personal connections of each member of your organization is a key first step in identifying possible donors.

Drawing circles of connections

Figure 14-1 represents a common brainstorming exercise that nonprofit organizations use to identify possible individual donors. This exercise is most effective if both staff and board members participate. Follow these steps:

1. **Identify the people who are closest to the organization — those within the "inner circle."**

   This includes staff and board members and may also include active volunteers or clients who frequently use its services.

2. **Identify those people who have the second closest relationship to the organization.**

   This second circle might include family and close friends of those in the inner circle, former staff and board members, neighbors of the organization and its inner circle, and clients and volunteers who sometimes use its services.

3. **Take one more step backward and identify the people who make up the third circle.**

   They may include grandparents or cousins of those in the inner circle, old friends whom they haven't seen recently, friends of former staff and board members, and former or infrequent users of the organization's services.

4. **Identify the friends, relatives, and other associates of those who make up circles #2 and #3.**

5. **Search for your cause-related friends and associates.**

   Who demonstrates an interest in the subject, the purpose your organization represents (as indicated by their memberships, their magazine subscriptions, or their contributing to other similar organizations)? Read local newspapers to find people who may take an interest in your cause because they have personal experience with the problem your agency addresses. For example, maybe their child was born with the congenital disease that your nonprofit is studying, or maybe they come from a beautiful, forested part of the state and care about the preservation of old-growth trees in that area.

You can continue enlarging your circle of connections, but with every step you take, the bond between the organization and the potential donors weakens. As the bond weakens, the cost of raising money from the people who inhabit those circles increases. Eventually, the cost of securing gifts from an outer circle becomes higher than the likely amount of income to be gained, and it's time to stop and focus on the names closer to the inner circle.

How do you know when it's time to stop and back-up? Your overall fundraising should not cost more than 20 percent of your organization's budget, and you should work to keep those costs within the 8 to 20 percent range. However, when you're starting out, your percentages may be higher and some types of fundraising — particularly special events, direct mail, and telemarketing — may cost as much or even more than they raise in the first year. These approaches generally begin to bring in significant contributions as they are repeated and donors' renew their gifts. If you are still just "breaking even" in year three, it's time to back up and refocus your approach.

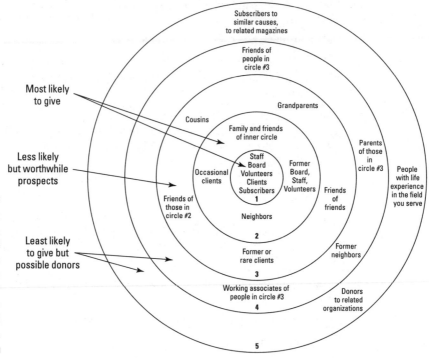

Most likely to give

Less likely but worthwhile prospects

Figure 14-1:
Drawing circles of connections helps you identify possible individual donors.

Least likely to give but possible donors

Once you start fundraising from individuals, always be alert to the identities and connections of possible donors. You and your volunteers become sleuths, constantly following clues, keeping track of people you meet at social gatherings or business meetings, clipping newspaper articles, and following the business and social pages and the obituaries. You want to identify not only the people who may be interested in your cause, but also the people who know those people — their families, business associates, and social contacts.

Getting a list of contacts from your board of directors

Every year, or before you start work on a special event or letter-writing campaign, ask each of your organization's board members to provide the names of ten or more people they know. This is a useful exercise for developing a solicitation list.

Most people can sit down and list ten friends and associates off the top of their heads. However, when asked to produce a list in that way, it's unlikely that they will exhaust all their connections and relationships. If you hand each board member a starter list of people he or she might know and then ask the board member to add to that list, you're likely to get many more names. To develop this "starter list," think ahead to whom your board members might know.

Say, for instance, that your nonprofit is lucky enough to have a local business leader on its board of directors. Scouring the local business pages to note this leader's business affiliations can bring up a variety of connections. If this person is quite prominent, your staff may also want to check *Who's Who;* but everyone, no matter how modestly he or she lives, has a web of professional or personal connections. Some connections to identify are

- ✔ Business partners or coworkers
- ✔ Leaders of banks, investment houses, or law firms that handle the company's money
- ✔ Auditors who prepare the company's annual financial reports
- ✔ Heads of printing companies that produce the company's brochures and annual reports
- ✔ Advertising, marketing, or design firms that do the company's public relations and advertising
- ✔ Members of social, athletic, and business clubs to which the board members belong
- ✔ College or university alumni affiliations
- ✔ Members of other boards on which your board members serve
- ✔ Close neighbors of your board members

As you get to know board members over time, you can develop profiles of their friends and professional relationships. A worthy next step in developing your organization's network of connections is to address personalized letters from your board members to the people on their lists of ten, asking each of those ten people for names of ten others who might be interested in learning more about your cause. When doing this, make it easy for your contacts to respond: Provide a form for them to fill out, a self-addressed, stamped envelope or postcard to convey their responses. You may also save postage by sending your query by e-mail.

On the CD accompanying this book we've included a sample letter from a board member asking associates for a list of ten possible donors.

The cause for which you're seeking money matters, your timing matters, and your organization's reputation matters, but the most important element in raising money from an individual is to have someone he or she knows and trusts ask for the contribution. This approach carries more weight in some fundraising contexts than others. The two types of fundraising in which it matters the most are

✔ **Special events fundraising,** particularly if an event involves an activity that takes several hours, such as a dinner. In this context, most people are more comfortable socializing with people they know. (If a serious runner is competing in a benefit marathon, for example, knowing other people who are involved may add to his or her enjoyment of the race, but is less significant.)

✔ **Major gifts fundraising,** where individuals ask other individuals (usually face to face) to make significant contributions.

Asking

According to marketing experts who study people's motivations for doing just about everything, the reasons people contribute to nonprofit organizations include the following:

✔ Wanting to feel generous

✔ Wanting to change the world

✔ Wanting to exercise compassion

✔ Wanting a sense of belonging (or acting out of a sense of duty)

✔ Wanting a sense of well-being

✔ Wanting to be recognized

Does it surprise you that belief in the work of a particular nonprofit agency is not on the list? By understanding these "hidden" donor motivations, you can learn to use them to raise money. We've already discussed how using board members' and current donors' influence with their friends and associates promotes the potential new donors' feelings of belonging; and how donor recognition can inspire larger contributions. Appeals to new donors often ask them to "join," "to become part of" a movement or cause in order to touch upon the desire for belonging. Appeals also call upon donors' compassion and idealism, and commonly link the needs of particular constituents served by a nonprofit to the well-being of an entire community.

Deciding who should do the asking

If at all possible, the board or staff person who knows the potential donor should make the visit. If that's not possible, the visiting team should be made up of two people who represent different aspects of the organization — maybe an administrator and a program staff person. Be careful not to overwhelm a potential donor with a huge swat team. Two or three people is plenty.

Ideally, the ask should be peer to peer. If the potential donor is a prominent member of the community, for example, a board member should do it if at all possible.

Note: For easier readability in the following sections, we're going to assume that the asker is you, whatever position you happen to hold in your organization.

Preparing to make a call

Gulp. It's time to ask someone for money. In preparing for this moment, you need to remember that you are not asking for something for yourself. You are inviting the potential donor to belong, to be a part of something worthwhile. This doesn't mean that you want to skip over the reason or purpose for the gift. You need to step back for a moment and remember why it's so important. How did you become involved? What lives (or lands, or seas) have you seen changed by the organization's work? Sally forth armed with your case statement, which will remind you of the key points you want to cover and — because you will leave it behind with the potential donor — covers any major information that you might forget.

Breaking the ice

Open the conversation with easy material. What did you find out about this person while conducting research, and how do you know him or her? Maybe your kids attend the same school or you attended the same college. Maybe you have a friend in common. Maybe you're both baseball fans. Try to use something low-key to open the conversation rather than forcing yourself on your "victim" with a heavy sales pitch. The key is creating rapport.

Getting to the point

Although brief small talk makes for a good start, you don't want to waste a potential donor's time. Bring him or her around to the point of the visit. Letting him or her know how you became involved can be a good approach. Then you can briefly introduce the agency and its current situation. Team members should take up different pieces of the conversation, remembering to let the potential donor talk, too, and paying close attention to the signals he or she sends. It's critical to keep the meeting comfortable for the prospect.

Many people do not believe asking for a specific contribution at the first business meeting. They believe in setting the stage by providing information and establishing rapport — letting the person know that a campaign or special program is coming up and that, in time, the organization will be asking him or her for a contribution. Maybe in a future visit you will try to get this potential donor to see a program in action or to meet other board members at an informal gathering. You're building a relationship with him or her, strengthening his or her feeling of belonging with others who lead the agency.

For some fundraising campaigns, the fundraisers use a feasibility study. This tactic combines research in which board members and potential major donors are interviewed. The process warns these "research subjects" that the agency plans to come knocking at their doors. Often, feasibility studies are conducted by consultants who determine whether an organization can meet a particular fundraising goal by testing the waters in advance.

Others believe in setting up the donor's expectations in a very direct manner. They may say something like, "This urgent situation will be upon us in nine months. We hope that you will become one of our $200,000 level donors." Notice here that the ask is nested within an invitation to belong, to be among others. The askers are courteous and to the point. They don't apologize for what they're doing. Then they leave behind the case statement and call later to ask whether the potential donor would like additional information.

When the time is right, you will ask. A part of knowing just when to ask has to do with the timing of other contributions. If potential donors seem to want to be ahead of the crowd, you might invite them to make a leadership gift that will inspire others to be generous. If they seem convinced but a bit reluctant, wait until their contacts within the organization have made their gifts and then let the potential donors know that they can join their colleagues.

Deciding what to ask for

Many theories address how much money to request. Before asking a potential donor for a contribution, find out everything you can about the person's gifts to similar causes. (To do so, you can scour donor lists and ask board members who know this person.) This will help you to ask for an appropriate amount.

Many people believe that you should ask for an amount that's somewhat higher than what you expect to get. However, you don't want to ask for so much money that the potential donor feels that whatever he or she gives will be a disappointment. It's common for a donor to say something like, "I can't do $200,000, but I will consider $150,000 if that would be a help." (Add or subtract zeros as appropriate.) In most cases, once the donor suggests a level, you don't want to haggle: You could become annoying and cause him to back out of contributing. Using the personal associations angle sometimes works — "We were hoping you might become one of our $200,000 donors, along with Joe Schmoe and Sally Smiley."

Adopting the right attitude

When soliciting gifts, be firm and positive, but not pushy. Pay attention to how the potential donor is acting or responding and step back if he or she doesn't seem to be feeling well or if his or her business has taken a difficult turn.

Just as it's critical to notice when not to press the case, if it's going well, you'll notice signs of readiness. The potential donor may bring someone else along to an event at the nonprofit. He or she will begin to tell others good things about the agency (some of which its board may not know)! He or she will display pride in the organization as if he or she is a part of it.

Setting a good example

It's easier to ask someone to contribute to an organization if you already have made a gift yourself. Even if you are a staff member and can't make a large contribution, you'll feel more confident about asking, and the potential donor will admire that you are willing to put your money where your mouth is.

In general, it's a good idea for the people in the agency's "inner circle" of staff and board members to contribute first, before you ask outside individuals to give. Sometimes potential contributors from outside the nonprofit will specifically ask if everyone on the board of directors has already given. If they haven't, the outsider may feel that the board is not as committed to the organization or project as they should be, and this is a sign of a potentially weak agency or a half-hearted project. We believe that all board members should contribute financially to the organization. It's surprising how often this is not the case.

Raising Funds by Mail

We hope that, after reading this section of the book, you will never again refer to the solicitation letters you receive from charities as junk mail. These letters may not be as welcome as personal letters, but they grow out of a sophisticated and fascinating area of fundraising.

Although much of the direct mail you receive is produced on a large scale, you can use some of the principles of this fundraising tool to develop effective letters to send to small, targeted lists of potential donors.

If your agency decides to fundraise with direct mail, you want to build a loyal cadre of direct-mail donors, or what's commonly called a *donor file,* gradually.

You can mail to the donors on your organization's donor file expecting a high rate of return. Commonly 50 percent of new donors will make a second contribution. If 55-65 percent of your new donors renew, you're doing great! Better yet, donors who give $25 or more are good candidates for upgrading to higher contribution levels over time. Once a donor has made a second gift, she (many more women than men contribute in response to direct mail) is likely to stick with you for between three and seven years, and it's likely that she'll contribute to you more frequently than once a year. Current direct mail wisdom suggests you can write to her monthly without growing annoying.

Before your donor file supporters develop into a significant and loyal group, you do well to break even on the cost of your direct-mail campaigns. Once you have a strong donor file, though, you should be raising significant money. The cost of securing a new donor is often $15-$25, while the cost of sustaining a donor on your donor file for several years is usually $5-$10.

In time, perhaps five to eight years, the people on your donor file will drift away. However, by continually testing and expanding your mailings, you can replace them with new contributors.

Looking at the basic process

How does an organization undertake a direct-mail effort? Here's a broad sketch of the steps you take:

1. **Analyze the cause.**

   Can it succeed as a direct-mail subject?

2. **Develop a written piece.**

   Your piece will include a letter, envelope, reply card, and reply envelope. It may also include premiums (free stuff) and other enclosures. (More about this below.)

3. **Collect lists of appropriate people to receive the piece.**

   This step often involves working with a specialized company called a list broker. It's likely if you're new to direct mail you are working with a consultant who can guide you through preparing your mailer and selecting lists. You can find leads for list brokers by skimming the ads in the *Nonprofit Times* and *Chronicle of Philanthropy*. You also may try out your letter at first on your organization's internal lists of board contacts, clients, and donors.

4. **Test the piece by mailing it to a large, yet limited, number of people (often 10,000 names and at least 1,000-2,000 names) and measuring their response.**

   A good response is when 1 percent or more of the recipients send back a contribution.

5. **Keep testing versions of the piece on different lists to find out which ones are most effective for your cause. To get a true comparison each "test" group should include 1,000-2,000 recipients.**

6. **As donors respond, take care to treat them well.**

   These folks are your donor file, and a donor file is gold. Guard it. Don't lend it to others. Don't neglect it. And send thank-you letters as soon as possible to acknowledge contributions.

Even if you don't launch a large direct-mail campaign (which requires the help of a professional), you can use some of the writing techniques and packaging approaches in this section to prepare fundraising letters for people close to your organization.

Deciding whether direct mail will work for your cause

Direct mail does not serve every cause. A direct-mail subject needs to have a strong degree of emotional appeal. Organizations that often use direct mail include, for example, programs focusing on

- ✔ Specific medical conditions
- ✔ Animal rights and protection
- ✔ Environmental protection
- ✔ Poor, ill, or abused children
- ✔ Civil rights
- ✔ International disaster relief

For obvious reasons, projects based in sparsely populated regions rarely get good results with direct mail. A complicated, academic, or highly technical activity may not be effective, either (unless you send the mailing exclusively to professionals who understand it). A direct-mail campaign needs to have the potential to appeal to a large number of donors to make it worthwhile.

You don't want to fail with direct mail. It can be very expensive.

Assembling the mailer

A direct-mail solicitation generally includes a mailing envelope, a letter (usually between two and four pages in length), a reply envelope and card, and sometimes a brochure, a copy of a newspaper clipping, or a short, "handwritten" note in addition to the longer letter.

Some nonprofits include *premiums* — little freebies — as well. Premiums we've received include pennies, pencils, stickers, transfers, and address labels. They're meant to urge recipients to open the envelope. *Involvement techniques,* such as surveys and contests, are meant to keep readers busy and encourage them to spend more time with the piece.

The more time a reader spends with the piece, the more likely he or she is to make a donation.

It's fun to look over a direct-mail piece and see how it was written. The following sections walk you through the various components of a direct-mail piece and give you some tips for making them enticing and effective.

The envelope

Start with the envelope. What makes you want to open it? Is there an intriguing headline running across it or a photograph on it? Does it mention a free gift? The recipient's name being printed in large letters is supposed to attract attention. The use of a real stamp (even a nonprofit bulk-rate stamp) makes the letter look more personal. In a recent trend, direct mail is being produced to look like bills or legal notices. The point is to get those envelopes opened.

The letter

Over time, trends in the length of direct-mail letters have changed. In the 1970s and '80s, direct-mail letters were long — six or eight pages. Currently, most are two or four pages. Market research demonstrates that people who pay attention to direct mail don't necessarily read every word but do note how much information is made available.

A direct-mail letter should be clear and timely. It shouldn't be melodramatic, but should generate an emotional response. To do so, include anecdotes and stories about real flesh-and-blood people (or animals). You want to create some drama.

The direct-mail writing style combines long and short paragraphs. Often, a long paragraph is followed by

A one-line paragraph that is underlined for emphasis.

This technique draws the reader-skimmer's attention to the points the letter's author wants to emphasize.

Most of the letter should be dedicated to describing the problem that the organization is trying to solve. After that, it discusses how things can be turned around for the better and the organization's specific method or program for doing so. It closes with a vision for how things will look if the plan succeeds.

When writing direct mail, in discussing your organization's method, you want readers to understand that your nonprofit has an urgent, yet reasonable and reachable, goal. You also want the reader to believe by the end of the letter that he or she is joining a winner.

Most direct-mail letters include a P.S. after the signature. Research demonstrates that most people read the P.S. first, before they read the salutation or opening line of the letter.

The reply envelope and card

The reply envelope and card should be easy to find and use, and the reply card should offer a variety of gift levels (appropriate to the probable giving levels of the donors you are approaching). Your nonprofit can get a permit from the post office to offer postage-paid envelopes.

At one time, reply envelopes printed in green ink led to a significantly higher return. Then, for a long period, blue and red were the preferred ink colors on outer envelopes. Now yellow and orange are beginning to work. Everything about direct mail has been studied in great detail, from the color of ink to the style of the signature to the type of postage used.

Using a mailing list

Who responds to direct mail? More women than men. People who are at home alone during the day. People over the age of 50. People who order things from catalogs. People who join clubs, churches, and other organizations.

How can your organization find these people? Other organizations serving similar populations may be willing to trade lists of clients, members, and donors if you promise to use the lists for only one mailing. (Of course, the people from their lists who respond to your letter will be added to your donor file.) Asking board members to secure lists of contacts from the professional organizations, clubs, and other boards that they belong to can be an effective and inexpensive list-development technique.

If your agency is serious about conducting a full-scale direct-mail campaign, work with a list broker to purchase the use of lists that are likely to work for your cause. When you purchase these lists, you can use them only once, and you must use them within a defined time period. If you skim the pages of professional newsletters like the *Nonprofit Times* or the *Chronicle of Philanthropy*, you will see ads for list brokers. You can also find them on the Web.

Some list brokers specialize in members of religious congregations (remember that wanting a feeling of belonging is one of the reasons people respond to direct mail). Others manage memberships and magazine subscriptions or track catalog shoppers. Still others organize lists based on geodemographic data. *Geodemography* assumes that you have a lot in common with your immediate neighbors because neighborhoods often are good indicators of socioeconomic backgrounds. These market researchers can analyze the people who currently support your organization and then come up with lists of other people like them living in similar neighborhoods across the country.

Part of a direct-mail manager's task is to test these different lists and find out which ones work for the organization. If less than 1 percent of the people on a list send checks, you may not want to use that list again. If the return exceeds 2 percent, the list is a winner: Your agency will want to use it again and seek other lists like it.

You definitely want to develop a good data base system for recording information about new donors in order to thank them, keep in touch with them, and ask for their support again in the future. In the meantime, keep testing, testing, testing, making your letters better, trying new ink colors on your envelopes, mailing to a new kind of list, and so on.

Telemarketing: Dialing for Dollars

In the mid-1980s, direct mail was a highly successful means of fundraising for many organizations. In the late 1980s, a sudden decline occurred. Households were receiving too much direct mail, making recipients less inclined to read it, and the costs of printing and postage rose. That's when the dinner hour began to be interrupted by incessant telemarketing calls.

Like direct mail, telemarketing is based on a directed message. The recipients are preselected for their potential interest in the topic of the call based on their behavior with other types of telephone marketing.

The advantages of telemarketing are the following:

- ✔ **It's hard to ignore.** A human voice engages you in a conversation, and you must respond. It's not like a letter that you can throw into the recycling bin without the author noticing.

- ✔ **It can be less costly than a mail campaign.** If you use trained volunteers to make the calls, you can manage a campaign at a very reasonable cost. Or — more costly but also potentially more effective — you can hire a firm to conduct the campaign for you.

- ✔ As with direct mail, you can effectively use the elements that shape a large-scale, professional telemarketing project for a modest campaign.

You may have to register

Many states and some local jurisdictions require organizations that solicit charitable contributions to register. The regulations differ from state to state. Typically, the rules don't apply unless the nonprofit raises more than a minimum annual amount. Check with your state's attorney general's office to be sure that your nonprofit is in compliance with all laws. It's especially important to check local laws when thinking about raising money through bingo games and raffles. Laws regulating these activities often differ from county to county and city to city.

The disadvantages? No one gets to have a quiet dinner any longer. For the callers conducting the campaigns, more and more potential donors use answering machines or services to screen calls. Plus, some commercial telemarketing firms take a very high percentage (as high as 75 percent!) of any funds raised, making it a poor return on investment for donors who want to keep fundraising costs low.

The key steps to beginning telemarketing are writing a script, training volunteers, organizing follow-up calls, and — of course — thanking, cultivating, and upgrading donors over time.

Writing a script

Every call should open with a clear, direct, personal greeting: "Hello, Mr. I'm-Getting-the-Person's-Name-Right, I'm Ms. Call-a-Lot and I wanted to talk to you about the Scenic Overlook Preservation Fund Committee's work."

Having connected with the call recipient, the caller then tries to link that person's interests and behavior to the reason for the call:

- ✔ If he or she is a past donor, begin with a hearty thank you.

- ✔ If he or she has been involved in a related cause or effort, mention how important that work is.

- ✔ If he or she lives near the scenic overlook, mention how beautiful it is and the community's concern for the fragile surrounding environment.

There's a tricky moment in the call when the caller wants the potential donor to relax and listen. At the same time, you want to tell your story and not be interrupted. To increase the caller's chances of keeping call recipients on the line, the script should be

    ✔ Brief (so as not to exhaust the listener)

    ✔ Upbeat about the possibility of improvement or change

    ✔ Deeply concerned about the current situation

    ✔ Specific about the time frame in which things need to change

    ✔ Specific about the amount of money the caller hopes the listener can contribute

On the CD accompanying this book we've included a sample telemarketing script.

Getting the callers ready

Telemarketing can be an excellent board or volunteer group effort. If someone involved with your organization works in an office that has multiple telephone lines, see if you can borrow the office for an evening. Early evening (6:00-8:30 p.m.) on week nights is generally considered the best time to call, but — as you've probably noticed from the sounds of your own telephone — telemarketers now frequently call during the day and on weekend evenings as well.

Gather your volunteer team an hour before beginning. Feed them a good meal and give them a pep talk. Building camaraderie among the callers can ease anyone who's nervous into the calls. Setting a group goal for the evening and mapping it on a big chart can build morale.

Inform the callers that they must deliver the message in a crisp, clear, and friendly voice. They shouldn't rush, but they also shouldn't leave holes in the conversation that the call recipient can close before the caller can ask for a contribution. They should ask for a specific contribution and confirm the amount.

As the development director, you provide your callers with information about each household they're calling, including a recommended gift request. You base your request on the potential donor's past contributions to your or other organizations. Sometimes you are just guessing. That's okay if your callers are also good listeners and deftly adjust the amount they're requesting in response to what they hear. If, after a gift is pledged, you feel that you asked for too little money, don't despair. You can ask the donor to upgrade his or her gift next time.

Collecting the pledge

If a pledge is made, the caller should thank the new donor and try to get him or her to promise to return the contribution within a certain time (or to give credit card information over the phone so that the gift can be charged then and there).

Confirm the spelling of the name and address before saying goodbye to the new donor. At the end of the evening everyone present should write brief, personalized thank you notes and send them with pledge forms (indicating the specific amount of the promised contribution) and return envelopes to the people they reached who promised to make contributions.

Every telemarketing campaign suffers from a percentage of unrealized promises, and callers want to keep that percentage as low as possible. You might ask a small number of your volunteers to re-convene for a short follow-up calling session two months after the initial campaign to jar loose any contributions that have not yet been received.

Using the Internet to Raise Money

Online fundraising is the newest way to raise money. Although it certainly shows promise, the art of raising money on the Internet is still being developed, so a nonprofit shouldn't worry too much about it until after it builds itself up and establishes other sources of income.

Any plan to raise money on the Internet should be part of a larger fundraising strategy. Nonprofits should not depend on any one technique for fundraising — especially not the Internet. Although the number of people who make online contributions is increasing, money raised on the Internet is still a drop in the bucket compared to more traditional ways of giving. And, what's more, surveys indicate that large national and international nonprofits receive nearly all funds raised online, and most of the money was given toward humanitarian relief.

It's a fact of life that some nonprofits have higher visibility, have more resources to take advantage of new technology like the Web, and, consequently, have more success raising money on the Internet than, say, a local childcare agency or modern dance company. When a devastating earthquake or a vicious hurricane strikes, the human impulse is to help. For most people, helping is sending money. The Internet makes it easy to respond quickly. So far, most money generated through the Internet comes in this way.

Using e-mail to build and maintain relationships

Fundraising is about building relationships with people. Individual donors want to feel that they're appreciated, so it's in a nonprofit's best interests to thank donors regularly and keep them informed about what the organization is doing. It can't hurt to get to know the people who give money to your nonprofit, either. This is where the Internet can be of help, even without great financial investments in fancy Web sites and complicated databases.

The most frequently used feature of the Internet is e-mail. E-mail is easy to use, you don't need the latest hotrod computer to use it, and it's cheap and fast. If you're keeping in touch with your mother through e-mail, you can keep in touch with your donors, too.

Your organization doesn't need a Web site to begin using e-mail to build and maintain good relationships with your supporters. Adding an e-mail address to your printed correspondence and newsletters is a good start. And, if you want to give people an opportunity to discuss issues important to your organization, you can start a mailing list (known as a *listserv*) for free at a Web site like Egroups (). It's a way to keep donors involved in your activities.

Don't add people to your mailing list unless they ask to subscribe, and always make it easy to unsubscribe from the list. Nothing kills a good relationship faster than unwanted e-mail.

Here are some other tips for using e-mail effectively:

- ✔ Answer your e-mail promptly, within 24 hours if possible.

- ✔ E-mail correspondence can be less formal than typed-on-paper business letters but shouldn't be overly familiar.

- ✔ Answer questions succinctly — don't ramble on and on.

  In fact, it's a good idea to have a short paragraph description about the organization already written and waiting to be cut and pasted. It can be added to and edited as needed. Figure 14-2 shows how a nonprofit uses e-mail to answer a question but then adds a bit more about the organization — and an offer to provide more still.

How does all this tie into fundraising? Consider it prospect development. If you're e-mailing a new correspondent, ask if he or she would like to be added to your mailing list. If the correspondent says yes, count one more new prospect. If he or she says no, keep the name and e-mail address in your To Be Pursued file. In two months, send an e-mail asking if he or she has any more questions about the project or organization. If the person responds, go back to Step 1 and begin again. If you don't hear from the correspondent again, put the person in a Maybe Someday file, and maybe someday when you have time, you can try again.

Bethseda Zoological Society

Dear Mr. Jones,

Thank you for your interest in the Bethseda Zoological Society.

Yes, we do operate the small children's zoo at Heathway Park. We are happy that your daughter enjoyed her visit this past Sunday.

BZS was founded in 1983 with the mission of providing information about the animal kingdom to residents of Bethseda County. We are supported by individual contributions, foundation grants and admissions to our small zoo. Besides the children's zoo, we work with elementary school teachers to provide curriculum materials and in-class presentations about wildlife in Bethseda County.

If you would like more information about BZS, please send us your mailing address, and we will mail you our annual report and a schedule of upcoming events. You can also visit our website at http://bza.org.

We also have an email newsletter that is sent once each month. If you would like to be added to the subscriber list, send email with the word "subscribe" in the subject line.

Thank you again for your question.

Sincerely,

Henry Peters

Executive Director

Bethseda Zoological Society

hp@bza.org

http://bza.org

Figure 14-2:
Using e-mail
to build a
relationship.

Using e-mail address lists to find prospects

E-mail address lists, like mailing address lists, can be purchased, traded, or borrowed. A nonprofit may be willing to lend or trade its list with another nonprofit with a similar mission.

When using a borrowed list, it's important to respect the privacy of the list names. Don't pass it along to others without permission.

Be extremely cautious when purchasing a list. E-mail addresses change as often as, if not more so than, street addresses. Finding a list of names who have expressed interest in specific causes also may be difficult.

You're on your way to accumulating the names and e-mail addresses of people who have expressed interest in what you're doing and even have asked to be kept informed of future developments. You can invite these people to special events, ask them for contributions, make available planned giving opportunities that will benefit them and your cause, and maybe even volunteer one day a week. You have prospects.

After your organization collects a lot of names and addresses (both e-mail and regular mail), you will need a database program. These programs come in various degrees of complexity and prices and are usually called fundraising or membership management software. You can download a free copy of Ebase at www.ebase.org. A good online directory for software options is William Keintop's *Nonprofit Software Index* (www.npinfotech.org/tnopsi).

Designing a Web site

Web sites come in many shapes, colors, and sizes. We have designed simple Web sites by learning some basic HTML and using an inexpensive WYSIWYG ("What You See Is What You Get") editor. It's not rocket science. But if time is a concern, you can find Web site designers just about everywhere these days. Shop around and look at their previous work.

It's hard to say what the cost for a professional designer will be — probably somewhere between $500 and $10,000. What we mean is, choose the designer carefully. Find a designer within your organization's budget and put a limit on how much can be spent. Once your site is complete and ready for the world to see, the designer and/or your Internet Service Provider can help you find Web hosting services.

Your organization can have a Web site for free if you want one. Just about all the big Internet portal sites, such as Yahoo!, MSN, and AOL, provide you with free space for a basic Web site and even give you step-by-step instructions on how to build it. Describe the organization and tell people how to contact the office by phone, mail, and e-mail. Keep it simple and clean. It's a way to get started.

However you decide to create your organization's Web site, make sure that it's easy to navigate, and keep it brief, just like e-mail. Reading on the Web is not like reading a book or newspaper. Describe programs in 150 words or less. Give people choices. Introduce programs on the home page. If you want to make available that four-page case statement you slaved over, add it as a link. Don't force all the information at once, which can make the site take longer to load and frustrate users. Instead, use the Web the way it was intended; use links. And don't forget to put your e-mail address on your Web site so that people (read: potential donors) can request more information.

Collecting money online

As people become more and more accustomed to spending money online, and as Internet use becomes second nature to more and more people, making charitable contributions while sitting in front of a computer will become even more common.

The Internet being what it is — that is, very changeable — online giving sites come and go as organizations test different business models. The Nonprofit Matrix (www.nonprofitmatrix.com) maintains an excellent online directory of all the options for online giving. Allison Schwein also provides a good online resource about online giving at www.internet-fundraising.com/home.html.

Chapter 15

Making the Most of Special Events

*F*rom glamorous dances under the stars to pancake breakfasts at the local firehouse, most nonprofits include social gatherings as part of the fundraising mix. But special events don't just raise money. They are often credited with raising friends as well as funds. New donors — who don't know the organization — may come forward because the event itself sounds fun and interesting, because of who invites them, or because someone they admire is being honored. Special events can be a wonderful catalyst for attracting businesses that like to be recognized when they make contributions or attracting people who like to socialize and be seen.

At their best, special events raise substantial amounts of money, draw attention to an organization's good work, and attract new volunteers. And they can be fun and inspiring. In fact, if fundraising is about cultivation, a special event can be a greenhouse for nurturing growth. You hope to create a special event that will become an occasion that people look forward to, an annual tradition.

Still, a special event can be one of the most expensive ways to raise money. Expenses may eat up half or even more of the gross event income. Less visible costs may rise as well — for example, parade permits, postage, printing, and advertising. And the staff time needed may be substantial.

Bottom line? Special events need careful planning. Putting together a special event draws upon all of your nonprofit management skills and can drain staff and board time and energy away from other important activities.

In this chapter, we show you how to plan a successful special event — and steer clear of obstacles.

Thinking through the Whole Event

If you think that a special event is in your future, we recommend sitting down with staff and board members and raising questions like these:

- ✔ What would our organization's followers enjoy doing and how much can they afford to pay to do it?

- ✔ What kinds of contacts does our organization have who can provide the key elements of an event, such as donated goods, celebrity auctioneers, entertainment, or printing services?

- ✔ When can we focus attention on a special event? The last six weeks before an event are generally the most labor intensive. Look for a relatively clear month-to-six-week block of time in which you don't have grant writing or other commitments.

- ✔ When can we hold an event without competing with our other fundraising drives? (If you have an annual fund drive in October, why not plan your special event in the spring?)

Deciding what the event will be

Special events can be produced on a bare-bones budget, for princely prices, or for any amount in between. As with most kinds of investments, event planners expect a higher return in exchange for a higher investment. But don't exceed your means. In this section, we outline some ideas for tailoring an event to the organization's budget.

Low-budget special events

Most nonprofit organizations have a wealth of talent simply waiting for a showcase. Some of the suggestions in the list that follows aren't going to work for your organization, but they can get you thinking about similar events that would be perfect for your nonprofit.

- ✔ **Children who use your services can be recruited for a community chorus or a dance troupe.** When the children perform, gear the venue, price, and other amenities toward the family and friends of participants. Sell concessions and flowers or other tokens for friends and family members to buy as congratulation gifts for the performers.

- ✔ **Sign up neighborhood children for a summer readathon that benefits the library or an after-school literacy program.** By sending forms home to parents in advance, secure their permission and help with collecting pledges. Write to your community newspapers inviting them to help you spread the word as event sponsors.

✔ **Invite potential donors to donate their time as an honorary employee of your nonprofit organization.** The donor can spend a day or a few hours working for your organization. This type of event can work well with glamorous causes, like conducting archaeological digs, but it can work equally well with less glamorous causes such as serving the food in a soup kitchen or working as a principal of a school for a day.

✔ **Offer a bake sale with a distinctive theme celebrating a cultural group or holiday.** Organize your volunteers around three primary activities: setting up and pricing, selling, and taking down the sale. Plan in advance what you will do with items that do not sell.

✔ **Hold a cocktail party in a board member's home focused on a theme that's related to your organization's work or honoring a special guest.** While single cocktail parties for 15 people may not raise much money, if every one of your board members signs up to host such a party over the course of a year, the cumulative amount raised may pleasantly surprise you.

Mid-budget special events

If the treasury is a bit fatter and you can afford a few more features in your special event, you may wish to do something like one of these:

✔ **Identify an up-and-coming performer or community musical group and ask for a donation of a performance in exchange for the promotion that your event will bring to him, her, or them.** The club or theater rental is likely to be your highest cost. If you choose an unusual site that is donated to you, make sure it can accommodate your performers' needs — acoustics, electrical outlets, and the like.

✔ **Sponsor a day-long cleanup of a coastal area, park, or preserve.** Volunteers can be sponsored by having their friends sign up to pledge a certain gift amount to the organization for each pound or garbage bag of trash that they remove. Offer prizes for the most unusual refuse items found and the largest numbers of sponsorship sign-ups.

✔ **Buy out an interesting new restaurant or a beloved community favorite for a night (usually a Monday or Tuesday when it otherwise would be closed) for your guests only.** Work with the restaurant to discount the cost charged your organization (but not to your guests!) by offering a more limited menu than usual (3 to 4 choices) and by promoting the restaurant through your public relations for the event.

✔ **Choose a popular board game and build a tournament around it.** Approach the game manufacturer for permission (and possibly sponsorship). Players pay a fee to play. They may also sign up sponsors to contribute according to the level they achieve in the game. Award lots of small prizes to contestants throughout the evening.

High-priced special events

If money is no object — at the front end, at least — these events may be of interest. All require lots of upfront cash.

- ✔ **Hire a major speaker or entertainer from a lecture bureau or through a theatrical agent and use that person as the focus of a dinner party or private concert.** Also honor one or more business and community leaders at the event. Form an event committee and have these people invite their friends and contacts and persons who would want to come for the sake of the honorees.

- ✔ **Host a telethon.** Present performances and appearances by local community leaders and television personalities. Include footage of behind-the-scenes work at your agency. Have on-air interviews with or stories about persons working at or benefiting from your nonprofit. A telethon can be very costly in major markets where charities usually have to pay for the airtime. If your nonprofit is based in a mid-sized city you may find stations willing to donate the airtime.

- ✔ **Present a costume ball featuring at least one live band.** Decorate elegantly. Make sure your crowd likes to dance and that the repertoire of your musicians suits the dances that the crowd knows! Because your board plays a key role in inviting the guests, ask their advice about their friends' tastes in music and dancing.

- ✔ **Organize an opportunity for amateur athletes to pay to play a sport alongside professionals or other kinds of celebrities.** Celebrity golf tournaments are popular. The idea can be applied to bowling, softball, pool . . . you name it. Create teams pairing professionals with amateurs or liberally handicap the amateurs so that everyone has a fair chance of winning. Provide trophies or other forms of recognition for many kinds of "achievements" — longest drive, bowling ball most often in the gutter, best break. Often these events end with celebratory dinners.

In deciding on an event, we recommend avoiding anything that can make your guests uncomfortable or deter them from coming, such as:

- ✔ Events that limit your guests' ability to come and go as they wish — like a soiree on a boat in the middle of lake.

- ✔ Events at which your intended audience finds the attire, time, or place awkward. If you're hoping to attract business people by holding your program downtown and right after work, make business attire the appropriate dress.

- ✔ Events that target an audience that is completely unknown to your organization or its supporters. Do you like to go to a party where you don't know anybody?

After you've sketched out an idea for an event, go to your staff and board members and ask them directly: Would you attend this event? For this price? At this time of year? If your core followers and supporters aren't enthusiastic, the event will not raise money. If they've had a central role in the event planning, you're on your way to success.

Budgeting for an event

The bottom line is very simple: Your total earnings from a special event must exceed your total cost — by a lot, you hope. But how do you get a handle on revenue? We have some thoughts.

If you are staging an event for the first time, it is particularly important *early in the process* to ask your core supporters — board, volunteers, and event leadership — how much they intend to give. Because these people are the most likely to give generously, knowing their intentions helps you forecast the overall results.

Another way to estimate the fundraising potential of an event is to check with organizations that produce similar events. If they have presented a program year after year and yours is a first-time outing, ask them where their income levels began. Try to objectively weigh your event's assets against theirs. Are your boards equally well connected? Is your special guest equally well known?

Figuring the income side

Try to design your event so that it creates income in more than one way. A rummage sale may also include a raffle and the sale of some baked goods. An auction may include ticket sales to the event and advertising in a printed program along with the income generated from the auction itself. Standard event income categories include:

- ✔ Individual ticket sales
- ✔ Table or group sales
- ✔ Benefactor, patron, and sponsor donations (for which donors receive special recognition in return for contributing higher amounts than a basic table or seat costs)
- ✔ Sponsorships of event participants (for instance, pledging to contribute a particular amount per mile run by a friend)
- ✔ Food and/or beverage sales at the event
- ✔ Sales of goods and/or services
- ✔ Advertising sales (in printed programs, on banners, and so on)
- ✔ Purchasing a chance (raffle tickets, door prizes, and so on)

The CD accompanying this book includes three sample special events budgets.

Capturing all expenses

Events produce expenses in a variety of ways. The general categories can include:

- ✔ Building/facility/location (space rental, site use permits, security guards, portable toilets, tents, clean up costs)

- ✔ Advertising and promotion (posters, invitations, publicist costs, postage, Web site development)

- ✔ Production (lighting and sound equipment, technical labor, stage managers, auctioneers)

- ✔ Travel and per diem (for guest speakers, performers, or special guests)

- ✔ Insurance (for example, liability should someone be hurt due to your organization's negligence or shipping insurance to protect donated goods)

- ✔ Food and beverages (including permits for sale or serving of alcohol, if necessary)

- ✔ Décor (flowers, rented tables and chairs, linens, fireworks, banners)

- ✔ Miscellaneous (prizes, awards, talent treatment, nametags, signs, tee shirts)

- ✔ Office expenses (letter writing, mailing list management, detail coordination)

- ✔ All other staff expenses

In spite of your careful planning, certain expenses can appear unexpectedly and cause you to exceed your budget. If you plan to serve food at your event, keep these tips in mind so that you can avoid surprise charges:

- ✔ Confirm whether or not all service and preparation charges are included in the catering budget.

- ✔ If you need to add additional meals at the last minute, find out whether your caterer charges extra.

- ✔ Similarly, if meals that you ordered aren't eaten, you will probably still need to pay for them: Check on your caterer's policy.

- ✔ If some of the wine that you've purchased is not consumed, find out whether the wine store is willing to buy it back from you.

- ✔ If wine has been donated to your event, serving it may not be completely free. Find out whether your caterer charges *corkage* fees for opening and serving it.

Non-food related expenses can sneak up on you too. Be sure to:

- ✔ Confirm whether or not you're expected to pay for the shipping costs for the items that are donated to your event.
- ✔ Ask whether tax and delivery are included with printing costs.

Soliciting in-kind gifts for your event

When you think about what your event will cost and how you can pay for it, think about the business contacts that your board, staff, and outside supporters have. Often, a business's contribution of *in-kind* (non-cash) materials will be more generous than any cash contribution to your event. You may need to be flexible about timing and willing to drop things off or pick things up, but don't overlook in-kind gifts.

- ✔ Businesses in your community that have in-house printing equipment may be able to print your invitations and posters, saving you thousands of dollars.
- ✔ A florist may contribute a roomful of valuable centerpieces in exchange for special recognition in the dinner program.
- ✔ A sculptor may contribute a small work you could give your honoree as a distinctive award.
- ✔ A donor may let you use her beautiful residence as your event site.

You may not want or need all the in-kind goods that are offered to you. Do look the gift horse in the mouth! Don't accept an in-kind contribution if it's not up to the standards that you need for your event. Also, consider fully the implications of accepting the gift. For instance, if your agency helps young people recover from drug or alcohol addiction, don't accept a sponsorship from an alcoholic beverage company.

Treating celebrities like . . . celebrities

Many special events depend heavily on the donated services of celebrities. Remember to treat them well so that you feel comfortable asking them to help again in the future. Some details to consider:

- ✔ Have flowers waiting for them in their hotel rooms.
- ✔ Find out in advance what foods or beverages they like to have backstage or in their dressing rooms.

- ✔ Plan in advance a place where they may get away from autograph hounds or other crowds if they want rest and privacy.

- ✔ Double-check your sound and lighting equipment with them to make sure they are presented under optimal conditions.

- ✔ If your honored guest is elderly or has a disability, double-check that any hotel, restaurant, or event site is fully accessible and that all elevators and other necessary aids are working.

Setting a date and location

Check around town to find out if you are planning to hold your event on the same date as a program by another nonprofit agency. Be as thorough as possible in this date checking. Competing for the same audience on the same date — or even dates that are close to each other — hurts both organizations' results. Also, in general avoid dates that are too close to holidays, as people want to be with their families.

Start the Countdown Six Months Out

Although events vary greatly in size and complexity, and although we have pulled off adequately successful events in two or three weeks, we recommend working against a six-month schedule. The following outlines such a schedule for a tribute dinner. It can easily be modified to fit other types of events.

- ✔ **First three months.** Develop the plan and pick the event's key leadership. Recruit co-chairs or hosts. Secure entertainment and a location. Select a theme and a caterer. The first three-month period is, not surprisingly, the slowest part of event planning. You can wait for several weeks to hear back from an invited celebrity, and you may need several more weeks to find a replacement if you get turned down.

- ✔ **Last three months.** Recruit an event committee or a core group of volunteers. Visit the site at which the event will be held, checking out all the regulations and recommendations for its use. Also, work on in-kind contributions of materials you need for the event. If your event is appropriate for a public relations drive, you should be sending out initial press releases and preparing public service announcements (PSAs) at this point too. (See Chapter 19 for PSAs and other parts of a marketing-PR program.)

As you come inside the two-month zone, you pass some additional checkpoints:

✔ **Two months before the event.** Call all potential committee members and develop your invitation design. All of the text on the invitation should be ready for final design and printing by six weeks before the event. Include a printed list of the final event committee members or core volunteers. Select your menu and start working on décor ideas.

✔ **Four weeks before the event**. Mail the invitations. A second batch of press releases should be mailed at this time. Make phone calls to the press and to invitees to confirm coverage and travel plans. Design the printed program to be passed out at the event. Assist honorees with their speeches (if necessary). Gather the elements — baskets, banners, confetti — needed for décor.

✔ **Last week before the event.** Confirm the number of guests that you expect, plan the seating at the event (if necessary), prepare place cards and table cards, and decorate the site. A few days before the party occurs, call *everyone* who has made a reservation and confirm they are coming. A few people will have had to change plans, increasing or decreasing the number of guests you expect. You don't want to pay for uneaten meals or to run out of food. In ordering food from your caterer, assume that, under normal circumstances, 5 percent of your guests will not attend. If the event is free, 10 percent of them will not attend.

You may think that nobody can rain on your parade, but you'll want to have emergency backup plans anyway. What if your performer is ill, a blizzard shuts down roadways, or your permits are not approved on time? You'll need to quickly move, replace, reschedule, or cancel your program. The faster you can communicate any changes, the better your constituents will feel about sticking with you and your cause.

Issuing a Memorable Invitation

Make your invitation something your potential guests will open and remember. Addressing the envelope by hand and using stamps rather than printed postage makes it look more personal, and an intriguing phrase or logo on the outside may lead to its being opened. If you can afford the increased printing cost, two colors of printing on the envelope can catch your potential guest's eye.

What do its recipients see first when your invitation is opened? Most invitations are made up of an outer folded piece, a reply card, and a reply envelope. Want some more attention? What if a pinch of confetti or glitter falls out of the envelope? Or a small black cat, spider, or bat falls out of your Halloween invitation? If you have a small number of invitees, roll your invitation into a small mailing tube and fill the tube with little prizes and surprises.

In spite of our recommending these bells and whistles, we are firm believers in clarity. Make sure that the reader of your invitation can easily see who is extending the invitation, what the event is, where and when it is being held, how much it costs, and how to respond to the invitation. If he or she has to search for these basics it will land in the recycling bin.

Print the address to which your guest should respond somewhere on the reply card, even though it is also printed on the reply envelope. Sometimes the pieces of an invitation become separated. You want your guest to readily know where to send his or her reply.

Media Coverage: Letting the Public Know

If the mantra of fundraising is "If you don't ask, you won't get," the mantra for special events fundraising is "Nobody will come if they don't know about it."

The advantage having your event covered in the media is that you reach a large number of people for a relatively modest cost. We emphasize the word *relatively*. Press relations work is not free.

If your event has a newsworthy angle, send press releases to the media in the hopes of their writing about it or broadcasting the news. (You can find information about writing press releases in Chapter 19.)

Finding a news angle

Think about all the angles you can exploit for publicity. Think through the attributes of your organization and of the specific event. Try to look at it from the point of view of every section of a newspaper or newscast. Modify your basic press release to suit the content of appropriate newspaper and magazine section editors, producers of radio feature shows, and TV news rooms. Follow-up your mailed release with a phone call. A few possibilities include:

- ✔ **Entertainment section coverage of performers.** You may be able to arrange interviews between your special guests and the local entertainment press that could run on radio, television, or in the newspaper prior to your event.

- ✔ **Business section coverage of your event chair or honoree.** Many papers run a column of activities of local business and corporate leaders.

- ✔ **Feature stories about the community improvements that your agency has helped to bring about.**

- ✔ **Food section coverage of your picnic lunch or outdoor benefit concert.**

- ✔ **Health advice connected to your event.** If your organization is sponsoring a 10K run, what's the current advice about dietary preparation for long distance running? Any medium can be appropriate, but what about a feature in a runners' magazine?

- ✔ **Society page coverage of your honorees, event committee members, or other guests at your event.**

- ✔ **Radio broadcast of your honoree or guest speaker's speech.**

- ✔ **Fashion page or television coverage of attire worn to your gala.**

- ✔ **Coverage in a small newspaper.** Many communities have newspapers that are focused on particular neighborhoods, suburbs, or cultural groups. Are any of your honorees, performers, or special guests from those communities?

The disadvantage of media coverage is that the relationship between your agency and the person receiving the message is indirect. The media outlet may not emphasize the aspects of your event that you want to convey. And you have no control over what the media does with the story: It may be hidden on the back page, announced at 2 a.m., or bumped by an urgent breaking news story.

Printing posters that announce your event or sending personal invitations by mail is more expensive than sending out press releases. But these methods have the advantage of being direct. You can mail invitations to the right individuals and post your posters in high visibility spots in the right neighborhoods.

Getting a mention on radio or TV

The mass media need great gobs of news, announcements, and other content every day. You can get some media exposure if you, for example:

- ✔ Prepare a prerecorded public service announcement (PSA) for broadcast by radio stations. (See Chapter 19 for guidelines on PSAs.)

- ✔ Donate free tickets to your event to radio stations to use as prizes of various kinds. If a station picks up on the idea, you get a free mention — maybe a number of free mentions.

- ✔ Invite live weather or traffic reporters to cover conditions from your location can be a novel way to draw attention to your event.

After the Ball Is Over....

Thank-you notes should be written soon after the event and should be as specific and personal as possible. They do not have to be long. Many people find hand-written notes of two or three lines to be much more sincere and memorable than boilerplate letters. Of course, if you have 1,000 donors you probably can't send personal notes to all of them, but a hand-addressed envelope with a stamp makes your thank-you personal.

We recommend holding a brief post-event gathering for your key organizers and volunteers a week or two after the event. You can thank them personally again for their effort, but the real purpose is to get their ideas about what worked, what needs to be improved, and what should happen in the future. Good records of this meeting are a jumping off point for planning the following year's program.

Now that you've gone to all the effort of attracting new donors, do your follow-up. Add any new supporters to your database. In recording the amount and occasion of their gifts, also indicate who invited them or who wanted to be seated with them. Print out your list of new donors for board and staff review. Are any of them known personally by people close to your organization? Do any of them have valuable skills that you need on your board? Are any of them capable of making much larger contributions to your organization? If so, turn the information over to your board recruitment committee or — if you have one — to your individual donor cultivation committee for additional research and future contact.

Chapter 16

Finding the Grant-Givers

· ·

· ·

This book emphasizes the major role that individuals play in supporting the work of nonprofit organizations. For some kinds of nonprofit programs, however, grants really are the primary source of support.

Great mystique has been woven around the writing of grant proposals. Consulting careers have been made based on that mystique. Don't be fooled by the smoke and mirrors! Yes, grants are very competitively sought, but small organizations with volunteer grant writers can succeed at securing them if they have good plans and sound organizations.

A classic rule for effective writing of any kind is to know your audience and keep that audience in mind. Grant writing is no different. In shaping a proposal, the grant writer considers the known and likely traits of the people he or she is addressing.

This chapter shows you how to find sources of grants and figure out your approach to a grant giver. Chapter 17 covers actually writing a grant request.

Planning a Grant Request to a Foundation

Grant sources can be grouped into two broad categories: private and public. Private sources are generally foundations and public sources are based within some level of the government — city, county, state, or national. We write about public sources later in this chapter. In this section, we give you the scoop on foundations.

In Chapter 15, we mention that foundations are accountable for only about 10 percent of contributions to charities. Because they don't shoulder much of the financing burden, many foundations see their role as supporting research and development activities at nonprofits. When your nonprofit has a new idea, wants to expand a program to a new location, or wants to compare and evaluate different methods, foundations are a likely source of support. Foundations typically emphasize short-term support that only lasts for one to three years.

The key to successful fundraising from any source is research, research, research.

Your time as a grant writer will be better spent if you use some of it to study the priorities and behaviors of the foundations you are approaching. *Shotgunning,* or sending the same proposal to a large number of foundations, is a waste of effort. *Targeting,* or focusing your attention on your most likely sources and writing to address their preferences, is much more effective.

Over the past fifty years, information about funding sources has become increasingly available to the public. One milestone in this movement was the creation of the nonprofit Foundation Center in 1956. Originally intended to collect information so that foundations could learn about one another, the Foundation Center quickly became a key source of information for grant seekers.

The Foundation Center manages five libraries across the United States and a number of official collections within other libraries and nonprofits. (See Appendix A for more information.) It also publishes several key directories in print, on CDs (FC-Search and FC-Scholar), and through a subscription service on the Web (`www.fdncenter.org`).

Foundation research generally has two phases: developing a broad list of prospects, and then refining that list until you find the likeliest sources.

In the first phase, you gather the names of foundations that meet three basic criteria:

- **Geography.** Does this foundation award grants in the area where your nonprofit is based?
- **Type of Support.** Does this foundation award the kind of grant that you want?
- **Subject.** Does this foundation award grants for the kind of project you're proposing or to the type of organization that you are?

If the answers are yes, good work! You have found an entry for your broad list of prospects.

Asking for a grant by name

Grant givers refer to their various kinds of grants by name. Grant seekers should use the same vocabulary. Here are the categories of the most common kinds of grants:

✔ Capital. For property and building purchases and/or renovations

✔ Endowment. Money the agency can invest to secure a stable source of operating funds

✔ General operating. For day-to-day operations

✔ Program related investment. A loan paid from the foundation's endowment to a non-profit organization at a very favorable interest rate

✔ Project grants. For short-term support of specific activities

✔ Seed funding. Money for starting a new activity or organization

✔ Technical assistance. Money for professional advice from experts

If you don't have access to FC-Search, we recommend you check these search criteria through the indexes at the back of The Foundation Center's *Foundation Grants Index.* This book lists and briefly describes thousands of grants for $10,000 or more that were awarded in the previous year. Grants from over 1,000 foundations are described. The *Index* also has the best, most detailed subject indexes of any of the Foundation Center's directories.

Jot down notes and questions on a prospective grantor evaluation sheet. Through cross-checking and deeper study — as we explain in the next section — you narrow your list to the five or six best potential sources.

Check the CD listings for Chapter 16 for a sample prospect evaluation sheet.

Digging deeper

Depending on your target prospects, you may want to consult one of the following references:

✔ If one of your prospects is among the 1,000 largest foundations in the United States, turn to *The Foundation 1000,* which provides a lot of helpful, detailed analysis. (We are sad to hear that the Foundation Center may stop producing this book.)

✔ If your prospect is not in the top 1,000 but fairly large, turn to *The Foundation Directory* or *The Foundation Directory, Part 2.*

✔ If your prospect is one of the thousands and thousands of small foundations, turn to the *Guide to U.S. Foundations, Their Trustees, Officers and Donors,* which briefly describes every foundation in the United States.

✔ If you are researching a corporate giving program or company sponsored foundation, you can get detailed information in the *National Directory of Corporate Giving.*

If you're rock climbing and save the life of someone wealthy who asks what they can do for you, you can find out if the person serves on a foundation board by checking the "Trustee, officer, and donors" index to *The Guide to U.S. Foundations: Their Trustees, Officers and Donors.*

The Foundation Directory profiles more than 10,000 foundations with assets of $3 million or more and that give away $200,000 or more. *The Foundation Directory, Part 2* lists some 7,500 foundations with assets of between $1 million and $3 million and that give away between $50,000 and $200,000 per year. Between them, *The Foundation Directory* and *The Foundation Directory, Part 2,* represent 90 percent of the foundation dollars awarded each year.

The above directories are all published by The Foundation Center. But Foundation Center books aren't your only option. We've identified many other choices in Appendix A, including:

✔ The *Taft Foundation Reporter* (The Taft Foundation) provides more-detailed profiles than those in *The Foundation 1000.* It analyzes about 650 foundations, including background information about trustees, such as where they went to college, professional positions, and board memberships.

✔ *The Directory of Research Grants* (Oryx Press) analyzes information about research funds from all kinds of sources — foundations, corporations, and government.

Two laws that apply to independent foundations are very important to grant seekers:

✔ Foundations are required by law to file annual tax returns (called *990-PFs*) with the IRS and to make them available to the public. These documents list every grant the agency awarded in that year.

✔ Foundations are required to meet a 5 percent payout requirement. They must spend 5 percent of the market value of a given year's investment assets in grants and allowable expenses (or average 5 percent in spending over several years).

In short, 1) grant seekers can find out about every grant a foundation awarded and 2) foundations are *required* by law to award grants!

Foundations must offer photocopies of their 990-PFs for the three most recent years, as well as their applications for tax-exempt status. To receive the photocopies, submit a request, either in person or in writing. Foundations that make their returns widely available on the Internet are exempt from this requirement. Foundation Center libraries (a complete list of these libraries is in Appendix A) have 990-PFs for the foundations in your region on microfiche.

See the sample 990-PF on the CD that accompanies this book.

If a foundation that interests you publishes an annual report, track it down. Not only is it likely to include guidelines and grant listings, annual reports often include essays or introductory letters by the foundations' trustees or executive directors that provide insight into the foundation's philosophy and current directions.

A growing number of foundations have Web sites that outline their funding priorities and list recent grants. Some, like the W.W. Kellogg Foundation (www.wkkf.org), post research they have conducted on their sites. However, fewer than 1,000 of the 50,000 U.S. foundations have Web sites. For some smaller foundations, the 990-PF is the only place you can find a grants list.

Going for a Government Grant

Before you start daydreaming about massive state or federal funding, it pays to compare the pros and cons of private foundation funding versus public funding. Table 16-1 sorts things out for you.

Table 16-1	Comparing Private to Public Grant Sources
Private Sources	**Public Sources**
The purpose of the grant-giving agency is set by donors and trustees.	The purpose of the grant-giving agency is set by legislation.
Most funders award grants to 501(c)(3) nonprofit organizations; some award fellowships and awards to individuals.	Most funders award grants, contracts, and loans to nonprofit and for-profit entities and to individuals.
Most grants are awarded for one year and, in general, grants are smaller that those awarded by public sources.	Many multi-year grants are awarded for large amounts of money.
The application process requires a limited number of contacts with individuals within the funding agency.	The application process is bureaucratic and may require applicants to work with staff at multiple levels of government.

(continued)

Table 16-1 *(continued)*

Private Sources	*Public Sources*
Grants are sometimes awarded in response to simple two-page letters with back-up materials.	Most proposals are lengthy (as long as 40 pages).
Agency files are private; applicants may not have access to reviewer comments or successful grants submitted by other agencies. Review panels and board meetings may be closed to the public.	Agency records must be public. Many review panels may be visited by applicants, reviewer comments must be provided, and successful proposals submitted by other agencies may be requested.
Foundation priorities may change quickly according to trustees' interests.	Agency priorities may change abruptly when new legislation is passed.
Developing personal contacts with trustees or with foundation staff may enhance the applicant's chances of securing a grant.	Developing personal contacts with senate and congressional aides for state or national representatives may enhance your application's chances.
After accepting a grant, in most cases the agency is required to file a brief final narrative and financial report.	In accepting a grant, agencies may be required to follow specified contracting and hiring practices and bookkeeping and auditing procedures. They may have to prove other compliance with federal regulations. Grants are more costly to manage.

Federal grants

If you decide to go ahead and pursue government funds, you'll probably want to start by checking out whether the federal government has any grant programs that meet your needs. What resources are there that can help you?

The federal publication that you're looking for is the *Catalog of Federal Domestic Assistance*. The bad news about the Catalog is that it's written in ponderous, bureaucratic language and has so much information that it can be overwhelming. The good news is that it opens with a very helpful introduction to guide new readers through its massiveness and it is available and searchable on the Web (www.cfda.gov).

You heard it here: Searching the *Catalog of Federal Domestic Assistance* on the Web can be a lot of fun. You can find federal programs for everything from eradicating blight in trout to rebuilding homes after hurricanes. Think of two or three topics of interest, dial up the Web site, and search for what's available. It's amazing!

In the section on foundation grants, we discuss the two-step process of making a list of potential funders and then narrowing that list down. When you get to the point where you need to select the best potential sources of federal grants, use the *Catalog* to check the:

- ✔ Applicant eligibility index. (Listing six different types of applicants — not all of whom are 501(c)(3) nonprofit organizations)

- ✔ Subject Index. (Listing more than 30 major subjects and many refinements on those broad categories)

- ✔ Type of Funding. Federal agencies provide six types of funding that foundations do not provide:

  - **Formula grants** are allocated to states and other geographic areas according to distribution formulas (commonly an area's population or size).

  - **Non-grant financial aid** consists of direct payments of things like college loans, and retirement and pension plans.

  - **Loans and guaranteed insurance** often are issued to cover losses sustained under specific conditions. (As when an area is declared a "federal disaster area.")

  - **Sale, exchange, and donations** transfer or sell federal property and goods.

  - **Special services** are similar to technical assistance grants and may include consultation, advice, or training.

  - **Research contracts** are payments for professional services of individuals or institutions and support study to create or improve products and processes for the public good.

The *Catalog of Federal Domestic Assistance* tells which agencies and offices manage the funds for different opportunities. After identifying federal programs of interest, experienced grant seekers always, always, always call, write, or e-mail those offices to confirm the information that's in the catalog. Information in the catalog may be slightly out of date.

Sometimes we've gotten excited about programs profiled in detail in the *Catalog* that were created by legislation — but have no money allocated to them! Bummer.

Another key resource is the *Federal Register* (www.access.gpo.gov/su_docs/aces/aces/40html). It's printed each business day by the United States government. Subscribing to the *Register* allows one to stay up to date on the latest federal grant-giving happenings. The Foundation Center library subscribes to the *Register* as do local government offices and major universities.

Lean on your legislators

Because members of the U.S. Congress are very interested in seeing federal money going to the people and places they serve, some make sure that their staff members keep up to date about available resources and help their constituents with applications. The staff members may review and assist with a proposal, write letters of support for a project, or place key phone calls in support of a project.

Also, these government offices receive frequent publications about new programs and — once they know of an agency's work — may refer other opportunities to the agency. The staff members who you'll be working with are very busy and you can't expect to sit back and let them do research for you, but they can be important allies.

After you identify a possible source for your project, we recommend that you read — well, skim — the legislation that created the program. Doing so lets you better understand why the program was created and helps you target your grant to the source. Also, you may want to check out regulations affecting the use of funds. To track this information, turn to the *Federal Publications Catalogue* (www.fhere.org/~grants/pubs.htm).

One great advantage of pursuing money from the government is that the money is public. That means that information of all sorts is also public. If grant seekers apply and are turned down, they can ask for (and get!) the comments of the grant readers. Sometimes they can see copies of successful proposals, or sit in on review panels to hear their proposals discussed.

Non-federal grants

In some cases, money for locally based programs is distributed by the federal government. You can find information about these programs in the *Catalog of Federal Domestic Assistance.* However, information about state and municipal grants (the money for which is generated by state or local tax dollars) can be trickier to find because it is not compiled in a central resource guide.

Checking the Web site for the state or local agencies related to a project (such as the Department of Education or the Office of Children and Youth) and visiting with local government officials and congressional office staffs are good steps in your research.

Finding government money sounds daunting, right? But remember that one or two major government grants may support most of the costs of your program for as long as five years. The time spent wading through bureaucratic offices and regulations can be very worthwhile.

In Your Neck of the Woods: Community Foundations

Key characteristics of community foundations are

- ✔ Their assets come from multiple sources.

- ✔ They focus their grantmaking on defined geographic areas (as specific as cities or as broad as a state).

- ✔ They are governed by a representative board, appointed from the community.

Community foundations are public charities. A few key features of public charities are interesting to grant seekers:

- ✔ They offer donors a better tax advantage than donors get when starting independent foundations.

- ✔ They do not have an annual payout requirement.

- ✔ To maintain their advantageous tax status, they have to continue to receive new support every year.

- ✔ Because they are required to fundraise, they generally have paid staff and produce annual reports, grants lists, Web sites, and other useful resources for grant seekers.

In short, community foundations are close to home, provide helpful information, and have professional staff to answer our questions!

Company-Sponsored Foundations and Corporate Giving

Corporate giving comes in many forms and sometimes keeping them straight is hard. Corporations may:

- ✔ Take part of their earnings and set them aside permanently to create an endowed, company-sponsored foundation.

- ✔ Set up a company-sponsored foundation but without an endowment. In a year when earnings are strong, the company can contribute a portion of its earnings to charity by passing them through the foundation.

- ✔ Make contributions of cash, goods, and/or services directly through the corporation's community affairs office.

> ✔ Sponsor or underwrite public events or specific programs through the corporation's marketing, advertising, or public relations department.
>
> ✔ A combination of any or all of the above.

Some fundraisers feel uncomfortable raising money from corporations. Their organizations may not want to be associated with a particular corporation because of its labor practices, environmental record, products, or investments.

Frankly, there is controversy and discomfort on the other side as well. Why should a corporation give away money to charity? Isn't its mission to earn money for its stockholders? Shouldn't that money be paid to its stockholders? And shouldn't those stockholders have a say in choosing those contributions? Or be informed about them?

These types of issues mean that a business expects to get something back for its charitable donations, whether its specific recognition or just goodwill. Businesses typically:

> ✔ Give in the communities in which they do business (and where their employees live). Because a large company can have many divisions and operating facilities, the company can give in a number of communities.
>
> ✔ Make an effort to include their employees in their contributions programs by making donations to organizations where employees volunteer or serve on boards, by matching employee gifts to charities with contributions of equal size, or by inviting recommendations from employees about nonprofits they should fund.
>
> ✔ Give grants to enhance education (which may, ultimately, improve their labor force).
>
> ✔ Like to be visibly recognized for their contributions.
>
> ✔ Focus their giving on nonprofit activities that relate to the purpose of the business — such as a major newspaper's awarding grants to enhance the teaching of journalism or a technology firm's giving money to enhance computer systems in public schools.

The CD contains an example description of a corporate giving program.

When analyzing the profile of a corporate giving program, note whether money is awarded directly by the company or through a foundation and whether that foundation has an endowment. If a company gives directly from its corporate office, or if it does not have an endowment, the amount of money that corporation may have to give away from year to year may fluctuate dramatically with the prosperity of the business.

Chapter 17

Writing a Grant Proposal

The hardest part about writing a good grant proposal is trying not to blurt out your brilliant project idea on the first page. Otherwise, there's nothing particularly mysterious or difficult involved. Grant proposals are a lot like basic business plans or even a simple scientific proofs: First you make the problem compelling, and then you set goals for improving the situation, and last, you propose a possible solution and a way to test the results of enacting that solution.

In the course of laying out the plan, you also want to assert the special strengths of the your organization and a sensible financial plan for the project, both in the near term and later.

Some proposals are quite long and elaborate. Some are just a few pages. Your research into the funding source (which we describe in Chapter 16) will guide you as to the appropriate level of detail. This chapter shows you how to write the grant.

The Windup and the Pitch

Generally a grant writer develops a proposal in one of two ways. Either she writes on behalf of an organization's analysis of a human need and great idea for addressing that need or she writes in response to one of two types of notices issued by a funding agency: a request for proposals (commonly called an RFP) or a program announcement. In those documents, a funder describes a problem or situation for which it is inviting applications from organizations whose work may lead to improvements. In the first kind of proposal, the grant writer's hardest job is making the problem compelling to the funding agency. In the second case, the funding agency has identified the problem and the grant writer, in responding to an RFP or a program announcement, resembles a job seeker who is convincing a prospective employer that she is the best person for the job.

Usually requests for proposals are issued by government sources, and program announcements are issued by foundations.

Deep down, every good proposal is based on a well-considered plan, and designing the plan is a creative, even fun, part of the job. The differences from source to source are in how to pitch that plan. But the parts — usually eight of them — and order of presentation in a proposal are fairly standard:

- ✔ **Summary:** Provides a brief overview of the entire project and its costs.

- ✔ **Introduction or background:** Discusses the applicants' strengths and qualifications.

- ✔ **Problem statement or needs assessment:** Describes the situation that the proposed project will try to improve or eradicate.

- ✔ **Goals, objectives, and outcomes:** Outlines a vision for success in both broad and pragmatic terms

- ✔ **Methods:** Describes the project idea and the actions that will be taken.

- ✔ **Evaluation:** Explains how the organization will measure whether it met its goals, objectives, and outcomes.

- ✔ **Budget:** Analyzes the project's costs and sources of income

- ✔ **Future and additional funding:** Discusses how the balance of funds needed will be raised if a grant is awarded (but doesn't cover the entire cost) and how its costs will be covered in the future.

Beginning with the cover letter and summary

Like many reports, a grant proposal begins with a cover letter and a summary — a brisk overview of its key ideas. The cover letter mentions any contact the organization may have had with the foundation before applying and draws attention to the proposal's key ideas. For example, you may want to say something such as "When I tripped over your feet and umbrella on the bus last Tuesday, I couldn't help but notice you were reading a book about frogs. Here at the city park aquarium, we have an astounding amphibian exhibition planned."

The letter provides an opportunity to speak about the project idea in a more personal voice than does the proposal. Its author should cover the key concepts covered in the proposal, but also may say something about his personal connection to the cause. It always should close with clear, specific information about whom the foundation should contact if its staff has any questions about the proposal.

A cover letter written by a member of the organization's board of directors is a good idea. Foundations like to know that boards are well informed about grant plans and fundraising. Board involvement makes a good impression.

Don't use the exact same wording to describe the project idea in the cover letter and in the project summary. Use the letter as an opportunity to represent a different point of view and speak in a more personal tone to the foundation.

The grant writer usually begins the summary section with a one-sentence overview of the project and how much money is being requested in the proposal. Next come key ideas (one or two sentences each) from every section of the proposal. The section closes with the prognosis for future funding for the program.

Gear the summary and cover letter to the foundation's priorities. This approach is helpful when a foundation program officer is reading only the summary and cover letter in trying to decide whether your proposal fits within the foundation's guidelines. Also be sure not to tell the reader anything in the cover letter that you don't also discuss somewhere in the body of the proposal in case the letter becomes separated from the rest of the document.

Introducing your agency

The introduction or the background information section of a proposal contains a description of the nonprofit organization that is seeking money. An introduction goes toward the front of a proposal, but a background information section is placed near the end of a proposal — after the discussion of future funding. Does it go without saying that the writer wants to put the agency's best foot forward?

Usually this section begins with a brief history of the nonprofit, its philosophy in approaching its field, and its major accomplishments. Then current programs are described as are the constituents served by the program. After these standard ingredients, the writer draws upon whatever other credentials recommend the organization for the work that is about to be proposed. Drawing attention to signs of outside validation is helpful. Here are some kinds of things the writer can mention:

- ✔ Reviews or coverage in the press
- ✔ Citations and awards presented to the agency or its leaders
- ✔ Credentials and/or experience of the nonprofit's leadership
- ✔ Other agencies that refer clients to the nonprofit
- ✔ Invitations extended to the nonprofit to provide expert advice or testimony
- ✔ Major grants received from other sources

Although the writer is not yet describing the project idea, items introduced here should back up the nonprofit's qualifications to do the proposed work. For example, suppose that an after-school program for inner city teenagers run by a nonprofit offers multiple programs — maybe athletics, arts, and youth-led volunteer work in the community. If the proposed project focuses on expanding the community service work to include teens from another agency, the writer can focus this section on how the service work began and evolved, where the teens have provided services, and who has praised it.

Grant writers are often tempted to write on and on (and on and on and on) (and on and on and on) about an agency's history or its philosophy. Generally, this information is more inspiring to the people working at the nonprofit agency than it is to outsiders. Don't drag this section down by including too many details or using too much eloquent verbiage.

Shaping the problem

A grant writer begins to shape the argument behind the proposal plan by introducing the problem in a section called a problem statement or a needs assessment. Generally a writer prepares a problem statement when proposing a new relationship with the constituents who would be served by the project. A needs assessment talks about the challenging situations of persons (or animals or environments) already served by the agency. If the problem is compelling and described well, the writer can capture the reader's attention.

An important way to strengthen this section is to describe the problem in terms of what threatens the constituents of the nonprofit organization. These constituents may be people, but they also can be trees in an old growth forest or salamanders by a polluted stream.

How do you know whether you need to write a problem statement or a needs assessment? Here are a couple examples. If someone notices (and writes about) a high crime and drug use rate among teenagers in a particular neighborhood, the situation of those teens might be described in a problem statement. If a writer from another organization already managing an after-school program serving teenagers in that neighborhood notices that they're not making progress in a tutoring program because they're too hungry after school to focus attention on homework, a needs assessment might discuss their eating habits and nutritional needs.

A common mistake made in a problem statement (or needs assessment) is to suggest the problem's solution. Wait! Hold off! The rest of the proposal will be boring if you propose the solution here.

At the most, the writer may want to plant the beginnings of an idea, lead up to the edge, and suggest a direction, but not a solution.

If the proposal is for a research project, this section is generally one of the longest and contains a literature review of other studies on the same or related subjects. This review describes other approaches previously taken to the research topic, setting the stage for the distinctive or tried-and-true approach about to be proposed.

Setting goals, objectives, and outcomes

Once the grant writer has set forth a compelling problem, the next tactic is to introduce what the nonprofit might achieve if it undertook the proposed project. Remember, the writer has not yet described the project and yet this section jumps ahead to the vision for results.

This may seem like a peculiar way to lay out an argument, but it follows up the bad news (the problem statement) with a description of the results the agency wants to achieve (the good news). It lays out the terms of the proposal's ambitions.

Goals, objectives, and outcomes are related but different terms. Goals are broad, general results. They may be somewhat lofty. Objectives should be measurable results. How much do you want to accomplish in what time frame, involving how many people (or trees or salamanders)?

Outcomes are the trickiest to state. An outcome is the answer to the question, "So what?" So what if you provide antismoking classes to middle school students, reaching every child in four districts? Well, the outcome may be that a lower percentage than average of those specific students gets hooked in high school. Or in college. Or ever.

The writer wants the outcomes to be compelling, measurable, and specific but also has to be careful not to overstate how much the project can claim or measure. What if the antismoking classes are one of a series of health classes and others also bear an antismoking message? How long do such classes hold sway over teenagers' behaviors? Over adult behaviors?

If the grant says the nonprofit intends to achieve a long-term outcome, the agency had better be prepared to conduct the research necessary to find out whether the outcome was achieved.

Presenting (ta-da!) your project idea

At this point the grant writer has held off long enough. It's time to explain the project idea. Who will do what to whom over what period of time? If a proposal is written for a research project, generally this section is called the procedures. For most other types of projects, it is called methods or methodology.

Although this section generally contains the idea that inspired the organization to seek funding, the writing can be dull. The content is similar to writing a list of instructions in which all of the information comes along at the same level of intensity.

To avoid the dullness trap, think about building the project idea, constructing an argument from beginning to end. A good methods section opens with an overview of the approach and then leads the reader through the project's development step by step. You include enough detail so that the reader can see the project clearly but not so much that you sink into the daily grind. Other techniques to preserve vitality include use of timelines, charts, and graphs — visual presentation of the information to break up and complement the text.

Most projects require a few months of preparation before they can be launched. Factor in time for hiring and training staff, purchasing and installing equipment, identifying research subjects, and performing other necessary preliminary steps.

Because this section contains all the project details, you may accidentally overlook or forget important information. Here are two tips to help you make sure that your project idea is complete:

- ✔ If you need to hire new staff to the project work, be sure to discuss the hiring process, job descriptions and qualifications, and the timeline for hiring.

- ✔ Just because you create something great doesn't mean that anyone will show up to take advantage of it. The proposal must explain how an organization plans to spread the word about this new project and entice the target population into becoming involved.

The proposal must do more than explain what the organization will do. It also must explain why it is taking that approach — the rationale. The reason may be that nobody has ever done it in this way before. The reason may be that the organization has tested the approach and knows that it works. The reason may be that another organization in another part of the country has tested the approach and the project proposes to try it in a new setting.

Include some information reinforcing points made in this section in the proposal's appendix. Staff resumes, job descriptions, and marketing materials are good appendix materials.

In an effort to raise as much money as possible to secure a grant, an organization may change its programs to match a particular foundation's interests. The organization's board and management should watch out for this potentially dangerous practice and carefully assess new project ideas to make sure they address the organization's mission. When the grant seeker feels like Cinderella's sister cutting off her toes to cram her foot in the shoe, he should stop and reassess whether receiving the grant is in the organization's best interest.

Explaining how results will be measured

If the grant writer has carefully shaped the goals, objectives, and outcomes section of the proposal, the desired project results are clear. The evaluation section, then, explains how the organization will measure whether it met those goals, objectives, and outcomes.

This section explains who will conduct the evaluation and why that person or organization is right for the job; what information already is known about the situation or population served; and what instrument(s) will be used to measure the project's results.

Different kinds of evaluation are appropriate at different stages of a project. In a project's first year, the most important question may be, "How can we make it run better?" A nonprofit with a brand-new effort may want to spend the first year analyzing its internal efficiency, balance of responsibilities, and general productivity before beginning an intense measuring of outcomes.

Some organizations evaluate all their projects with project staff. Who is better suited to understand the details and nuances of the work? Who else can grasp the purpose and objectives of the project so quickly?

Of course, the opposing view is that one gets biased results by asking staff members, whose livelihood may depend upon continuation of the project activity. Yet, outside consultants may be much more expensive, and they, too, are employed by a nonprofit agency. While working at an arm's length, they're likely to have some bias about the project. (They, too, may want future work from it.)

Don't let catchy titles trip you up

Many grant writers believe strongly in giving a project a short, catchy name. After all, it is much quicker and livelier to talk about "Backstroke" or "Upstart" than droning on about the "Community Planners' Planning Process Planning Analysis," a fictitious example of terminal title syndrome.

But a project needs a good name, a fitting name. It must capture the spirit of the organization and project. If the subject is medical research, for example, the project title should not be cute. If the title can be shortened into an acronym, be careful about what the acronym spells.

Also, just as fads for the naming of children arise so that whole generations are made up of Judys and Shirleys, Zacharys and Justins, fads arise in the naming of projects. Keep an eye out for vogue titles that say little.

Evaluation of nonprofit activities has evolved over the past several decades. Here are some common questions (roughly listed in the order of their evolution) used in evaluations:

- Were project funds spent according to the proposal plan? Did the grant recipients do what they said they were going to do?

- What is the project's cost per unit (or person)? How do its costs compare to those of other approaches to the same problem?

- How many units of service (hours of counseling, copies of publications, and so on) is the project producing?

- How satisfied are consumers of the agency's services with the quality of those services?

- How does this agency's work compare to industry standards for an effective work of this type?

- What measurable outcomes is the agency's work accomplishing?

A nonprofit often can learn a lot about the effectiveness of its work by evaluating information it already gathers and has at hand. For example, individual public schools in a system may be required to submit an annual plan to the school superintendent's office to qualify for special forms of funding. A researcher interested in understanding how many schools in a district were trying a particular approach to school reform probably could find out by reviewing these plans that already are on file in the school offices.

Other kinds of data a nonprofit may have on file include names and addresses of persons participating in public programs, intake and exit interviews with staff and clients, or questions submitted by e-mail in response to a Web site.

If the agency plans to gather data from new sources (such as through surveys, interviews, and focus groups), the proposal should explain what those sources are, who will design the instruments to be used, who will gather the information and input the data, and who will analyze the results. If you already have designed your survey, it may be another useful appendix item.

Talking about the budget

Because a proposal is a request for money, at some point your proposal needs to get around to talking about how much the project costs.

If the organization offers one service for which the nonprofit is seeking money, the organization's budget is the same as the project budget. If the project is one of many things the nonprofit does, it will be presented as a smaller piece of the overall budget.

 Chapter 10 discusses how to compute indirect costs. Don't forget to include such costs in a project budget. Projects genuinely do cost agencies money in staff time, space use, utilities, accounting, and other areas. Different foundations have different attitudes about covering the indirect costs associated with projects. Check with the foundation to which you are applying to see whether it limits how much can be charged to indirect costs or management expenses. Thirty-three percent is a common figure, but some foundations set lower or higher standards.

The project budget should be clear, reasonable, and well considered. The grant writer should keep a worksheet of budget assumptions with the grant file in case anyone asks questions about the basis for computing items. Foundations don't want to believe that an organization is inflating the budget, nor do they want to think that the applicant is trying to low-ball them (making their proposal seem competitive by requesting less than they really need). Either approach — budgeting too high or too low in relationship to the cost of a project — can lead to a wasting of resources.

Unless the foundation is willing to consider a proposal for 100 percent of the project costs, the proposal budget should include both income and expenses. Some foundations ask for the information in a particular format.

For those foundations that don't require a special format on the budget, some general standards apply to the presentation:

- ✔ Income should head the budget, followed by expenses.
- ✔ If the organization has multiple income sources, contributed sources should be listed apart from earned sources. Within contributed sources, government grants and contracts usually are listed first, followed by foundation grants, corporate gifts, and contributions from individuals.

✔ All expenses related to personnel costs — salaries, benefits, and consulting fees — come first in the expense half of the budget. Usually personnel costs are subtotaled.

✔ Non-personnel costs follow and also are subtotaled.

✔ Some kinds of project budgets allow for contingency funds of a certain percentage of the project's projected costs. These are usually listed last among expenses.

✔ The budget's footnotes should explain anything that may be difficult for a reader to understand.

The budget is like a spine for the rest of the proposal. It should support every aspect of the plan. Costs of every activity in the methods and evaluation sections must be considered.

Some project budgets seem simple and straightforward. An agency wants to purchase a piece of equipment. It researches the costs, which become the main (and sometimes only) budget item. The agency should remember, however, that some other costs are involved. These may include shipping and installation, training of staff, and maintenance and supplies.

At some foundations, all project budgets and financial reports are analyzed by staff with expertise in that area. They may be separated from the rest of the proposal for this reading. Therefore, a budget should be clear even if it is read on its own — apart from the narrative part of the proposal.

You can find sample foundation budget forms on the CD with this book.

Explaining where the rest of the money comes from

In Chapter 13, we introduce the age-old concept of not putting all of one's eggs in one basket. Between many foundations' reluctance to pay for 100 percent of a project's costs and their preference for offering short-term project support, if you start a new project, you'll want to know how you'll cover the balance of the costs in the present and all of the costs when project support has run out.

Foundations reviewing grant proposals want to know the same information. What resources, other than the grant that the foundation is considering, are available to the project? And how will the agency sustain the project in the future?

Willingness to cover the full cost of a project varies from foundation to foundation and agency to agency. Some like to "own" a project and have their names strongly associated with it; therefore, they may be willing to cover full costs. Some like to be one of several supporters so that if they can't continue to support the project in a future year, the nonprofit hasn't been entirely dependent upon them and has other possible resources to count on.

An additional funding plan should be clear and reasonable. Because a nonprofit can't assume it will receive every grant for which it applies, a foundation understands if a nonprofit has applied for more grant funding than the full cost of the program. If a nonprofit lists another foundation as a possible source of income for a project, it doesn't necessarily have to have received that grant, but the prospect should be plausible. The size of the grant should be appropriate to others awarded by the agency, and the focus of the foundation should be aligned with the project request.

Foundation staff members talk with colleagues at other foundations. Never lie about having submitted a proposal or having received a grant from another foundation. That lie can undermine your request (and future requests, too)!

Guidelines for future funding are similar to those for additional funding. The plan should be reasonable and well considered. Other foundations may not be the most appropriate means of future support. Generally, foundations hope to see agencies growing less dependent on grants over time and are happy to see proposals projecting future increases in earned revenues. For instance, if a project is designed to market a theater's season and increase subscriptions, in future years increased subscription income may cover some of the costs.

Here are some other possible sources for future funding:

- Government contract to sustain a valuable service once it has been developed and tested
- Sale of publications, recordings, or services based on the project
- A membership drive
- A major donor campaign

Some proposals don't need to address these concerns. They begin and end in a short period of time. For example, a proposal to publish a report based on an agency's work may continue to bear modest marketing costs in the future, but once the printing and production of the report are done, future funding is a minor concern. For others, future funding is very important. For example, you wouldn't want to start a recreation center for low-income youths and have to close it after a few years. The lack of program continuity can have a negative effect on the clients and on the community.

Having the last word

Not all proposals include a conclusion. Some writers feel that a conclusion simply repeats points already covered in the cover letter and summary. Proposal readers face vast piles of paper every day: Why make those piles higher? On the other hand, if the proposal ends with a discussion of future and additional funding, the last thing the reader may recall is all about financial planning. This part of the proposal may seem remote from the passion that fueled the project in the first place and from the distinctive approach the project intends to take.

We recommend taking a bow: A brief concluding section may bring the reader back to the point of the proposal, leaving a compelling finale as the last thing the reader remembers about your proposal.

The first time we ever made a personal visit to a foundation, we were invited to take a seat on the couch in the program officer's office. Unfortunately, there was no place to sit on the couch; it was covered with four-foot-high stacks of proposals. In preparing grant proposals, we think back to this couch and to the person at that foundation who was going to have to read our materials. Make sure that your proposal is written in a clear, inviting format and uses clear, succinct prose so that, even while surrounded by clutter and distractions, the reader won't have any trouble understanding your proposal.

We highly recommend against what is called "shotgunning" — writing one proposal and sending the exact same document to all of the foundations on your target list. A good grant writer conducts research into the foundation's interests and goals, makes an effort to thoroughly understand those interests and goals, and then addresses the proposal to those interests and goals.

P.S.: The appendix

A proposal always needs an appendix. Four key items are routinely included in the appendix (and often identified by foundations as required enclosures):

- ✔ Proof of nonprofit status
- ✔ List of the board of directors (and of any advisory boards)
- ✔ Current year's budget
- ✔ Prior year's financial statement

Other common, but not mandatory appendix items include the following:

- ✔ A list of major grants received in recent years
- ✔ An organizational chart outlining staff and board roles

✔ A time line of the organization's history

✔ Copies of newspaper clippings about the agency

✔ Job descriptions and/or resumes

✔ Samples of evaluations or reports

✔ A copy of a long-range plan (or its executive summary if the plan is lengthy)

✔ Agency brochures and program announcements

✔ Letters of support

On the CD accompanying this book we've included a few sample application forms from foundations, demonstrating different proposal requirements and approaches.

Trolling for Corporate Funds with a Two-Page Letter

Proposals addressed to corporations and company-sponsored foundations generally are brief. A two-page letter is an excellent approach. If an employee of the corporation is involved with your organization, say so in the first paragraph.

Businesses care about how well nonprofit organizations are managed: Clear budgets and financial statements are critically important.

Here's what to do in your letter proposal:

✔ Ask for a specific contribution early in the letter. If you've had prior contact with the funder, mention it.

✔ Describe the need or problem to be addressed.

✔ Explain what your organization will do if the grant is awarded.

✔ Provide information about your nonprofit organization, its strengths and accomplishments

✔ Include appropriate budget data. If the budget is more than a half page long, include it as an attachment.

✔ Discuss how the project will be sustained in the future.

✔ Make a strong, compelling closing statement.

A two-page letter outline also can be used when a foundation asks for a "letter of inquiry." Such letters enable foundation staff to become somewhat familiar with the project so that they can judge whether it's worthwhile for the applicant organization to submit a full proposal. If the project doesn't seem to be a good match with the foundation's interests, the foundation may be saving the nonprofit (and itself) time and money.

A letter of inquiry follows the same outline you use for a letter proposal, with one twist at the beginning (and perhaps at the end). Rather than asking for money, the writer is asking for an invitation to apply for money. An example of wording this "twist" might be taken from the following opening paragraphs:

> Children First! has provided emergency health services in rural Iowa for the past 20 years. Based in the renowned research hospital in Ames, it manages four satellite clinics across the southern half of the state. Medical specialists are dispatched within three hours to serve chronic and emergency needs of children and families at clinic sites that are within one hour of their homes.

> Children First! seeks $3 million to establish three additional clinics in central and northern Iowa. I very much appreciated the time you took to talk to me last week about our shared interests in providing excellent medical services in rural communities and am writing to see if your foundation would consider a request for $100,000 towards this project.

Pitching a Research Project

Research proposals are often longer and more elaborate than proposals for other kinds of projects. They present a lot of detailed information and vary from grant proposals and letters in the following ways:

- ✔ The problem statement or needs assessment includes a literature review of other research that has been conducted on the topic at hand. Different approaches are compared to one another (leading up to the approach the proposal will take).

- ✔ The introduction is more often placed at the end of the document and called "background information." This section includes detailed information about the research credentials of the principal investigator and the research team and institution. If several institutions are cooperating on the project, this section describes all partners.

- ✔ The methods section is called procedures, and each approach to be taken is compared to others outlined in the literature review.

Deliverables, included at the end of the procedures or the evaluation section, are "end products" of the research such as published reports, books, or articles.

Dissemination, a section following "Deliverables" describes the ways that the nonprofit will share the research with others. These methods may include presenting papers at research conferences, and distributing published reports, or posting new discoveries on a Web site.

Seeking General Operating Support

If you're seeking funds for general operating support, your proposal needs to make an argument for the work of the entire agency rather than for a specific project. In this type of request, some of the information about current activities, often included in the introduction or background information sections, should be moved to the methods section. The grant-making organization judges the application based on overall organizational strength and its role in its field. Increasingly, foundations consider the ability of an agency to cooperate or work with others an important criterion. If you're tailoring a proposal for general operating support, we recommend the following:

✔ Prepare an introduction that very quickly introduces the problem that the agency was created to solve, the goals it addresses, and its current programs. Give some attention to describing its leadership (board and staff), its history, and how its activities may have evolved over time.

✔ In the problem statement, discuss the human needs implied by the agency's organizational mission.

✔ When preparing the section on goals, objectives, and outcomes, address the external goals (how the nonprofit plans to serve its constituents) and internal goals (such as expanding the board of directors or changing the accounting system).

✔ Use the methods section to describe the agency's current programs.

✔ In the evaluation section, describe various means the agency uses to understand and improve its programs.

✔ Include the entire annual budget for the organization in the budget section. This is the budget that often is placed in the appendix.

✔ In the section on future and additional funding, briefly describe fundraising or earned income areas the organization is working to increase. Mention major grants being submitted for all aspects of the organization or include them as a list in the appendix.

Seed Money: Proposing to Form a New Agency

A writer presenting a proposal for a brand-new organization that doesn't have a history, a staff, or any accomplishments faces a particular writing challenge. What is there to say?

Writers of such proposals should take heart. Some foundations specialize in "seed proposals" for new projects and new organizations, specifically inviting such proposals. A seed proposal has two key ingredients: 1) careful assessment of the problem to be addressed; and 2) special qualifications its founders bring to its creation.

Here's a quick outline of a proposal for a new endeavor:

- ✔ Background information introduces the people who are creating the organization, their vision, how they identified the idea, and steps they've taken to date to realize their ideas.

- ✔ The problem statement should be a strong, convincing presentation of what the founders have observed and learned about the needs to be addressed.

- ✔ Goals, objectives, and outcomes should be carefully stated. The goals may be lofty, but the founders need to realize they'll take baby steps before they run. Objectives and outcomes should be reasonable considering the developing state of the organization.

- ✔ Methods should be plans for the first year or two of activities. Include discussion of how the organization will be structured and how services will be offered.

- ✔ Evaluation plans may "go easy" during the organization's initial phases. Founders may be testing basic ideas for their feasibility and efficiency for a year or two before studying an approach in depth.

- ✔ The budget is likely to be the entire organizational budget. Some seed grant funders don't mind helping to set up the organization and are willing to cover costs such as equipment purchases or deposits for renting an office.

- ✔ Future and additional funding should outline basic plans for supporting the nonprofit in the future (unless it addresses a discrete problem that may be solved within a few years).

A foundation may be willing to support a feasibility study for a new idea. Such a grant funds interviews and research into how distinctive the idea is, what the likeliest sources of support are, and how much funding the new organization may expect from such resources. Such a plan arms the seed project in applying for other start-up grants.

Chapter 18

Capital Campaigns: Finding Funds to Create a Home Base

· ·

In This Chapter

▶ Developing the campaign plan and budget

▶ Figuring where gifts will come from

▶ Understanding the drawbacks of capital campaigns

· ·

*F*or many nonprofit organizations, finding and keeping the right home base is critically important to success. The right kind of space is easy for the nonprofit's clients or patrons to get to and use, whether they're bird callers, clay potters, recyclers, kindergartners, or any of the myriad other people who benefit from a nonprofit's programs.

Great space? Think of an acoustically perfect concert hall awash in lights, or a restored Georgian home, or a sweep of preserved coastal land, or a multi-story medical facility. Each one can be a magnificent, memorable site whose beauty, setting, authenticity, or technical capabilities inspire awe, evoke memory, or ease pain, among the many missions of nonprofit organizations. Such sites are created through capital campaigns to acquire land, construct buildings, or restore or renovate existing buildings.

Some organizations don't have an "edifice complex," as the need for places or buildings is sometimes called. Those organizations can fit easily into standard offices, storefronts, or mini-malls. If that sounds like your group, you may want to skip this chapter. But if you have any designs on grander designs, this chapter shows you how to turn the dream into reality.

Beginning the Funding Plan

You've found the building of your organization's dreams. It's just around the corner from where you currently serve clients. It's bigger and better than your current building and comes with a parking lot and garden. Better yet, it's for sale at a reasonable price.

You need money to buy it and money to make repairs. Where do you begin?

Taking steps toward acquiring or making improvements to your building requires you to analyze your organization's situation and to plan carefully and thoroughly. One issue you need to be aware of is that a real estate deal can arise and disappear quickly. Sometimes you have to take these initial steps at the speed of a contender in the Olympic 100-meter race.

Preplanning your move

Once your organization begins thinking that it may want to move or build or restore, you can begin some of this planning. Here are some preliminary steps that we recommend:

✔ Take advantage of technical assistance. Find out whether the Nonprofit Finance Fund (www.nonprofitfinancefund.org) has a program set up in your area. It offers low-cost consultations, small grants for planning, low-interest loans, and excellent one- and two-day workshops about understanding and planning capital projects. If these services and program aren't available in your area, check into other nonprofit management classes and consulting offered in your community. A program officer at your local community foundation should be able to suggest nearby resources. Your chamber of commerce or board of real estate companies or professional service clubs may send retired business executives into the community as volunteers, and they may be able to assist you.

✔ Check your board for expertise. Board members with professional experience in financial lending, construction, real estate, city government, and law all can provide valuable assistance. If your board doesn't include such expertise, its members may know professionals who could provide advice and assistance on a short-term basis.

✔ Summarize your organization's primary sources of contributed income. Who has been donating money to your cause and at what level?

✔ Gather information about major capital resources in your area. Which foundations' names appear on the walls of many nonprofits' buildings? Which individual donors?

Loans may be an important part of your capital plans. Many organizations borrow some of the money they need to finish construction while waiting for capital campaign pledges to be awarded. Does your area have a community loan fund? Do any local foundations make program-related investments (low-interest loans) to nonprofits? Do any local foundations guarantee bank loans for nonprofits?

Developing your capital campaign budget

Before you test your project to find out whether it's feasible, you'll need assistance figuring out what it will cost. Planning and building codes vary greatly across the country. A local architect or city appraiser/inspector should be able to tell you what your building will need based on how it will be used.

Just because a building is currently in use doesn't mean that you can move right in and begin operating your programs there. The current occupant may have complied with all the regulations that were in force at the time that occupant began using the building. Building codes often change over time, however, and whenever a building changes hands or its use is changed, it then must be brought up to code so that it complies with the most recent requirements.

Building codes are closely tied to the building's function. Rules for classrooms sometimes change according to the age of the children. Rooms in which large numbers of people may gather — those used for public assembly — are likely to have stricter safety requirements than those used by individuals as offices.

Also to be considered are any regulations tied to your nonprofit's funding sources. For instance, programs accepting money from government sources are required to comply with the Americans with Disabilities Act (ADA). They must offer ramps and elevators for wheelchair users; appropriately placed plumbing, railings, and equipment; and large-print signs or audible signals. (We'd like to see all nonprofits comply with the ADA requirements, regardless of whether they receive government money.)

Once you go through a building with an architect or inspector, you'll realize that there are regulations for just about everything you can imagine, from the height and depth of stairs to the amount of steel rebar in the poured concrete. You may have thought that you were just going to paint a new sign for the door and find that you need to pour a whole new foundation.

Your architect can help you develop a list of major projects to be done. At this point, you may be able to get a contractor to give you a ballpark estimate of the cost. Nobody can make a firm bid on your project or make a clear cost estimate until after you have hired an architect, obtained detailed drawings, and have those drawings approved by the city or county agency that issues building permits in your area.

In addition to architectural and construction costs, your capital campaign is likely to have eight major kinds of expenses:

✔ **Real estate fees:** Purchase of real estate often includes fees for inspections, closing costs, and other charges paid to banks, realtors, and other professions involved in the transaction.

✔ **Fees and permits:** These are charged by local building or planning departments for approval of your architect's plans. Some projects require multiple permits, such as one for construction, another for specific safety features, and yet another for any signs, exterior lights, or awnings.

✔ **Financing costs**: If you borrow money, your organization will need to make mortgage payments, which include interest and other financing costs.

✔ **Fundraising costs:** Your capital campaign will take time as it, in effect, doubles your fundraising expenses. You'll need to continue to cover the costs of current programs while also raising funds for construction and moving. This may mean assistance from an outside consultant to plan the campaign, extra staff in your fundraising department, printed materials, and special events costs.

✔ **Technical costs:** Rarely does your old technology neatly fit into a new building. If you have expanded, you may need more phone lines or more computers. Your new theater may need a state-of-the-art sound system. You also may need to adjust the location of the building's cables and wiring to accommodate your equipment.

✔ **Furnishings and fixtures:** Placing your funky old couch in the lobby of your elegant new lobby detracts from the value and impact of your renovation project. Your old furniture may fit just fine into your new building, but an organization often needs some new furniture and fixtures to fit into and take advantage of its new location.

✔ **Moving costs**: You may remember to budget for the moving van, but that's just the beginning of the moving costs. You'll need to have services — phones, utilities, trash pickup, and others — transferred from your old location to your new one. And you'll need to let everyone know where you've moved, so you'll want to send change-of-address cards and newsletters. Stationery, brochures, invoices, and other printed materials will need to be reprinted with your new address.

✔ **Maintenance:** If your new building is bigger and nicer, taking care of it will cost more. Not only do you need to raise funds for janitorial services and lightbulb replacements, you also need to have enough money put aside to take care of routine maintenance and unexpected repairs to the building. What if the radiator blows up? Or the pipes freeze? Or the sprinkler system leaks? Protect your investment by creating a cash reserve for the building's care and maintenance.

Failing to create a plan and budgeting for building maintenance is one of the most common mistakes made by nonprofit organizations undertaking capital projects.

Organizations often think that owning a building is the only way they can protect themselves from rapidly rising real estate costs. But building ownership is not the only solution and, indeed, may not be an ideal solution for a small or mid-sized organization because it may not have the staff or resources to become a building manager. If you can't afford to own a building, here are some other ways to secure reasonably priced real estate:

- ✔ Negotiate a long-term lease at a reasonable rate with a landlord in exchange for making some building improvements.

- ✔ Find a foundation that buys and develops properties and then leases to nonprofit organizations at reasonable rates.

- ✔ See whether you can find a nonprofit community development organization that purchases, renovates, and manages real estate for other nonprofits at reasonable rates.

The CD includes two sample capital project budgets — one for a modest project and one for a large-scale project.

Testing Feasibility

You've figured the general costs of your project. Now your feasibility study will test the hypothesis that you can raise the amount of money you need for your land or building.

Remember that tried-and-true method for buying a used car? The one where you circle the vehicle, kicking all the tires? An organization's capital campaign starts with that kind of tire kicking, except that it's called a "feasibility study." These are the four essential feasibility study test points:

- ✔ Tire One: How much money does this organization have the capacity to raise?

- ✔ Tire Two: For this particular building?

- ✔ Tire Three: At this location and at this time?

- ✔ Tire Four: Is that enough money to pay for what it needs to do?

A member of the organization's staff or board may be able to conduct the feasibility study, but nonprofits often hire consultants with expertise in this arena. The study involves interviewing key leaders in the organization, its current supporters, and others whose involvement in supporting the project is critical to its success.

The accuracy of the feasibility study is critically important to the capital campaign. Whoever conducts it has to have enthusiasm for the project, yet still be able to speak honestly about the organization's position and listen carefully to the direct and indirect messages conveyed in the interviews. This is one reason a consultant often is used: She is a step removed from the organization. If a consultant is used, interview subjects are more likely to be frank, and the consultant can interpret their answers without bias.

In hiring a consultant to conduct a feasibility study, talk to some of her past clients about the relative accuracy of studies conducted for them. Some consultants write encouraging feasibility studies in spite of discouraging findings, hoping that the organization will undertake and hire her to advise or even manage the project.

Starting with the board

Whether or not an organization's board includes wealthy individuals, all members of an organization's board members should contribute to the campaign. When talking to a foundation, you may be asked whether you have 100 percent board participation. Essentially, the foundation is asking whether all board members have given a gift or made a pledge to the campaign.

Board members are expected to lead the way. Theirs may not be the largest contributions, but they should be made or pledged in the campaign's earliest phases.

Why is this step so important? A charismatic executive director may be able to stir up enthusiasm about a building project, but most capital projects require broad-based support and the assistance of all levels of leadership in the organization. If not everyone on the board of directors has given to the campaign, it suggests that only a few people really support the idea and that the board may not be committed to assisting with the fundraising.

People asking other people to make contributions are in a much better position to ask if they, themselves, have given. Board members must be willing to be involved in the campaign fundraising.

All that matters is that everyone on the board gives. Well, that's true and it isn't. The size of a donor's gift (in relation to what the donor can afford) is some indication of enthusiasm. If a penniless playwright who serves on the board gives $100 toward a capital campaign for a theatre, it is as clear a sign of that enthusiasm as a wealthy banker on the board who makes a gift of $1 million.

If the wealthy banker makes the $100 gift, it suggests that either the board has one malcontent (who, perhaps, should be asked to resign) or that the project is unsupportable.

When organizations have limited money or time to invest in a feasibility study, sometimes only the board members are interviewed. Although this isn't the optimal approach, such a study can reveal a great deal: The members' opinions and behavior set the standards that shape the entire campaign.

Feasibility study interviews

A typical feasibility study interview opens with an overview of the proposed project, emphasizing why the building or location was selected, how in finished form it can enhance the organization's programs, and the features it will have when built. Next, the interviewer describes how much money is needed and how, in general, the organization plans to raise it. If any major donors already are involved, their levels of support are mentioned. Finally, the interviewer suggests a possible donation to the potential contributor and makes note of whether that person is likely to give to the campaign and how much the contribution may be.

The interview should be a conversation among the parties in the room rather than a one-sided presentation. The more the interviewer can engage the interview subjects in discussion, the more the interviewer learns about how outsiders view the organization and about the fundraising potential.

At the point of the feasibility study, most contributors aren't making promises to the campaign, but rather stating their intentions and probable levels of support. The study, therefore, is very important for two reasons:

- ✔ It gathers information that informs the organization's capital campaign goal.
- ✔ It begins the process of "cultivating" contributions to the campaign.

On the CD accompanying this book you can find sample outlines of a capital campaign feasibility study interview and a finished study.

If we continue with the used car metaphor, perhaps a feasibility study is like finding out — after talking to your parents, spouse, or the bank — how much you can afford to pay for a car.

Sometimes your parents may say that they'll give you money for a small sedan, but not for that red sports car, and the same is true for a feasibility study. Board members, community leaders, and/or potential donors may tell you that they would support the project if it were in a different neighborhood, if the building didn't need a new foundation, or if the building didn't seem so extravagant. They may change an organization's plans.

If the feasibility study suggests that you can raise more than the cost of your planned purchase and renovation, you may consider increasing your capital campaign goal to include a larger cash reserve or an endowment whose earnings can be used for building maintenance.

If the feasibility study suggests that you can't afford a "champagne" version of your building plans, you may have to settle for a serviceable "house wine" edition. If your plans already were of the house wine variety, you may want to break the capital campaign into phases. Over the first two years, you could make major safety and structural changes or renovate one of several floors. Then maybe three or four years later you could launch the second phase of a capital campaign to cover the balance of the costs.

You also may learn that you need to wait. Perhaps a few potential major donors gave recently to another campaign, and although they like your project, they were recently tapped (to borrow a maple syrup metaphor). You may be able to come back to them in a year and receive a major contribution. Or maybe potential donors voiced concerns about your organization. You don't have good records about past donors. Your board has dwindled in size. Your executive director just accepted another job. When you organize, recruit, and hire anew, your campaign can proceed.

And you may find out that it's not a good idea to undertake the project at all. Period. Time to start over and plan a different project that you can afford — or stay put.

Although it may seem romantic and courageous to forge ahead against all odds, ignoring a critical feasibility study's recommendations, don't. A failed capital campaign can hurt your organization's reputation even if your programs are good. And what can you do inside of an unfinished building? You may have to suspend operations. You may be shut down by the fire marshal. You may be sued or lose funding for not providing access for persons with disabilities. Worst of all, you may endanger the lives of your clients.

Building the Pyramid of Gifts

You've sketched out your budget. You've set your sights on a reasonable goal. How do you set goals for individual grants and contributions to your campaign?

When it comes to capital campaigns, there is a lot of conventional wisdom. Each campaign develops its own strategies. Each organization has distinctive strengths to call upon. But the same diagram is used by most of them. It's called a gift table, and it looks like a pyramid (see Figure 18-1).

Remember the old saying, "Ten percent of the people do ninety percent of the work"? A capital campaign works that way. Only a few donors are able to contribute large gifts. They go at the top of the pyramid. Smaller gifts from many other donors fill in the lower levels as the campaign moves forward and the pyramid takes shape.

Starting at the top

We know you don't start at the top when building a pyramid but that's where you begin with a capital campaign.

The math for structuring a gift table is easy:

- Ten percent of the money to be raised will come from a single gift, known as the lead gift. This large donation crowns the tip of the pyramid.

- Fifteen percent of the money to be raised will come from two gifts.

- Fifteen percent of the money to be raised will come from four gifts.

- More than one-third of the money to be raised will come from these donations, usually ten or fewer donors. You've put the top on your pyramid.

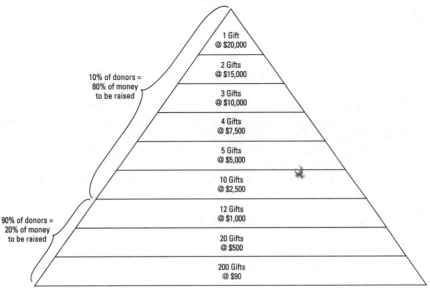

**Campaign For $200,000
Sample Gift Table**

10% of donors =
80% of money
to be raised

1 Gift
@ $20,000

2 Gifts
@ $15,000

3 Gifts
@ $10,000

4 Gifts
@ $7,500

5 Gifts
@ $5,000

10 Gifts
@ $2,500

12 Gifts
@ $1,000

90% of donors =
20% of money
to be raised

20 Gifts
@ $500

200 Gifts
@ $90

Figure 18-1:
The gift "pyramid": 80 percent of donations come from 10 percent of donors.

You're driving across town and pass the Janice Knickerbocker Symphony Hall, the Engin Uralman Medical Center, and the Jerome Kestenberg Museum of Natural History. What do Janice, Engin, and Jerome have in common? Generally, those whose names adorn buildings are those who made the contribution of 10 percent or more of the campaign total. They are what is called the "lead donors."

When you conduct your feasibility study, one thing you're trying to determine is the size of the campaign's largest gift and whether it totals 10 percent or more of the campaign total.

Your lead gift becomes one of your campaign's attractions. Some contributors may support a capital project because they like or admire the person after whom the building is named even if they have little connection to the cause or organization contained within its walls.

In general, capital campaigns start at the top of the pyramid and work down. Once the lead gift is in place, your organization begins seeking the other major gifts that make up the first one-third of the funds to be raised. These lead gifts usually are given by individuals and raised through personal visits. (See Chapter 14 for more about raising money from individuals.)

Filling the pyramid's mid-section

Continuing down the pyramid's structure to the widening middle:

- ✔ Ten percent of the total comes from eight gifts.
- ✔ Ten percent of the total comes from 16 gifts.
- ✔ Ten percent of the total comes from 32 gifts.
- ✔ Ten percent of the total comes from 64 gifts.

By the time an organization hits the gift table's mid-section (the middle of the pyramid), all board members should have made their gifts or pledges. Foundation and corporate grants may play an important role at this point. Some foundations, such as the Kresge Foundation in Michigan, specialize exclusively in capital grants. Kresge tries to help organizations attract new donors to their capital campaigns by awarding matching grants. Generally, if Kresge participates in a campaign, it steps in at this mid-section.

See the CD for the Kresge Foundation guidelines, which provide detailed and explicit information about what it requires in a proposal, an excellent guide for developing other capital proposals to foundations and corporations.

Ending the quiet phase

Generally, up to this point, the organization's capital campaign has been conducted among trustees, close friends of the nonprofit, past donors, and foundations. This early period in a capital campaign is often called the "quiet phase." All along the way, the staff is monitoring the campaign's success, noting how it is progressing in relationship to the feasibility study's predictions and the gift table's structure. Because falling short of the campaign goal can appear to be a terrible public failure for an organization, capital campaigns don't leave the quiet stage until 75 to 80 percent of the fundraising goal has been attained. At that point, those managing the campaign are confident that it can succeed.

Then the campaign is announced to the general public through a press conference, tour, gala party, or cornerstone-setting event.

This is the time to seek smaller donations from lots of people — neighbors, friends of friends, and grandparents. Most often these contributions are raised through special events, special mailings, or even phone-a-thons to individuals and smaller foundations and businesses.

The base of the pyramid is constructed from smaller gifts from many people. Don't discount these gifts. They're important financially to close out the campaign and also to build a feeling of participation in all your donors.

- ✔ Ten percent is raised from 128 gifts.

- ✔ The final ten percent is raised from 266 gifts.

   Ta-da! You can raise the roof, dance on the floor, dig into the soil, or knock down the back wall: You have the money you need.

Annual campaigns and other focused fundraising drives are structured along the gift table pattern. Whether you're raising money for your child's school, an election, or a community fair, a gift table can help to shape and focus your plans.

Return of the case statement

In Chapter 14 on raising money from individuals, we outline steps in writing a case statement. A capital campaign cries out for a case statement — a brief, eloquently stated argument on behalf of the capital project. Sometimes these are produced as fancy brochures with drawings of the future building, maps of the land to be purchased, or clients of the future taking advantage of new opportunities that the building makes possible. Sometimes they are simple typed and copied statements.

Selling immortality on a brass plaque

Many capital campaign case statements offer their donors "naming opportunities." Names of new buildings are often synonymous with the names of the campaign's lead donors. One of the great things about most buildings is that they offer so many other opportunities for donor recognition, often expressed on brass plaques.

Rooms, suites, floors, grand pianos, and stained glass windows can bear the names of donors of large gifts. Those who contribute mid-sized gifts can be recognized on walls, passageways, fountains, and gazebos. Theater seats, lobby sofas, garden benches, desks, trees, and trellises are suitable places to recognize donors of small gifts. For still smaller gifts, consider plaques on floor tiles, wall panels, bricks, and planters.

A capital campaign case statement should incorporate the following elements:

- ✔ Mission and brief history of the organization
- ✔ Major accomplishments
- ✔ Compelling information about constituents served
- ✔ Vision of how the mission can be served better as a result of the capital project
- ✔ Vision for the finished building or acquired land
- ✔ The campaign's leadership and goals
- ✔ Naming and giving opportunities

Shaping a campaign proposal

Grant proposals for capital campaigns follow the general outline of a standard grant proposal (see Chapter 17), with some important variations and additions. The grant writer needs to include parallel discussions of the organization's problems, goals, and activities; how its current building furthers those problems, goals, and activities; and how a stronger organization with stronger capital assets will better serve the organization's goals and clients. Your proposal may focus on purchase of land or open space, but we use a standard bricks-and-mortar building project in the following outline of a grant proposal for a capital campaign:

- ✔ The introduction includes general information about current facilities and leads up to a discussion of the need for a new or renovated building.
- ✔ The problem statement describes needs of clients or potential clients and how satisfaction of those needs is hindered by the organization's current building (or lack of a building).

✔ The goals and outcomes section discusses aspirations that the organization holds for serving its clients and its goals for the capital project (the building's dimensions and amenities) and for the capital campaign.

✔ The methods section briefly touches on how services are delivered but primarily focuses on how the capital campaign is being conducted, how construction will proceed, and activities undertaken to connect current and future clients to the building. Organizations often include a discussion of the results of the feasibility study in this section as a rationale for how goals were set and how the campaign was shaped.

✔ The evaluation section should focus both on whether the building project will meet its goals (such as achieving all city fire and safety code standards) and on how clients are served by the improved building.

✔ The cost section should be presented in categories, just like a budget. See the section "Developing your capital campaign budget," earlier in this chapter.

✔ The section on future and additional funding should discuss how the capital campaign is progressing and where the organization anticipates raising the necessary funds to complete it. This section also should provide information about how the finished project will affect the organization's operating costs and how those changes in expenses will be covered in the future.

Recognizing the Risks of a Capital Campaign

Although the need for capital may be described to potential supporters as a one-time need, many campaign donors will continue to give after the campaign project is finished. They've been introduced to the agency, they've left their names in its lobby, and they want to be sure that it will succeed. In the best situations, capital campaigns strengthen the nonprofit organization's programs both by improving the place in which it offers services and broadening its donor base. A capital project also can be good for staff morale because it improves physical working conditions.

But capital campaigns also have their drawbacks:

✔ Campaigns that do not succeed or that drag on for a long time can damage an organization's reputation.

✔ Because buildings tend to be visible entities, the public may be more aware of an organization's building crisis than of a problem with the programs or services.

- ✔ Capital campaigns may double, triple, or quadruple an organization's fundraising needs while they're being conducted.

- ✔ More staff may be needed.

- ✔ Time will be committed and material costs — such as printing — will be incurred.

- ✔ Organizations often have turnover in their development offices after a capital campaign is completed. Employees may stick around to achieve the end of the project, but they often are burned out by a crippling workload and quit soon after it is finished.

- ✔ Capital campaigns detract from organizations' basic fundraising. If an annual donor is asked to contribute to a building project, he may or may not contribute to the organization's ongoing programs in the same year.

In short, capital projects offer both opportunities and pitfalls, buy-in and burn-out, new donor development and loss of current annual fund donors. But when the building rises out of the empty field, or the gold leaf is restored to its original luster, or the land trust secures a vast swath of horizon, the specific, visible accomplishment is worthy of celebration.

Chapter 19

Marketing: Spreading the Word about Your Good Work

. . . .

. . . .

*Y*ou may think that marketing has no place in the nonprofit sector. After all, if an organization's work isn't driven by the dollar, and if its focus is entirely on meeting a community need, why does it need to sell its services? If your motivation is to do good, isn't it crass to toot your own horn? Doesn't *humility* go along with charity?

Whoa there, all you saints! Before you go marching into the nonprofit cloister, consider this: Marketing — the process of connecting consumers to services and products — is just as critical to the success of most nonprofit organizations as it is to commercial enterprises. Both nonprofit and commercial organizations depend on getting the word out, and the message from both is the same: Here we are. Come and check us out.

This chapter shows you what goes into a marketing plan. You can go far if you have the "goods" — good planning, good stories, good will, and good luck. And persistence.

Discovering Who You Are: First Steps to a Plan

Your organization finishes a year with healthy finances and public accolades, but as its director you sense that something is wrong. You know that you are addressing a need and that your agency is highly regarded. But why aren't all of your programs full? How can you engage more people in the important work that you do?

If a marketing plan is what you need (and we believe it is), the first step is recognizing your current situation — what you do, who you serve, who admires your work and is willing to support it. When you know the answers to these questions, you can begin to build a marketing program that is tailored to all your key audiences — the people who walk through your doors every day to receive your services, your board members and staff, your donors and volunteers, and the community at large. Blend in your budget constraints (we all have to do that!) and you're ready to roll.

Having made an honest assessment, you gradually develop marketing strategies, craft your message, and decide on what steps to take. You brainstorm, consult with experts, talk with peers in your field, test key ideas at a small scale, and do research. You'll want to measure how much money and time you can afford to invest in this effort. Put it all together with a timeline, and voila! — you have a marketing plan.

Defining your current market

If you want to improve the way you reach your public, first you need to know how your current marketing works. Whom are you currently reaching? How did they learn about your organization? Why do they make use of your programs?

You may never learn who reads about you in the newspaper or sees your sign every day on the bus, but some constituents — those with whom you directly communicate — can be identified. As with a fundraising plan, start by defining your core group — your most important constituents — and work out from there.

Suppose that your organization is a small historical society presenting exhibits and panel discussions at three small libraries in your town, publishing a quarterly newsletter, and maintaining a Web site featuring news and information about its collection. Your current customers (working from the core to the outer connections) are

- Your board and staff (and their friends and relations)
- Families and organizations donating materials to your historical collection
- Your trained docents and volunteers
- Local library staff and board members
- Persons signing your guest books at panel discussions

✔ Schools and other groups touring your exhibits

✔ Scholars and other archivists writing to ask about your holdings

✔ Patrons of the three libraries

✔ Subscribers to your quarterly newsletters

✔ Persons visiting your organization's Web site

Thinking up this list of constituents is easy enough. For marketing purposes, you need to know as much as possible about their characteristics, backgrounds, and interests. Some things you can do to collect this sort of information include

✔ Gather names and addresses from every possible source within your organization–items like checks from donors, subscription forms from newsletter subscribers, and sign-up sheets from volunteers. Enter these names and addresses in a computer database or word processing program that can sort them by postal or zip code. (Many mailing list, database, and even word processing programs have sorting options. Filemaker Pro, Access, Word, and Word Perfect are all widely available choices.) Review the zip codes appearing most frequently on this list. If you're in the United States, you can visit the United States Census Bureau Web site (www.census.gov) and receive detailed demographic information about residents in those that zip code areas. If you're patient and take your time to explore the Web site, you can find helpful information, profiling your constituents.

✔ Ask the three libraries if they collect demographic data when visitors apply for library cards and whether they can share that information with you. (Also, some public agencies have information about their constituents on their Web sites.)

✔ When schools or other groups call to sign up for a tour, interview them briefly over the phone as part of the registration process. Find out how they learned about your program, why they want to visit it, and whether they have other needs you may be able to address.

✔ Insert clearly worded and inviting surveys in the programs at your public events. At the beginning and end of an event, make a brief public pitch explaining why it's so important for people to respond to the surveys. Make pencils or pens available. Create incentives for completing the form, like a free museum membership to be given to a person whose survey will be drawn at random.

✔ Include the same survey as part of your mailed newsletter. Provide a return envelope to make it easy for readers to respond, and — again — explain the purpose of the survey and include incentives for completing it.

✔ Ask visitors to your Web site for their e-mail addresses and send a brief survey to them by e-mail. Make the survey inviting, make a pitch for why the information is important to your organization, and provide a prize or incentive for returning it.

Once you have survey results you can create a simple check sheet to compile the responses. Or you can use a database program and create a record for each person who responds or for each event at which surveys are gathered. (See Appendix A for the names of databases.)You may learn that you serve several distinct groups of people. Low-income teenagers use the library after school and visit your exhibits while they are there. Middle-income mothers from the immediate neighborhood bring their toddlers to the library for afternoon stories and take advantage of your programs. And wealthy older adults volunteer as patrons, serve on your board, and attend your organization's panel discussions.

With this valuable information you should be able to recognize ways to reach more people who resemble the ones you already are serving. The more challenging task will be to reach and entice new groups of people.

Do people gather at your organization's programs but you don't know who they are? Sponsor free drawings in which contestants compete for prizes by filling out forms with their names, addresses, and phone numbers.

Designing a useful survey

Developing a picture of your current clients is critically important to creating a marketing plan, and a good survey can be your camera.

If you are going to go to the effort to conduct a survey, it should have a purpose and be based on questions you want to explore, such as why the people who currently use your services find them worthwhile. If you can get to the root of why others value you, you have learned a lot about how to talk about your work to your future constituents.

The survey should not be too long or people won't complete it, but you'll want to explore different kinds of information, such as: How convenient and appealing are your events and services? and What other kinds of programs would your followers enjoy? Also, ask your current consumers how they found out about you. That tells you which forms of your current marketing are effective and begins to suggest how you may most effectively spread the word further about your programs.

If the responses tell you that your clients like your programs but not the current schedule of offerings, should you experiment with new times and formats? For instance, would consumers find Sunday afternoons (when the library is closed) to be more convenient? What other barriers inhibit their involvement? Maybe mothers with toddlers would like to come to your lectures but need childcare. Perhaps you charge a modest amount for lectures but teenagers find that charge to be too high.

Your A to Z references on marketing and public relations

Whole books — hundreds and hundreds of whole books — have been written on the topic of marketing and the related field of public relations. Our job in this chapter is to take you on a quick fly-over of marketing for nonprofit organizations so that you get the big picture and know where to turn for details. And for all the details on marketing plans, surveys, public relations, press releases, and related topics, we recommend three other books from Hungry Minds: *Marketing For Dummies, Small Business Marketing For Dummies,* and *Public Relations Kit For Dummies.*

One of marketing's hardest disciplines is analyzing the very basis of what you do and how you do it. You may feel that your historical society's close working relationship with libraries is its greatest asset, but the surveys may point out that those libraries are cold and musty during winter months. You may do better by taking over a neighborhood restaurant, creating a "warmer" atmosphere — even offering hot gingerbread and beverages.

To succeed at reaching and serving more people, you will want to keep an open mind, be observant, and test your hunches.

The Web site `zoomerang.com` provides assistance with online surveys. You also can find many sample surveys on the Web that give you ideas about wording questions. And an excellent survey package, ADIS, is available to anyone through the Association of Performing Arts Presenters (`www.artspresenters.org`).

On the CD accompanying this book, you can find two sample surveys that may suggest wording for your survey questions.

Defining whom you want to reach

Armed with information about the people who already know about your nonprofit, you're now ready to extend your reach by defining target groups you want to serve and learning how best to reach them. In general, it's wisest to begin with your current constituents and work to expand within their demographic group or to others who are similar to them.

The less the people you want to reach resemble the people you now serve, the more difficult and expensive your marketing task will be. As you shift your attention to reaching new groups, be cautious. You may alienate and lose current followers.

Sticking with the earlier example of the local history archives and its audiences of low-income teenagers, middle-income mothers of toddlers, and affluent docents and volunteers, logical target audiences are

✔ Family members and classmates of the teenagers using the libraries

✔ Mothers and toddlers from a wider geographic area surrounding the libraries

✔ Docents and volunteers who assist other local cultural institutions

✔ Friends and acquaintances of the docents

Your marketing plan then would be tailored to reach these groups. Attempting to reach these groups may require changes both in how you present your work and in how you spread the message about that work. Some ideas for achieving this goal through key audiences are:

✔ **The teenagers' classmates and friends.**

- Contacting local high-school history teachers and working with them to link their lessons to archival materials in your collection. Invite them to bring their classes to see your exhibits and involve the teenagers who are familiar with the collection as docents for the school tours.

- Inviting the teenagers who currently use the library space to join your organization in planning, researching, and presenting an exhibit. Honor them for their involvement at the exhibit's opening and provide them with invitations for their friends and acquaintances.

✔ **The teenagers' families.**

- Working with local teachers and your teen-aged audience, design family-friendly weekend events on the library's grounds. You could offer a variety of activities for different age groups — puppet shows, art projects, scavenger hunts, and picnic meals — based on themes in your historical materials.

✔ **More mothers and toddlers.**

- Advertising or placing articles about your organization's work in local newsletters for parents of young children.

- Posting flyers about your organization's work at parks, playgrounds, local stores that sell goods for small children, and at other cultural institutions with children's events.

✔ **Docents and volunteers who also help other organizations.**

- Advertising or placing articles in your local volunteer center's newsletter.

- Exchanging mailing lists of docents and volunteers with other local cultural organizations, then using the new lists to extend invitations to a special get-acquainted-with-us event.

✔ **Friends and acquaintances of your current docents.**

- Holding a volunteer recognition party and providing each of your volunteers with ten or more invitations for friends and acquaintances.

Marketing to achieve your mission

What if, after analyzing your current audience, your organization realizes that it's not fulfilling its mission? To continue with our example, what if the historical society's mission is to inform and improve professional scholarship? Reaching its current audiences may be worthwhile, but reaching these audiences isn't advancing professional scholarship.

How market research can open your eyes

A small nonprofit alcoholism treatment center for women was started in San Francisco in the late 1970s in response to studies that demonstrated multiple programs existed to help alcoholic men but few focused specifically on women. No local service of this type focused on helping Spanish- speaking immigrant women.

The program's mission was to provide comprehensive counseling and alcohol treatment services to low-income women, particularly those originally from Mexico or Central America.

Four years into the nonprofit's history, its programs were full and effective, and it had won prestigious contracts from the city. The center had even launched a capital campaign to create a permanent home. The center looked very successful.

With one exception. The women being served were mostly middle class and white. A few were African American. None came from the neighborhood where the program was based.

The board realized that the center needed to change its image and marketing strategy.

Through interviews with women from the center's target population, board and staff realized the stigma associated with alcoholism was particularly strong among Mexican and Central American families and women from these cultural groups were struggling with alcoholism in private.

The center began a multi-faceted campaign to change this situation, beginning with cultural sensitivity training for counselors. When new staff was hired, an aggressive effort was made to find Chicanas and Latinas to fill positions. All brochures and other informational materials were published in Spanish. Press conferences were held for the Spanish-language press. A Chicana outreach counselor was hired to meet with community groups, churches, and schools and develop connections and a system of referrals to the agency.

Within two years, more than one-third of the women served were Chicanas and Latinas. The marketing aimed at this community was well worth the investment. Fulfilling the organization's mission depended on it.

The historical society's target audiences might be librarians, archivists, historians, and graduate students. The nonprofit has to figure out how to reach these groups. It should ask itself: How do they get information? What do they read? Who and what influences their decisions and behavior? With the answers to these questions, your nonprofit can retool its marketing plan.

Taking Care of Basics

You've analyzed your current followers' demographic profiles, opinions, and preferences. You've planned ways to reach new and larger constituent groups. You've written a marketing plan. Yes, marketing is about the "big picture."

It's also about attending to every day needs. In reaching the public, your organization will make use of a set of marketing tools. If you're starting out you'll need to assemble your toolbox. If you're working to reach new audiences, you may want to adjust some of its contents.

As a rule, you will invest most of your public relations time and money in reaching the people who are closest to your organization. Does that seem peculiar? After all, they already know about you, right? Yes, but your loyal customers — board members, long-time volunteers, and past donors — are the people who *deserve* your time. They are also the members of your organization who are the most interested in reading your marketing materials. And they're the folks who are most likely to be inspired by your accomplishments and send money.

Design a logo

A good logo suits the tone of your organization. Many people remember pictures more vividly than words. They may remember your logo more easily than they remember your organization's name! You won't want to grow tired of it, or for it to be confused with the logo of another group in your community.

If you need to create a logo, try not to resort to standard computer font symbols or clip art. Do you know a graphic artist or a printer with a good eye who can help you create something original? If not, we recommend choosing an attractive typeface in which to present your name. You can get fancier later.

If your organization is small and your resources are limited, don't design a logo that has to be printed in more than one color of ink. Using just one color helps to control your printing costs.

Select stationery

Your stationery should include your organization's name, address, phone number, fax number, e-mail address, and Web site (if you have one). Many organizations also list their board members on the stationary. Doing so is a great way to highlight board members' affiliation with your organization, but if your board is rapidly changing and growing you'll be reprinting the stationery every few weeks. You may also want to include a tag line, briefly identifying what your organization does, like *Feeding the hungry in Tuborville.*

In selecting stationery, choose paper that makes clear, readable photocopies (avoid dark papers or those with lots of flecks and spots).

Print a background sheet or brochure

A background sheet is a one-page typed overview of your organization's purpose and programs. You may enclose it with press releases, grant proposals, and fundraising letters. You may leave copies of it in your lobby for visitors to read.

As you grow, your organization may want to get a little bit fancier and move beyond a simple typed sheet to invest in a folded brochure with photographs or drawings. A brochure should clearly convey the essence of your organization. You want it to be inviting and readable. Visual elements, if you can afford them and they're appropriate, help to make a more attractive document and tell your story in fewer words.

Post your sign

How do people find your physical location? An attractive sign can be an important part of your image. In some cases, banners can be printed more easily and cheaply than many other kinds of signs. Consider all the options for price, image, durability, flexibility, and visibility — awnings, quilts, stencils on glass, neon, LED, flags. And consider the sign's placement. We once had a great sign behind an enormous oak tree. Nobody could find our organization.

Produce an annual report

Begin producing an annual report after your first year of operating. It may be a letter, brochure, pamphlet, or even a book. Usually, the annual report includes a financial statement for the year along with an overview of recent accomplishments. It may also include letters from the president and executive director of your organization.

Proving that you're still in business

Once we worked for an organization that had to shut down for awhile because its building was damaged in an earthquake. We wanted to write to our constituents to tell them that we still existed and what we were doing. A consultant recommended that we produce a newsletter rather than a letter. She said, "A letter will say you exist, but a newsletter proves that you exist." She was right. We produced a newsletter and our followers were reassured, volunteered to help with our move, and gave money.

Issue a newsletter

A newsletter offers four, eight (or more) pages of background stories and information about your organization. Issuing a newsletter is a great way to keep in touch with your organization's constituents and it can take them behind the scenes of your organization. You may use it to profile members of your staff, board, and constituents, alert followers to coming events, summarize research, and announce news about your organization's work.

Marketing on a Shoestring

Effective marketing doesn't have to be expensive. It can be based on multiple grassroots efforts that are small in scale and very specifically targeted. *Guerilla marketing* is the term for marketing that's on the cheap, creative, and effective. (You may also see it spelled *gorilla*.)

The guerilla approach may use stickers affixed to parking meters, cards tacked on the bulletin boards at local health food stores, flyers mailed along with supermarket coupons, bookmarks stacked by checkout counters, and e-mail discussion groups.

These efforts work if they are based on knowing the habits of the people you want to reach. Using them, you can reach some of the people all of the time. Do a Web search for guerilla marketing (or gorilla marketing) to get more information.

Saving money at the printer's

Printing costs can eat a hole right through your nonprofit's wallet. If you print postcards, odd-sized announcement cards, bookmarks, or other smaller marketing pieces, talk to a local printer about including your job around the edges of a larger piece being printed or on odd-sized paper trimmed from larger jobs. This type of printing can be very inexpensive.

Talk to other organizations that print materials on a similar schedule to yours (such as a calendar of events that gets printed every month). By processing your print jobs at the same time and using the same paper, you may be able to save money for all parties.

Taking Good Care of Customers Every Day

We've been writing a lot about ways to reach new users of your services. But taking good care of your current "customers" is an equally important part of your marketing plan. If your constituents, audiences, patients, clients, volunteers, and board members are not treated well, you can make major investments in advertising and public relations without sustaining their interest or reaching new people. Small adjustments in customer service can make a big difference to your organization's image.

The trick is to attend to service in little ways all of the time. Every staff member should be aware the importance of customer service. We offer five key areas to address to improve (or maintain) your service levels.

The telephone

Talk to all staff and volunteers about how to answer the phone politely and otherwise use it to maximum effect. Provide a cheat sheet with lists of extensions, instructions on how to forward calls, and anything else that would be useful. Simple additions to a greeting, like, "May I help you?" or telling the caller the receptionist's name can set a friendly, professional tone.

Make a rule for yourself to return all calls within 24 hours or, if that's not possible, within one week. Let callers know, through your voice mail greeting, when they may expect to hear from you.

If you're selecting a voice mail system, make sure it is user friendly to callers. We prefer a small number of transfers within the system and options for modifying standard recorded announcements with more personal and pertinent messages.

If your agency is likely to receive calls from people requiring counseling or emergency assistance, make sure that everyone answering the phone is thoroughly trained in how to calm a caller and provide a referral.

The door

Someone needs to (cheerfully) answer the door. If you're in a small office without a receptionist and the interruptions are frequent, you can rotate this task among staff members.

If visitors must use a buzzer or pass through a security system, try to balance the coldness of that experience with a friendly intercom greeting and pleasant foyer.

The sale

If you have something to sell, make it easy to buy. Accepting only cash is far too restrictive. The banker managing your business account can help prepare you to accept credit card orders. Also, consider selling over the Web; more and more sites are available on the Web to assist small businesses with Web sales.

If a customer is not satisfied with your product or service, invite the customer to give feedback and listen carefully. Offer a partial or complete refund. Doing so wins loyalty.

The note

Keep some nice stationery and postcards handy so that writing personal notes is easy. Hand-written notes are more personal and often make a stronger impression than formal, typed letters.

Write thank-you notes within a few days of any contribution.

If your organization receives *things* — like a theatre group that receives play manuscripts or a natural history museum that receives research — have pre-stamped postcards ready that acknowledge the item's receipt and state when the person submitting it can expect to hear from you.

The details

An old saying suggests that the devil lurks in the details, but that's also where you'll find the heart and soul of hospitality and service. Keep notes in a database or on file cards about the interests, connections, and preferences of your board members, donors, and frequent customers, if appropriate helps you master those details. Learn the names of your board members' significant others and be prepared to greet them personally at events and on the phone.

Reaching Your Audience through Mass Media

What if you want to reach all the people some of the time? (Sorry, you can't reach all the people all of the time.) That's when you're likely to move to the mass media — newspapers, magazines, radio, television, and the Web.

Planning for effective publicity and PR

Guess what? Before you try to get the media to cover your work, you'll want to create a plan. If you've put the time into developing an overall marketing plan (a topic we discuss earlier in this chapter), you've got a head start in creating a public relations plan for targeting the mass media. After all, you already know how people learn about your work and how media has or has not played a role in their awareness.

Before contacting the media, first decide what story you want to tell and who you want to reach with that story. What is distinctive and important about your organization's work? Why is it newsworthy? Be honest: Analyze your idea as if you are a news editor who has to choose among many different stories from many sources. How does yours stand up in the competition?

Developing a media list

A media list is a compilation of names, addresses, e-mail addresses, and phone numbers of contacts at local (and maybe national) newspapers, radio and television stations, magazines, and Web sites. The list also should include wire service contacts in your area, such as Associated Press and Reuters.

Like your donor list, a media list is a valuable tool that you refine and expand over time. Some metropolitan areas have press clubs and service organizations from which you can buy membership lists, providing a basis for your list. If there's no such service available, you can begin building your media list at the public library, using *Broadcasting Yearbook, Editor and Publishers Yearbook, BPI Media Services* and other reference books. In a pinch, you can use the classified pages of the telephone book.

For all the nuances of media list development and management, we recommend that you take a look at *Public Relations Kit For Dummies,* published by Hungry Minds, Inc. In general, your objective is to build two working lists, one that you use with practically every press release you send out and the other for specific opportunities for publicity. The latter group may include

- ✔ Social and entertainment editors to whom you send news of your annual benefit gala

- ✔ Social and business editors to whom you announce new members and officers of your board

- ✔ Opinion page editors for letters to the editor

- ✔ Sunday magazine supplement editors for in-depth profiles of leaders in your field of work

- ✔ Features columnists for amusing anecdotes or unusual news

- ✔ Internet chat room hosts to whom you give your organization's perspective and who you use to test public response to news and ideas

Starting to work with media

Here's our advice for getting started with the mass media:

- ✔ Pay attention to the areas of interest of different media outlets, writers, and reporters and match your story to these interests.

- ✔ Analyze your program or event as if you were a news editor. Is there a human-interest story? What's newsworthy?

- ✔ Write (or record or film) a basic document and vary it to address the different media interests that you appeal to, making use of your multiple story angles.

- ✔ Persist in following-up on every item you send to the press, but don't become annoying.

- ✔ Keep the press fully informed about any changes in your story. Printing incorrect information makes them look bad and may hurt your chances of future coverage.

- ✔ Prepare for a visit to your program or orchestrate other forms of direct interaction.

- ✔ Take no graciously when media decide not to use your story. You need to be able to go back to these people in the future.

Different media outlets require different amounts of lead time. In an ideal situation, you will want to begin your efforts to reach the media four or five months in advance of that hoped-for coverage. The first two months will be spent creating press releases and public service announcements, shooting and developing photographs. Then you'll start distributing the materials:

- ✔ Most monthly magazines need to receive your press release and photographs at least three months in advance of publication (even earlier if they are quarterly or bimonthly).

- ✔ At the same time that you're mailing to magazines, you'll want to send advance notice to your most important daily and weekly outlets.

- ✔ We recommend sending public service announcements (see the section on PSAs later in this chapter) two to three months prior to the time when you hope they will be used. While most stations have set aside time for broadcasting nonprofits' announcements, they need time to rotate through the many announcement materials they receive.

- ✔ Press releases to daily or weekly papers should be sent four-six weeks in advance of the event you want covered. You also may send follow-up releases approximately ten days prior to the event. You'll certainly want to make follow-up phone calls.

- ✔ Releases inviting members of the press to a press conference or to witness a special event or announcement may be sent close to the event (three to ten days in advance). Generally such announcements are conveyed with a sense of urgency.

Reaching your media contacts

Each section of a newspaper and each part of a TV or radio program is made up of materials from multiple sources that are competing for time and space. You improve the odds of receiving attention in the media by providing clear, accurate, and provocative materials in time for consideration and possible use by reporters and broadcasters.

We recommend the following steps when you submit material to the media:

1. **Call to identify the most appropriate contact person at the newspaper, radio station, or TV station, and ask about the format that you should use in your submission.**

    The better you get to know your contacts, the less frequently you'll be taking this step.

2. **Submit clear, accurate written materials, labeled photographs, or recorded audiotapes, videotapes, or compact discs, as is most appropriate.**

3. **Call to see if your materials have been received.**

   Take this opportunity to ask whether more information or a different format is needed.

4. **If requested, submit additional information and call to confirm its receipt and clarity.**

5. **If you do not receive a clear response (either "Yes, we'll cover it" or "Sorry, I don't see the story here") to your initial release, update it, resubmit it, and call again.**

6. **If a member of the press comes to cover an event you've announced, have a press packet ready.**

   A press packet is usually a press release with background information and photographs. The packet briefs the reporter about your event and makes it easy for him or her to combine notes and materials from the event with your organization's official overview of the story.

   Introduce yourself and be available to answer questions or to introduce the reporter to key spokespeople, but don't be a pest: Let a reporter find his or her own story.

7. **If your situation changes and the press release is no longer accurate, immediately call in the change and, if necessary, revise and resubmit your original release.**

Sample press releases, press alerts, calendar releases, photo captions, and public service announcements are on the CD. They can help you understand the approaches and formats to use.

Getting listed in the calendar

Getting your organization's events listed in newspaper calendars and broadcast on TV and radio can be critically important to attracting a crowd. Readers, viewers, and listeners use these calendars to help decide how they are going to spend their time on, say, a Thursday night. If your event is listed clearly and accurately, you're in the running.

Larger newspapers and many other media outlets assign the preparation of calendar sections to specific editors. When you put together your media contact list, make sure you identify the calendar people. And to improve your access to this important source of publicity, contact the calendar specialists in advance and ask for instructions about how they prefer calendar listings to be formatted and how much in advance of the event they want to receive your information.

The art of shaping a news story

A few years ago we were involved as grant-makers in supporting the creation of a mural on the exterior of a community center next to a small urban park. One of San Francisco's best-regarded mural artists led the project. She spent a great deal of time talking to the park's neighbors and people who used the building about images to use in her mural. While not originally her subject idea, those she talked to kept mentioning a young couple who had been killed in the park in a random, accidental shooting several years earlier. She included their portraits in the painting surrounded by images representing peace and renewal.

The story of the mural's unveiling was presented to the media as a public memorial event for the neighbors and families of the young couple. Front page, color images of the piece appeared in both the morning and evening papers the next day and five television stations covered the event that evening. An acclaimed artist's completing another mural wouldn't have been a story, but a neighborhood's mourning two lost teenagers was hot news.

We hope your nonprofit is never thrown into telling the story of a tragedy, but we give this example to show that not all good work is news. Tragedy is news. Drama is news. Breakthroughs are news. Surprises are news.

Preparing public service announcements

Many radio and television stations allot a portion of their airtime to broadcasting public service announcements (PSAs) on behalf of nonprofit causes. In some countries and regions, their receiving a license to broadcast requires them to provide this service.

Although these stations rarely give away their best viewing and listening hours to this free service, sometimes they do tack PSAs onto the end of a newscast or special program during prime time. But even an announcement played during the morning's wee hours can reach many people.

Public service announcements are brief. Most are 15, 30, or 60 seconds long. You may submit them as written text to be read by the stations' announcers, or you may submit them recorded or filmed on audiotape, CD, or on videotape for direct broadcast. Many stations are more willing to use PSAs that are already recorded or filmed, but this isn't true all of the time and if you submit a pre-recorded PSA, also include a print version of the text. Some stations string several announcements together in a general public announcement broadcast, and it's easier for them to work from text.

If you choose to submit a fully completed PSA, make sure that it is of broadcast quality with excellent sound and/or images. If you're the narrator, spit out your gum! If you mumble or if the videotape is blurry, stations cannot use it.

The challenge to writing public service announcements is to convey a lot of information in a short time and to be very clear. Write your message and test it against the clock. If you're rushing to finish it in time, it's probably too long. Ask someone else to read it back to you and time that person. You don't want to be the only one who can finish it in 15 seconds.

Table 19-1 summarizes an appropriate format for presenting a public service announcement.

Table 19-1	Presenting a Public Service Announcement
Placement	*Content*
Left top of page	"For immediate release to public service directors for use between [identify dates during which the release is timely]." Also clearly indicate the length of the release (15, 30, or 60 seconds).
Right top of page	"For further information contact:" followed by name, phone number, and e-mail address of a person who can answer questions about the announcement.
Centered	Brief headline that both orients the reader to the subject of your story and that can become part of the reading of the release.
Below headline	The announcement in large print (sometimes all caps), double-spaced. Make sure that your release can be read within the length of time that you specify and that it flows well. If it includes names or words with unfamiliar pronunciations, spell them phonetically in parentheses next to the challenging words.

Developing a Web site

More and more nonprofit organizations feel that having a presence on the Web is as important as being listed in the telephone book or printing a brochure. A basic Web site need not be difficult to create. You may want an overview of your agency on the home page, and a few additional pages where people learn about your organization's leaders and programs.

For complete instructions on developing a Web site, we recommend *Small Business Marketing For Dummies,* published by Hungry Minds, Inc. Take a look at Chapters 18 and 19 in that book.

Part IV
The Part of Tens

The 5th Wave   By Rich Tennant

Every nonprofit organization needs someone who can help hammer out a clear mission statement.

In this part . . .

*H*ere's a place to turn for some quick reminders and
encouragement. We debunk some common biases,
prejudices, and misconceptions about nonprofit organizations. And we return to the theme of money raising, sum-
marizing our experience and advice into easy-to-follow tips.

Chapter 20

Ten Myths about Nonprofit Organizations

In This Chapter
▶ Saintly workers poor as church mice, and all that nonsense
▶ Other misconceptions smashed to smithereens

*I*n this chapter, we expose common myths about nonprofit organizations. Here are our favorites. Let the truth be told!

Nonprofits can't charge for their services

We think that this myth came about because of the word *charity*. Most people think of charity in the same way they think about the custom of giving alms — giving money or assistance to those in need without expecting anything in return.

Some nonprofits do give free services to the poor, the homeless, and others less fortunate than themselves. Food and clothing programs, legal services, and advocacy for certain groups generally are provided without billing those who benefit. But many nonprofits do charge fees for their services or charge for tickets to performances or museum exhibits, for instance.

It's typical for nonprofits that provide programs such as counseling or health-related services to have sliding-scale fees. In other words, the amount you pay is based on your income and the number of people in your family. Contributions to the organization make up the difference between the cost of providing the service and the fee received.

Nonprofit workers can't be paid (or can't be paid very much)

This myth brings up the image of a dedicated worker toiling away for no remuneration. You *do* find a lot of these people in nonprofit organizations — they're called volunteers. And many paid nonprofit staff members work for less than they might make in the private sector.

But many nonprofit staff members are well compensated, especially those who work for the larger nonprofit organizations. A 2000 survey undertaken by the Center for Nonprofit Boards and the Stanford Graduate School of Business found that 18 percent of nonprofit chief executives earned $100,000 or more. Thirty-four percent reported salaries of between $50,000 and $75,000. Now, the nonprofits surveyed did have larger budgets than most, and we suppose that $100,000 a year isn't that extravagant these days. But the belief that nonprofit workers can't be paid, or even paid fairly well, just isn't true.

Nonprofit board members can't receive compensation

This claim is actually more or less true in practice. Very few board members receive payment for serving on nonprofit boards. But board members can receive compensation for services provided to the organization. For example, some nonprofits have a paid staff member serving on the board.

We don't recommend that nonprofits pay their board members, but that doesn't mean there isn't a good reason for doing it sometimes. If an organization serves low-income clients, for example, having representation from that group on the board is a good idea. The offer of a stipend in exchange for board attendance and service might encourage more people to be actively involved.

In its Standards on Philanthropy, the National Charities Information Bureau comes out against paying board members but does allow one paid staff member to serve on a board. Of course, board members can be reimbursed for reasonable expenses associated with serving on the board such as travel costs.

Nonprofits can't make a profit

Many people think that nonprofits can't end the fiscal year with money in the bank. Not true. Nonprofits should end the year with extra money if possible.

It's true that nonprofits can't distribute surplus funds (profits) to board members or staff, although this doesn't mean that nonprofits can't pay salary bonuses. But surplus funds can be kept in reserve for a rainy day, invested in a variety of ways, or used to start new programs.

Nonprofits can't own and operate for-profit businesses

Nonprofits *can* own for-profit businesses. A good example of nonprofit success in business is Minnesota Public Radio, or, more properly, its parent organization, American Public Media Group. In 1981, Minnesota Public Radio began selling posters associated with its successful *Prairie Home Companion* radio show. This mail-order business grew into a multimillion-dollar mail-order operation that was sold to the Dayton-Hudson company for an estimated $120 million. The sale generated $90 million for Minnesota Public Radio's endowment and generated cash reserves approaching $20 million to invest in new programming, new equipment, or just kept for a rainy day.

Generating income does come with a downside, though. Nonprofits that generate income from activities unrelated to their charitable purpose must pay taxes on that income. It's known as Unrelated Business Income Tax (UBIT). We cover the topic in Chapter 2.

Nonprofit organizations aren't run as efficiently as businesses

If the Minnesota Public Radio story didn't convince you that this is a myth, we're not sure what will. What we want to attack with this myth, however, is the idea that nonprofit managers are less effective than managers in the private sector.

This myth is hard to dispel because you can find nonprofits that are poorly managed almost as easily as you can find sand on a beach. But you have to keep in mind that the IRS has approximately 650,000 charitable nonprofit organizations in its database. That doesn't include the organizations that are too small to file regular tax returns. Our point is this: Nonprofit organizations abound, and making generalizations about them is dangerous.

Consider the manager of a nonprofit organization that has a budget of, say, $350,000. Depending on the type of programs the organization offers, the manager may have three to five staff members. About half of the organization's income comes from program services, and the other half comes from individual contributions and grants from foundations and corporations. Any new equipment acquired to improve efficiency must be paid for by writing a grant or by scrimping and saving from meager surplus funds. This manager is no doubt doing six things at once — raising money, communicating with the board of directors, supervising staff, developing new programs, meeting with foundation officials, and writing a publicity brochure.

This scenario is typical for nonprofits, certainly more typical than the Minnesota Public Radio tale. So although this manager may not be privy to the latest organizational management theory, he or she is juggling enough balls to make a cat dizzy. How can you say that this isn't good management?

All people who work for nonprofits are saints

We think that the saint myth comes from the same place as the nonprofits-as-charities myth — the idea that charities are full of selfless people who sacrifice themselves for others.

You *can* find saints in nonprofits, of course. You can find examples of everything in the nonprofit sector. But by and large, the nonprofit workforce is a fair sample of the general population. Some people are more committed to the missions of their organizations than others; some nonprofit managers could be CEOs of Fortune 500 companies if they wanted to be; and some are just marking time until their retirement.

Nonprofit fundraising costs are too high

According to one poll, 43 percent of Americans agreed that nonprofits are wasteful with their funds. But we are with the 57 percent who didn't agree that nonprofits are wasteful. At least we're in the majority.

Take fundraising as an example, because fundraising costs receive the most criticism. Let's talk about what most people call junk mail. In the fundraising business, it's called direct mail (see Chapter 14) and, believe us, you wouldn't receive so much of it if it didn't work.

The simple truth about fundraising is that few people donate to charity without being asked. If nonprofits waited patiently by the mailbox for unsolicited gifts, they would soon be out of business. Raising money costs money, for paying fundraising staff, preparing brochures and fundraising letters, and postage. These efforts aren't wasteful; they're necessary.

Most agencies that issue standards for nonprofit organizations say that fundraising and management costs together should be less than 40 percent of a nonprofit's total costs. We think that 30 to 35 percent is a better target, especially for larger, more established organizations. The larger the nonprofit, the easier it is to control management and fundraising costs.

Working for a nonprofit is easy

Working for a nonprofit isn't any easier than working anywhere else. Work is work, after all. Nonprofit employees work long hours, take work home, and suffer sleepless nights just like everyone else does. Of course, nonprofit workers do have one advantage: They work for a double bottom line. Yes, the organization's books need to end up in the black instead of the red, *but* they're making progress toward accomplishing the organization's mission. Maybe this is the reason people think that nonprofit work is easy — they want to be doing something they believe in.

All nonprofits are essentially the same

People sometimes talk about the nonprofit sector as if it were one homogeneous entity.

In fact, there is more variation in the nonprofit sector than there is similarity. There is tremendous variation in the size of nonprofits, for example. Kaiser Permanente, one of the largest health care operations in the world, is a nonprofit organization. Compare Kaiser's operations with the church around the corner from your house or your local PTA chapter. Think about Harvard University, with an endowment of $14 billion or so (yes, we mean billion), and then think about the Head Start program in your town or the group that's trying to raise money to protect wetlands from a housing development.

Chapter 21

Ten Tips for Raising Money

In This Chapter

▶ Popping the question

▶ Being prepared

Raising money is essential to managing a successful nonprofit organization. There's nothing easier than knowing you should be raising money — and nothing harder than asking for it. In this chapter are our ten tips for that all-important task.

Ask

One of fundraising's oldest adages is "If you don't ask, you won't get."

Developing fundraising plans, compiling lists of potential donors, and designing invitations are labor intensive. But those aren't the things that slow you down. Many people pause when it comes to picking up the telephone or ringing the doorbell — when it comes to "the ask." Then, when it's a little too late for the prospective donor to make a decision, write a check, or forward a proposal to a board meeting, they make their move and stumble over their own procrastination.

We repeat, "If you don't ask (and ask at the right time), you won't get."

Ask people you know

Some fundraisers believe that the entire money-raising game is in knowing people with money and power and working those contacts — charming them to bend their wills and write those checks. To be honest, if yours is a good cause, that approach isn't bad. But what if you don't know wealthy people? Does that mean you can't raise money?

No, it doesn't. Begin with people you know. Don't be afraid to ask your friends and associates. It's harder to say no to someone you know than it is to say no to a stranger.

Tell your story

The best way to write an effective fundraising letter or make a successful presentation to potential donors is to tell a story. You don't have to explain how your organization was founded and everything it has done since then (although that history may be worth a brief mention). The best stories focus on the constituents you serve and how they benefit from your efforts. They are free of jargon, direct, and compelling. They're hopeful stories that paint a picture of a better future and describe what "better" would look like in clear, specific terms.

Pace the story so that it has a bit of drama (but don't stoop to melodrama or hyperbole). Include facts. Recognize and discuss the complexity of the field in which you work, but don't drone on and on about technical matters.

Tell how you are improving lives

In grant-writing terms, this piece of advice would be worded as "clearly describe your outcomes." Providing training about nutrition to a group of 50 seniors is not enough if those seniors don't change their eating patterns and live longer, healthier lives. Removing toxins from a lake is not enough if its fish population and ecosystem are not revived. Exposing 500 children to formal music lessons is not enough if none of them can read a simple score later.

Outputs is the word used for the quantity of work that a nonprofit organization produces — the number of meals served, shelter beds offered, workshops led, miles covered, or acres planted. *Outcomes* is the word for the changes that occur as a result of those outputs. Well-defined outcomes are the hallmark of a good proposal, fundraising letter, or pitch.

Don't leave potential donors thinking, "Sounds nice, but so what?"

Make the numbers sparklingly clear

Effective requests for money include information about how much is needed to achieve change or to test an idea. Make sure to present any data you cite in clear terms. In most cases, letting your reader or listener know how much it costs to make a needed change — the cost per child to participate in a special classroom for a year, the cost per injured sea mammal rescued, the cost per village to provide emergency food for a week — helps to make your point.

Nothing undermines a well-written proposal or case statement faster or more thoroughly than a confusing budget or a muddled financial statement. Double-check your presentation to make sure that every activity in your proposal is represented in the budget and that every item in your budget can be traced easily to the work outlined in your proposal. If some items may be confusing to your reader, include budget notes. In all cases, check your math.

Research, research, research

We told you to ask people you know. We're not taking back that advice, but at some point you will need to move beyond your immediate circle of acquaintances. That's where doing your homework pays off.

Before you send a fundraising letter, submit a proposal, or visit with a corporate giving director, find out as much as you can about the prospective contributor. Do you have anything in common on a personal level? Maybe the foundation director you're meeting recently published an article. If you read it, you'll have a conversation topic to break the ice. This advice holds true even when your approach is a direct-mail appeal: You want to know as much as you can about the people whose names are on the lists you borrow or purchase.

More important, you want to learn as much as you can about your potential donors' giving behavior. Does this person give small amounts of money to a wide array of organizations or generous gifts to a few selected agencies? Does the foundation like to be the only contributor to a given project, or does it prefer to support an activity along with others? Does the corporate giving program prefer a low-key style, or does it like to have the company's involvement highlighted?

You can turn to many sources for this information. Much assistance can be found in the Foundation Center library and in its published and online resources. Other helpful directories are available from the European Foundation Centre, Oryx Press, Taft, and others (see this book's appendix). For personal information about individuals, check the *Who's Who* directories, local newspapers, and college alumni associations. Follow business and social news along with obituaries to keep track of people's families, professional developments, and affiliations. When you attend events at other nonprofit organizations, pay close attention to their contributor lists. Make research a habit.

Think like a trout (know your donors)

Remember the old saying, "To catch a trout, think like a trout"? The point of conducting research is to be able to talk or write about your organization in ways that are compelling to your listener or reader. You don't want to warp your message or change your mission, but you do want to think about it (and talk or write about it) in ways that respect your audience's point of view. To do so, you need to think about your organization as if you were a prospective donor yourself.

People have different personal giving styles. You don't want to offer to hold a tribute dinner in honor of someone who contributes anonymously. And you don't want to downplay a gift from a contributor who relishes public acknowledgement. Some donors prefer the sociability of supporting a cause through a special event, others respond to direct-mail appeals, and still others like to see as much of their money as possible going directly to the service being provided. (If possible, let them see that service with their own eyes!)

Often, development directors forget that foundations are nonprofit organizations with mission statements. Their job is to support proposals that further their missions. Your job as a grant-seeker is to measure how your goals align with their purposes. For example, many corporate giving programs and company-sponsored foundation programs work to improve the conditions in which their employees live and work. When they learn that their employees are involved in or contribute to a given cause, they may be more inclined to support it.

Government grant-making programs are created through legislation. If you find a program that seems well suited to your organization's work, it's worth your time to go back and review the legislation. Doing so will help you fully understand the program's context and intentions. You'll be able to think like a legislator trout!

Build a pyramid

Earlier in this chapter, we suggest starting by asking people you know. As a next step, you want to enlist those donors to ask their contacts to support your organization. Then ask those donors to ask their friends. Keep building the pyramid.

Make it easy to respond

You've written a brilliant appeal letter. You've created a compelling Web site. You've delivered a compelling speech to a room full of prospective donors. You've got them hooked. They want to contribute. But they're glancing around the room with confused looks on their faces. You blew it. You didn't give them an easy way to respond.

Always suggest a specific amount for donors to consider contributing. Connect that amount to what you need and to their potential giving levels (which you can estimate from your research). And always make it easy for them to respond. Provide an addressed envelope and reply card with each mailing, a Contribute button on your Web site, or a labeled box by the exit where they can leave contributions. Provide pens, stamps, e-mail addresses, pledge cards — any tools to help potential donors respond when you have their attention.

Keep good records

Once you begin attracting contributors, your donor records become your most valuable fundraising tools. Individuals who give to your organization once are likely to continue giving for between three and seven years. If you thank them, address them as if they are part of your organization, and generally treat them well, the size of their gifts is likely to increase over time.

In the realm of direct mail, your donor list is gold. When you first start a direct-mail campaign, the costs often exceed your income. Sounds like a bad idea, doesn't it? But direct mail can be an effective way to raise money because the cost of securing renewed and enlarged gifts from your growing donor list is modest — significantly less than the cost of attracting new donors. As your donor list grows, you can raise significant amounts of money. (See Chapter 14 for more on direct mail.)

Working with foundations, corporations, and government sources is a different story. In their case, you want to keep clear records of your original project goals and outcomes, project budget, and due dates for any required reports. Although these sources may not be willing or able to support your organization year after year, their future support is more likely if you are a conscientious grantee who submits reports on time and keeps clear records.

You can create a simple database on a set of index cards by recording names, addresses, phone numbers, and e-mail addresses, patterns of giving, and personal information (such as whether a donor knows one of your board members or whether he or she is married and has children).

Of course, these days we like to keep databases on computers. You can spend lots of money on commercial database programs known as "fundraising software," but these probably aren't necessary unless you have thousands of donors. One inexpensive option is eBase (www.ebase.org), a free program based on FileMaker Pro. You don't need FileMaker Pro to run the program unless you want to customize it. The Nonprofit Software Index (www.npinfotech.org/tnopsi) provides helpful software information.

However you keep it, guard this database carefully. It's one of your organization's most valuable resources.

Part V

Appendixes

The 5th Wave   By Rich Tennant

"Jerry! Bad news! Some of the cuttlefish lapel pins are leaking!"

In this part . . .

*H*ere we provide some useful tools, including a
glossary of nonprofit terms and a selection of
print and Web references for further reading. Appendix C
is your introduction to using the CD that accompanies
this book.

Appendix A

Nonprofit Resources

· ·

*H*ere, arranged in order of the parts of the book, is a cornucopia of reference materials. It doesn't list every book, magazine, or Web site that may be of interest to nonprofit folks, but these resources will get you started in the right direction.

We organized the resources as we organized the parts of the book; however, many references easily could have been placed in more than one category. We include Web site addresses where appropriate. Keep in mind that Web site addresses change frequently, so if the page isn't where we say it is, use your favorite search engine to track down the new address.

Part 1: Getting Started with Nonprofits

Organizations

The Aspen Institute: Nonprofit Sector Research Fund, www.nonprofitresearch.org

Center for Civil Society Studies at the Johns Hopkins University Institute for Policy Studies: www.jhu.edu/~ccss

Civicus World Alliance for Citizen Participation: www.civicus.org

Independent Sector: www.independentsector.org

Indiana University Center on Philanthropy: www.philanthropy.iupui.edu

Web resources

Giving USA 2000/AAFRC, Trust for Philanthropy: www.aafrc.org/giving

GuideStar: www.guidestar.org

Helping.org: helping.org

Internal Revenue Service: Information about nonprofits, `www.irs.ustreas.gov/prod/bus_info/eo/index.html`

Internal Revenue Service: Forms for filing for nonprofit status, `www.irs.ustreas.gov/prod/bus_info/eo/eo-tkit.html`

Internal Revenue Service: Form 1023 application package in PDF format, `www.irs.ustreas.gov/prod/forms_pubs/forms.html`

Internal Revenue Service: IRS Publication 557 for filing 990 tax forms, `www.irs.ustreas.gov/prod/forms_pubs/pubs.html`

Books and print materials

Colvin, Gregory L., *Fiscal Sponsorship: 6 Ways to Do It Right*, Study Center Press, San Francisco; `www.studycenter.org/scp.fs.html`

Hodgkinson, Virginia Ann et al, *Nonprofit Almanac 1996-97, Dimensions of the Independent Sector,* Jossey-Bass Publishers, San Francisco, 1996

Hopkins, Bruce, *Starting and Managing a Nonprofit Organization: A Legal Guide,* 3rd Edition, John Wiley & Sons, 2000

Mancuso, Anthony, *How to Form a Nonprofit Corporation,* 4th Edition, Nolo Press, Berkeley, 2000; `www.nolo.com/product/NNP/summary_NNP.html`

Renz, Loren et al, *Foundation Giving: Yearbook of Facts and Figures on Private, Corporate and Community Foundations,* The Foundation Center, New York; `http://fdncenter.org`

Salamon, Lester, *America's Nonprofit Sector, A Primer,* 2nd Edition, The Foundation Center, New York, 1999; `http://fdncenter.org/learn/bookshelf/salamon/summary.html`

"What You Should Know About Nonprofits," brochure, a joint project of the National Center for Nonprofit Boards and Independent Sector, 2000

Print and online periodicals

Chronicle of Philanthropy: `philanthropy.com`

Foundation News and Commentary: `www.cof.org/foundationnews/index.htm`

The Nonprofit Quarterly: `www.nonprofitquarterly.org`

The Nonprofit Times: `www.nptimes.com`

Philanthropy: `www.philanthropyroundtable.org/`

Part 11: Managing a Nonprofit Organization

Organizations

Alliance for Nonprofit Management: www.allianceonline.org

American Society of Association Executives: www.asaenet.org/main

Peter F. Drucker Foundation for Nonprofit Management: www.pfdf.org/index.html

The National Center for Nonprofit Boards: www.ncnb.org

National Charities Information Bureau: www.give.org

National Council of Nonprofit Associations: www.ncna.org

Nonprofit Finance Fund: www.nonprofitfinancefund.org

Web resources

About Nonprofit Charitable Organizations: nonprofit.about.com

Charity Channel: http://charitychannel.com/forums

CharityVillage: www.charityvillage.com/charityvillage/main.asp

CompuMentor: www.compumentor.org

Graduate programs for nonprofit managers: pirate.shu.edu/~mirabero/Kellogg.html

Internet Nonprofit Center: www.nonprofits.org/index.html

Kent Information Services for links to information about tax laws and forms in each U.S. state: www.kentis.com/siteseeker/taxusst.html

NetPoint Center for Nonprofits and Technology: www.netpointcenter.org

Nonprofit Genie, CompassPoint Nonprofit Services: www.genie.org

Nonprofit Management Library: www.mapnp.org/library

Web surveying: www.zoomerang.com

Books and print materials

Carver, John, *Boards That Make a Difference,* Jossey-Bass, San Francisco, 1990

Duca, Diane, *Nonprofit Boards: Roles, Responsibility and Performance,* John Wiley & Sons, 1996

Messmer, Max, *Human Resources Kit For Dummies,* Hungry Minds, Inc., 1999

Olenick, Arnold J. and Olenick, Phillip R., *A Nonprofit Organization Operating Manual: Planning for Survival and Growth,* The Foundation Center, New York

Seltzer, Michael, *Securing Your Organization's Future, Revised Edition,* The Foundation Center, New York, 2001

Tracy, John A., *Accounting For Dummies,* 2nd Edition, Hungry Minds, Inc., 2001

Part III: Raising Money and Visibility

Organizations

AAFRC Trust for Philanthropy: www.aafrc.org

Association of Fundraising Professionals: www.nsfre.org

The Council on Foundations: www.cof.org

The Foundation Center: fdncenter.org/grantmaker/contents.html

Government Printing Office (for regulatory guides): www.gpo.gov

The Grantsmanship Center: www.tgci.com

Indiana University Center on Philanthropy: www.philanthropy.iupui.edu

Web catalogs and databases

The Catalog of Federal Domestic Assistance (a comprehensive directory about federal funding opportunities): www.cfda.gov/

Commerce Business Daily (for information about federal contracts): cdbnet.access.gop.gov/index.html

Congressional Record: www.access.gpo.gov/su_docs/aces/aces150.html

Federal Assistance Monitor (a privately produced guide to federal and foundation programs): www.cdpublications.com/cdpubs

Federal Register (for daily news about federal funding opportunities): www.access.gpo.gov/su_docs/aces/aces140html

Federal Research in Progress: www.ntis.gov

The Foundation Directory Online (available for a monthly fee): www.fconline.fdncenter.org

U.S. Census Bureau: www.census.gov

Web resources

ETapestry donor management software: www.etapestry.com

FundClass: www.fundraiser-software.com/fc-ance.html

Fundraising Forum: www.raise-funds.com

Grant Advisor: www.grantadvisor.com/tgaplus/links

Grassroots Fundraising Journal: www.chardonpress.com/titles/gr_journal.html

Internet Prospector: www.internet-prospector.org

Nonprofit Matrix: www.nonprofitmatrix.com

Taft Directories: www.taftgroup.com/taft/contents.html#directories

Books and print materials

Carlson, Mim, *Winning Grants Step by Step,* Jossey-Bass Publishers, San Francisco, 1995

Corporate Foundation Profiles, The Foundation Center, New York, 2000

The Directory of Research Grants, Oryx Press, Phoenix, Arizona, 2000

Geever, Jane, C., *The Foundation Center's Guide to Proposal Writing,* 3rd Edition, The Foundation Center, New York, 2001

Hiam, Alexander, *Marketing For Dummies,* Hungry Minds, Inc., 1997

Mixer, Joseph R., *Principles of Professional Fundraising: Useful Foundation for Successful Practice,* Jossey-Bass Publishers, San Francisco, 1993

FC-Search, CD-ROM, The Foundation Center, New York, 2001

The Foundation Directory, Directory Part 2, and *Supplement,* The Foundation Center, New York, 2001

The Foundation Grants Index, 2001 Edition, The Foundation Center, New York, 2001

The Foundation 1000, 2000-01 Edition, The Foundation Center, New York, 2001

The Grants Register, St. Martin's Press, New York

The Guide to U.S. Foundations, Their Trustees, Officers, and Donors, The Foundation Center, New York, 2001

Hall, Mary, *Getting Funded: A Complete Guide to Proposal Writing,* Continuing Education Publications, Portland, Oregon, 1998

Miner, Lynn E., Miner, Jeremy T., and Griffith, Jerry, *Proposal Planning and Writing,* Second Edition, Oryx Press, Phoenix, Arizona, 1998

National Directory of Corporate Giving, 6th Edition, The Foundation Center, New York, 1999

Appendix B

Glossary of Nonprofit Terms

● ●

*H*ere, for handy reference, is a glossary of terms used by and about nonprofit organizations.

annual report: A voluntary report published by a nonprofit organization, foundation, or corporation describing its activities and providing an overview of its finances. A foundation's annual report generally lists the year's grants.

articles of incorporation: A document filed with an appropriate state office by persons establishing a corporation. Generally, this is the first legal step in forming a nonprofit corporation.

bylaws: Rules governing a nonprofit organization's operation. Bylaws often outline the methods for selecting directors, forming committees, and conducting meetings.

capital campaign: An organized drive to raise funds to finance an organization's capital needs — buildings, equipment, renovation projects, land acquisitions, or endowments.

capital support: Funds provided to a capital project.

case statement: A brief, compelling statement about an organization's projects, accomplishments, and vision.

challenge grant: A grant that's made on the condition that other funds must be secured before it will be paid — usually on a matching basis and within a defined time period.

charitable contribution: A gift of goods, money, property, or services to a nonprofit organization.

charity: The word encompasses religion, education, assistance to the government, promotion of health and the arts, relief from poverty, and other purposes benefiting the community. Nonprofit organizations formed to further one of these purposes generally are recognized as exempt from federal tax under Section 501(c)(3) of the Internal Revenue Code.

community foundation: A grantmaking organization receiving its funds from multiple public sources, focusing its giving on a defined geographic area, and managed by an appointed, representative board of directors. It's classified by the Internal Revenue Service as a public charity.

community fund: An organized community program making annual appeals to the general public for funds that are usually disbursed to charitable organizations rather than retained in an endowment. Also sometimes called a federated giving program.

company-sponsored foundation: A private foundation that derives its grantmaking funds primarily from contributions of a profit-making business.

corporate giving program: A grantmaking program established and managed by a profit-making company. Unlike a company-sponsored foundation, gifts of goods and services go directly from the company to grantees.

demonstration grant: A grant made to experiment with an innovative project or program that may serve as a model for others.

designated funds: Restricted funds whose use is defined by those contributing the money. Also called donor designated funds.

distribution committee: The board responsible for making grant decisions. For community foundations, this committee must be broadly representative of the community to be served by the foundation.

donee: A recipient of a grant. Also called a beneficiary or grantee.

donor: An individual or organization that makes a grant or contribution (also called a grantor).

donor advised fund: A fund held by a community foundation for which the donor, or a committee appointed by the donor, may recommend charitable recipients for grants from the fund.

donor designated funds: A type of restricted funds in which those contributing the funds specify the beneficiaries.

endowment: Funds intended to be kept permanently and invested to provide income for continued support of an organization.

excise tax: An annual tax of net investment income that private foundations must pay to the IRS.

family foundation: Not a legal term, but commonly used to describe foundations that are managed by family members related to the person or persons from whom the foundation's funds were derived.

federated campaign or federated giving program: Raising funds for an organization that will redistribute them as grants to nonprofit organizations. This fundraising often is led by volunteer groups within clubs and workplaces. United Way and the Combined Federal Campaign are two examples.

fiscal sponsor: A nonprofit 501(c)(3) organization that formally agrees to sponsor a project led by an individual or group from outside the organization that may or may not have nonprofit status. If the outside individual or group receives grants or contributions to conduct an activity, those funds are accepted, approved, and managed on behalf of the project by the fiscal sponsor.

foundation: A nongovernmental, nonprofit organization with funds and a program managed by its own trustees and directors, established to further social, education, religious, or charitable activities by making grants. A private foundation may receive its funds from an individual, family, corporation, or other group consisting of a limited number of members.

gift table: A structured plan for the number and size of contributions needed to meet a fundraising campaign's goals.

grantee: An individual or organization receiving a grant.

grantor: An individual or organization awarding a grant.

independent sector: The portion of the economy that includes all 501(c)(3) and 501(c)(4) tax-exempt organizations as defined by the Internal Revenue Service, all religious institutions, all social responsibility programs of corporations, and all persons who give time and money to serve charitable purposes. It's also called the voluntary sector, the charitable sector, the third sector, or the nonprofit sector.

lobbying: Efforts to influence legislation by influencing the opinion of legislators, legislative staff, and government administrators directly involved in drafting legislative policies. The Internal Revenue Code sets limits on lobbying by organizations that are exempt from tax under Section 501(c)(3).

matching gifts program: A grant or contributions program that matches employees' or directors' gifts made to qualifying nonprofit organizations. Each employer or foundation sets specific guidelines.

matching grant: A grant or gift made with the specification that the amount contributed must be matched with revenues from another source on a one-for-one basis or according to another defined formula.

mission statement: A statement of the purpose and key activities of a nonprofit organization.

nonprofit: A term describing the Internal Revenue Service's designation for organizations whose income is not used for the benefit or private gain of stockholders, directors, or other owners. A nonprofit organization's income is used to support its operations and further its stated mission. Sometimes referred to as an NPO (nonprofit organization).

outcome evaluation: An assessment of whether a project achieved the desired long-term results.

program officer: A staff member of a foundation or corporate giving program who may review grant requests, recommend policy, manage a budget, or process applications for review by a board or committee. Other titles, such as program director or program consultant, also are used.

proposal: A written application, often with supporting documents, submitted to a foundation or corporate giving program in requesting a grant.

public charity: A type of organization classified under Section 501(c)(3) of the Internal Revenue Service. A public charity normally receives a substantial part of its income from the general public or government. The public support of a public charity must be fairly broad, not limited to a few families or individuals.

restricted funds: Assets or income whose use is restricted by a donor.

social entrepreneurism: Creating and evaluating programs in a way that considers social benefits as well as financial results.

tax exempt: A classification granted by the Internal Revenue Service to qualified nonprofit organizations that frees them from the requirement to pay taxes on their income. Private foundations, including endowed company foundations, are tax exempt; however, they must pay a modest excise tax on net investment income. All 501(c)(3) and 501(c)(4) organizations are tax exempt.

unrelated business income: Income from an activity that's not within the scope of the organization's mission.

unsolicited proposal: A proposal sent to a foundation without the foundation's invitation or prior knowledge. Some foundations do not accept unsolicited proposals.

venture philanthropy: A style of grantmaking drawing on the business practices of venture capitalists.

Appendix C

About the CD

. . . .

In This Appendix:

▶ System Requirements

▶ Using the CD with Windows and Mac

▶ What You'll Find on the CD

▶ Troubleshooting

. . . .

System Requirements

Make sure that your computer meets the minimum system requirements shown in the following list. If your computer doesn't match up to most of these requirements, you may have problems using the software and files on the CD.

- ✔ A PC with a Pentium or faster processor; or a Mac OS computer with a 68040 or faster processor

- ✔ Microsoft Windows 95 or later; or Mac OS system software 7.6.1 or later

- ✔ Some files require Microsoft Excel 97 or higher

- ✔ At least 32MB of total RAM installed on your computer; for best performance, we recommend at least 64MB

- ✔ A CD-ROM drive

- ✔ A sound card for PCs; Mac OS computers have built-in sound support

- ✔ A monitor capable of displaying at least 256 colors or grayscale

- ✔ A modem with a speed of at least 14,400 bps

If you need more information on the basics, check out these books published by Hungry Minds, Inc.: *PCs For Dummies,* by Dan Gookin; *Macs For Dummies,* by David Pogue; *iMacs For Dummies* by David Pogue; *Windows 95 For Dummies, Windows 98 For Dummies, Windows 2000 Professional For Dummies, Microsoft Windows ME Millennium Edition For Dummies,* all by Andy Rathbone.

Using the CD with Microsoft Windows

To install items from the CD to your hard drive, follow these steps:

1. **Insert the CD into your computer's CD-ROM drive.**

2. **Click the Start button and choose Run from the menu.**

3. **In the dialog box that appears, type** `d:\start.htm`.

   Replace *d* with the proper drive letter for your CD-ROM if it uses a different letter. (If you don't know the letter, double-click My Computer on your desktop and see what letter is listed for your CD-ROM drive.)

   Your browser opens, and the license agreement is displayed. If you don't have a browser, Microsoft Internet Explorer and Netscape Communicator are included on the CD.

4. **Read through the license agreement, nod your head, and click the Agree button if you want to use the CD.**

   After you click Agree, you're taken to the Main menu, where you can browse through the contents of the CD.

5. **To navigate within the interface, click a topic of interest to take you to an explanation of the files on the CD and how to use or install them.**

6. **To install software from the CD, simply click the software name.**

   You'll see two options: to run or open the file from the current location or to save the file to your hard drive. Choose to run or open the file from its current location, and the installation procedure continues. When you finish using the interface, close your browser as usual.

Note: We have included an "easy install" in these HTML pages. If your browser supports installations from within it, go ahead and click the links of the program names you see. You'll see two options: Run the File from the Current Location and Save the File to Your Hard Drive. Choose to Run the File from the Current Location and the installation procedure will continue. A Security Warning dialog box appears. Click Yes to continue the installation.

To run some of the programs on the CD, you may need to keep the disc inside your CD-ROM drive. This is a good thing. Otherwise, a very large chunk of the program would be installed to your hard drive, consuming valuable hard drive space and possibly keeping you from installing other software.

Using the CD with Mac OS

To install items from the CD to your hard drive, follow these steps:

1. **Insert the CD into your computer's CD-ROM drive.**

   In a moment, an icon representing the CD you just inserted appears on your Mac desktop. Chances are, the icon looks like a CD-ROM.

2. **Double-click the CD icon to show the CD's contents.**

3. **Double-click** `start.htm` **to open your browser and display the license agreement.**

   If your browser doesn't open automatically, open it as you normally would by choosing File⇨Open File (in Internet Explorer) or File⇨ Open⇨Location in Netscape (in Netscape Communicator) and select *NonprofitKit FD*. The license agreement appears.

4. **Read through the license agreement, nod your head, and click the Agree button if you want to use the CD.**

   After you click Agree, you're taken to the Main menu. This is where you can browse through the contents of the CD.

5. **To navigate within the interface, click any topic of interest and you're taken to an explanation of the files on the CD and how to use or install them.**

6. **To install software from the CD, simply click the software name.**

What You'll Find on the CD

The following sections are arranged by category and provide a summary of the software and other goodies you'll find on the CD. If you need help with installing the items provided on the CD, refer back to the installation instructions in the preceding section.

Shareware programs are fully functional, trial versions of copyrighted programs. If you like particular programs register with their authors for a nominal fee and receive licenses, enhanced versions, and technical support. *Freeware programs* are free, copyrighted games, applications, and utilities. Unlike shareware, these programs do not require a fee or provide technical support. *EULA software* is governed by its own license, which is included inside the folder of the EULA product. See the EULA license for more details.

Trial, demo, or evaluation versions are usually limited either by time or functionality (such as being unable to save projects). Some trial versions are very sensitive to system date changes. If you alter your computer's date, the programs will "time out" and will no longer be functional.

CD Contents — Samples, Forms, References — Listed by Chapter Number

Use the following list to find materials referred to in chapters and for numerous additional resources related to the chapter topic. Each form is available to you as a PDF file and almost every form is available as a Rich Text File (.rtf). You'll need Adobe Acrobat Reader (available on this CD) to view and print the PDF files. You can use your favorite word processor to view, print, and edit the .rtf files. Links to resources on the Web are included for each chapter. You must be connected to the Internet to use the links.

Chapter 1: Tuning In to the World of Nonprofit Organizations

Form 1-1 Web resources

Chapter 2: Deciding to Start a Nonprofit

Form 2-1 Sample Fiscal Sponsorship Agreement

Form 2-2 Web resources

Chapter 3: Writing Your Mission Statement

Form 3-1A Sample Mission Statement for Artspace Projects, Inc., Included with Permission

Form 3-1B Sample Mission Statement for the Bay Area Discovery Museum, Included with Permission

Form 3-2 Web resources

Chapter 4: Incorporating and Applying for a Tax Exemption

Chapter 5: Safeguarding Your Nonprofit Status

Chapter 6: Building Your Board of Directors

Chapter 7: Getting the Work Done with Paid Staff

Chapter 8: Getting the Work Done with Volunteers

Chapter 9: Planning: Why and How Nonprofits Make Plans

Form 9-1 Sample Planning Retreat Agenda

Form 9-2 Sample Needs Assessment Questionnaire

Form 9-3 Outline of an Organizational Plan

Form 9-4 Web Resources

Chapter 10: Showing the Money: Budgets and Financial Reports

Form 10-1A Sample Organization Budget, Photography Workshops for Teenagers

Form 10-1B Sample Organization Budget, Mid-sized Sheltered Workshop for Persons With Disabilities

Form 10-1C Sample Organization Budget, Education/Recreation Program for Homeless Children

Form 10-1D Tracking Actual Income and Expenses: Sample Organization Budget and Monthly Report of Budget vs. Actual Income and Expenses

Form 10-1E Tracking Actual Income and Expenses: Sample Organization Budget and Monthly Report of Budget vs. Actual Income and Expenses

Form 10-2 Cash Flow Worksheet

Form 10-3 Sample Cash Flow Projection

Form 10-4 Sample Audited Financial Statement, Community Health Fund Network

Form 10-5 Web resources

Chapter 11: Creating a Home for Your Nonprofit and Insuring It

Form 11-1A Planned Change and Facilities, Included with Permission from the Nonprofit Finance Fund

Form 11-1B Change, Facilities & Program Choices, Included with Permission from the Nonprofit Finance Fund

Form 11-1C Questions to Ask Yourself About Your Program, Included with Permission from the Nonprofit Finance Fund

Form 11-1D Common Project Justifications, Included with Permission from the Nonprofit Finance Fund

Form 11-1E Your Project's Relative Size, Included with Permission from the Nonprofit Finance Fund

Form 11-1F Costs Your Capital Campaign Should Include, Included with Permission from the Nonprofit Finance Fund

Form 11-2 Facilities Requirements Checklist, Included with Permission from the Nonprofit Finance Fund

Form 11-2A (Excel file) List of Required Spaces

Form 11-3 Web resources

Chapter 12: Finding Help When You Need IT

Form 12-1 Web resources

Chapter 13: Crafting a Fundraising Plan

Form 13-1A Sample Fundraising Plan, High School Music Awards Program

Form 13-1B Sample Fundraising Plan, Neighborhood Park Coalition

Form 13-2A Sample Fundraising Budget, High School Music Awards Program

Form 13-2B Sample Fundraising Budget, Neighborhood Park Coalition

Form 13-3 Web Resources

Chapter 14: Raising Money from Individuals

Form 14-1 Board Member Contact Letter

Form 14-2 Sample Donor Information Record

Form 14-3 Telemarketing "Dos" and "Don'ts" and Two Sample Telemarketing Scripts

Form 14-4 Sample Case Statement, Bay Area Discovery Museum "My Place by the Bay" Capital Campaign, Included with Permission from the Bay Area Discovery Museum

Form 14-5 Web resources

Chapter 15: Making the Most of Special Events

Form 15-1A Sample Special Events Timeline: Tribute Dinner or Luncheon

Form 15-1B Sample Special Event Timeline: Benefit Concert

Form 15-1C Sample Benefit Auction Timeline for a Combined Silent/Live Auction

Form 15-2 Sample Special Event Committee Invitation Letter, Save Our Lakeshore Awards Dinner

Form 15-3 Sample Special Event Solicitation Letter, Save Our Lakeshore Awards Dinner

Form 15-4 Special Event Invitation, International Children's Relief Committee Dinner

Form 15-5A Sample Budget for a Tribute Dinner

Form 15-5B Special Event Budget Form for a Concert or Performance

Form 15-5C Sample Benefit Auction Budget

Form 15-6 Web resources

Chapter 16: Finding the Grant-Givers

Form 16-1 Foundation Research Checklist

Form 16-2 Federal Government Program Research Checklist

Form 16-3 Foundation Prospect Evaluation Sheet

Form 16-4 Web resources

Chapter 17: Writing a Grant Proposal

Form 17-1 Sample Foundation Application Form

Form 17-2 Sample Foundation Budget Form

Form 17-3A Sample General Operating Grant Proposal, Included with Permission from Kevin Walsh

Form 17-3B Sample Project Grant Proposal, Included with Permission from Jerome Moskowitz and the San Francisco Mime Troupe

Form 17-4 Final Report to Equity Grants Program

Form 17-4B San Francisco Project Budget Notes

Form 17-5 Sample Letter Proposal to a Corporation, Tech Re-use Center

Form 17-6 Sample Letter of Inquiry, Save Mount Artemis

Form 17-7 Sample Company-Sponsored Foundation Guidelines and Application Information

Form 17-8 Finishing and Submitting Your Proposal

Form 17-9 Web resources

Chapter 18: Finding Funds to Create a Home Base

Form 18-1 Capital: Hard and Soft Costs, Included with Permission from the Nonprofit Finance Fund

Form 18-2 Feasibility Study Overview

Form 18-3 Feasibility Study Interview Outline

Form 18-4A Sample Capital Campaign Budget, Constructing a Youth Center within an Existing Building

Form 18-4B Sample Capital Campaign Budget, Constructing a Small Theater Within an Existing Building

Form 18-4C Sample Capital Campaign Budget, Constructing a Child Care Center Within an Existing Building

Form 18-5 Pyramid of Gifts

Form 18-6 Capital Campaign Costs

Form 18-7 Web resources

Chapter 19: Marketing: Spreading the Word about Your Good Work

Form 19-1 Sample Public Service Announcement

Form 19-2 Sample Audience Survey, Neighborhood Historical Society

Form 19-3 Sample Participant/Volunteer Survey

Form 19-4 Sample Press Release, Included with Permission from Carla Befera

Form 19-5 Sample Press Alert

Form 19-6 Sample Calendar Release

Form 19-7 Sample Photo Caption

Form 19-8 Sample Photo Use Permission Form

Form 19-9 Web Resources

IRS Forms

Form SS-4

Form 1023

Publication 557

Form 990-EZ

Form 990

Instructions for Completing the Form 990

Schedule A

Schedule A Instructions

Schedule B

Software

Acrobat Reader

Evaluation version.

For Macintosh and Windows. Acrobat Reader , from Adobe Systems, is a program that lets you view and print Portable Document Format, or PDF files. The PDF format is used by many programs you find on the Internet for storing documentation, because it supports the use of such stylish elements as assorted fonts and colorful graphics (as opposed to plain text, or ASCII, which doesn't allow for any special effects in a document). You can also get more information by visiting the Adobe Systems Web site, at www.adobe.com.

Internet Explorer

Commercial version.

For Macintosh and Windows. Internet Explorer, from Microsoft, is one of the best-known Web browsers available. In addition to the browser, this package includes other Internet tools from Microsoft: Outlook Express 5, a mail and news reading program; Windows Media Player, a program that can display or play many types of audio and video files; and NetMeeting 3, a video conferencing program.

If you have a version of Windows 98, 2000, or NT that already includes Internet Explorer 5.5, don't install the CD-ROM version. Instead, go to Microsoft's Web site at www.microsoft.com/windows/ie/download/windows.htm and see what updates are available to fix errors and security problems in the version you have.

MindSpring Internet Access

Commercial version.

For Macintosh and Windows.MindSpring is an Internet service provider (ISP) that has local telephone access from most areas of the continental United States. The software provided by MindSpring on the CD-ROM includes and easy-to-use interface to the Internet programs you will want to use, as well as some useful Internet client -programs. Visit the MindSpring Web site at `www.mindspring.com`

Before you sign up for an account with MindSpring, check whether it's accessible from your location as a local telephone call. You can check MindSpring availability in your area through their Web site or call their customer service department at 1-888-677-7464.

MindSpring has several plans you can choose from, depending on how much time you need to spend connected. At the time this book was written, MindSpring offered unlimited 56K dial-up Internet access for $19.95 per month. MindSpring also offers residential and business ISDN and DSL service.

If you already have an Internet service provider, please note that the MindSpring software makes changes to your computer's current Internet configuration and may replace your current settings. These changes may stop you from being able to access the Internet through your current provider.

Netscape Communicator

Commercial version.

For Macintosh and Windows. Netscape Communicator, from Netscape Communications, is one of the best-known Web browsers available. The CD-ROM installs Netscape Communicator Version 4.7. You also have the option of installing Real Player G2 (to play streaming audio and video files) and Winamp (to play MPEG3 files).

You can find information about Netscape Navigator from its Help menu or at its Web site, `home.netscape.com`.

Troubleshooting

I tried my best to compile programs that work on most computers with the minimum system requirements. Alas, your computer may differ, and some programs may not work properly for some reason.

The two likeliest problems are that you don't have enough memory (RAM) for the programs you want to use, or you have other programs running that are affecting installation or running of a program. If you get an error message such as `Not enough memory` or `Setup cannot continue`, try one or more of the following suggestions and then try using the software again:

- ✔ **Turn off any antivirus software running on your computer.** Installation programs sometimes mimic virus activity and may make your computer incorrectly believe that it's being infected by a virus.

- ✔ **Close all running programs.** The more programs you have running, the less memory is available to other programs. Installation programs typically update files and programs; so if you keep other programs running, installation may not work properly.

- ✔ **Have your local computer store add more RAM to your computer.** This is, admittedly, a drastic and somewhat expensive step. However, if you have a Windows 95 PC or a Mac OS computer with a PowerPC chip, adding more memory can really help the speed of your computer and allow more programs to run at the same time. This may include closing the CD interface and running a product's installation program from Windows Explorer.

If you still have trouble installing the items from the CD, please call the Hungry Minds, Inc. Customer Service phone number at 800-762-2974 (outside the U.S.: 317-572-3993) or send email to `techsupdum@hungryminds.com`.

Index

• D •